Frank Hird's
Lancashire Tales

Previously published as "More Stories of Old Lancashire"

SELECTED BY
CLIFF HAYES

AURORA
PUBLISHING

© AURORA PUBLISHING

ISBN: 1 85926 040 3

Selected from: "Lancashire Stories", Published c. 1911, - Frank Hird.
                     Previously published as "More Stories of Old Lancashire".

Stories selected by: Cliff Hayes.

Distributed by: Aurora Enterprises Ltd.
                     Unit 9C, Bradley Fold Trading Estate,
                     Radcliffe Moor Road,
                     Bradley Fold,
                     BOLTON BL2 6RT
                     Tel: 0204 370753/2
                     Fax: 0204 370751

Printed
and bound by: Manchester Free Press,
                     Unit E3, Longford Trading Estate,
                     Thomas Street,
                     Stretford,
                     Manchester M32 0JT.

06248789

Front cover illustration: Preston 1796 - W. Orme.

Contents

Other books in the
Stories & Tales
series...

Stories and Tales of
Old Manchester

Selected and Edited by
CLIFF HAYES

Stories and Tales of
Old Merseyside

Selected and Edited by
CLIFF HAYES

Stories and Tales of
Old Lancashire

Selected and Edited by
CLIFF HAYES

**STORIES & TALES OF
OLD YORKSHIRE**

Originally edited by William Smith in 1883

Selected & Edited by Dawn Robinson-Walsh

This classic story of Lancashire's dark past is now reissued.
You will be spellbound by these tales of the county's
most infamous characters: Alizon Device,
Mother Chattox, Alice Nutter and Mother Demdike
— and perhaps horrified by their fate!

£3.99 from all good bookshops

Hobson's Choice
THE NOVEL

by **Harold Brighouse**
and **Charles Forrest**

£4.95

**The classic tale of Salford life, now
available in this new edition.**

GRANTED by Henry II. in 1179, the Preston Guild Merchant has been in existence for over seven hundred years. In the thirteenth century every town had its Merchant Guild, but the feudal lords. These guilds laid the foundations of the middle class.

The men of Preston had to pay King Henry II. the sum of one hundred marks for the privilege of the Guild; and upon

6 *The* MARSHAL

W Williams Inv.t Darly Sculp

Pub acc.t to Act.762
by T Anderton.

Preston is the only town in the country in which it still exists. It has now been merged in the municipality, but in its earliest beginning, and for centuries afterwards, the Guild was the protection of the townspeople against the tyranny of an old and much dilapidated sheet of parchment called the "Custumal or Ordinances of the Preston Guild," carefully preserved in the town records, is set forth all the benefits it conferred upon them. To begin with, only burgesses could belong to the Guild, these being either merchants or holders of land, and no man could be a burgess unless he had a burgage, as property in a town was called, of twelve feet frontage. The working man, the man " with blue nails," " with dirty hands," or " who hawked their goods in the streets," received no privileges under the Guild. An important clause in the Ordinances directed that no one who was not a master of the Guild should sell any merchandise in the town without the consent of the burgesses ; it was also enacted that no stranger should sell in the town. As a matter of fact the origin of these Guilds was trade protection, each town being anxious to protect its market against the underselling or competition of neighbouring places. In the course of time powers were given to the Guilds to inflict fines upon burgesses for offences outside matters of trade. Thus, in the Preston Ordinances there is this clause :—

" Also if a burgess wound another, and they shall be willing to agree, friends appointed between them may require for every hidden cut of a thumb's breadth 4*d.* ; for every open or visible wound 8*d.*; and he who is wounded may prove what he has lost by the wound, and the other shall pay him, and in like manner he shall repay what the wounded has paid to the surgeon for healing the wound, and the arms shall be brought to him, and he shall swear upon his arms that he has been wounded and that such things have been done to him, so that if his friends consent and approve he may take what is offered to him." Another ordinance was that if any one called a married woman or a widow a particularly offensive name, he could clear himself by his oath if no witnesses appeared. If he could not deny the charge upon oath he was fined 3*s.* But full pardon was granted if " he by whom

it was said took himself by the nose and said that he had spoken a lie."

The " reeve " filled the place now occupied by the mayor, and in the twelfth century in Preston personal violence would seem to have been of frequent occurrence between the holders of the office and the burgesses, since a clause is specially devoted to the matter :—

" Also if a burgess shall strike the reeve, or the reeve a burgess in court, and shall be convicted he shall henceforth be at the mercy of the court for the offence. Also if the reeve shall strike anyone out of court he shall be liable to 40*s.*"

It was in the reign of Edward III. that the Guild Merchant was ordered to be held every twenty years, but it was not until 1500 that the procession, which became such an important ceremony in the Guild Merchant, was inaugurated. A Guild was held in 1542, and it was then quoted as a precedent that in 1500 it had been ordered " that all burgesses shall be ready at the Guild Merchant to go with procession from the Maudlands throughout the town as the procession is wont to be of old times, that is to say the first day of the foresaid Guild." As Colonel Fishwick points out, there is no evidence of a Guild being held between 1500 and 1542. The intermediary Guild would have fallen at a time when war had just been declared against France, and Henry VIII. was claiming a tenth part of the movable goods of all those who were worth a hundred pounds ; the Preston merchants, therefore, would not be in a position to meet the royal demand and hold their Guild. By the middle of the sixteenth century, the rule that burgesses must be inhabitants of the town had been relaxed, and we find most of the leading families in the neighbourhood

THE CORPORATION

represented upon the list—the Stanleys, Hoghtons, Heskeths, Fleetwoods, Bartons, Farringtons, etc.; and a hundred years later the number of "foreign" burgesses outnumbered the in-burgesses by some two hundred. But in 1662, the town had increased so much in size that there were fourteen hundred in-burgesses to twelve hundred "foreign" burgesses.

In the reign of Charles I. the Guild seems to have lost some of its ancient authority, probably owing to a visitation of the plague. The Guild Order Book records "that the great sickness of the plague of pestilence wherein the number of eleven hundred persons and upwards died within the town and parish, began about the tenth day of November in Anno 1630, and continued the space of one whole year." The terrible epidemic of plague had given strangers the opportunity of carrying on the various trades, and the Guild was apparently helpless to enforce one of the most important of its rules, for we find the mercers, drapers, grocers, and salters of Preston petitioning Charles I.'s Privy Council in this wise: "Your petitioners at the present doe con-

THE CLOTH WORKERS

9

THE TAILORS

sist of very neere 80 poore persons which doe bear Scott and Lot with their neighbours, etc. But nowe so it is that the said Burrough haveing beene visited with the plague and pestilence which infec'con continued amongst them for a whole yeare, and thereby your petitioner and others of the surviving inhabitants for that time were altogether barred from the exercise of their trades, and so are become very much impoverished and weakened in their estates, and divers persons . . . have sett up and do take upon them to exercise and employ themselves in your petitioners' several trades, having never served any apprenticeshipps to the said trades and

THE TANNERS

THE CORDWAINERS

misteries . . . to the general impoverishment and discountenancing of the inhabitants of the borough which since the late visitation amongst them (through the usages aforesaid) lost a great part of their former trading and their markets are become small . . . Your petitioners pray, etc., Your Honors to direct some speedy course for suppression." This petition was presented in 1633.

A twenty-year celebration of the Guild fell in 1662, two years after the Restoration of Charles II., and on this occasion the statutes were entirely revised. Of the next celebration, in 1682, a full record has been left by Kuerden, and is preserved in the Heralds' College. The date was the 4th of September.

" About eight in the morning all the Company of Trades with the wardens of

THE MASONS

THE SMITHS

each company in their gowns and long white rods ranged into two fyles, the flags of each company displayed and variety of musick . . . marche regularly up and down the street singing, wayting for the Guild Mayor's attendance. And the young men within the town not being as yet free to trade of themselves have a captain and leftenant of their own, their ensign being the town's arms, a flagg with the Holy Lamb, and they marche and attend in like order with their drums and music. After them marched a proper man bearing the great banner with the King's arms : and after that following in rank, the mayor's pensioners or guard before the banner with partizans (these were short pikes), and those after with halberds, after which singly the black sargeant with his halberd, and then the town sergeants with

THE VINTNERS

THE CARPENTERS

their maces, the two balives with their white rods, and the aldermen in their robes, and after them the Guild Mayor with his great staff of authority, and attended on each side with nobility and gentry of the country as well as with the gentry of the town." The procession then passed from the mayor's house to the Town Hall, which Kuerden described as a "well-beautifyed gylde or town hall." From here the procession "with sound of trumpet," marched to the High Cross in the market place where a proclamation was made "that the Guild is now to be opened." Thence they all repaired to the church, where after prayers, "a learn'd sermon was preached by the Guild Mayor's chaplain." Divine service over the pro-

THE SKINNERS AND GLOVERS

cession was re-marshalled and marched to the Churchgate Barrs, where the Mayor listened to a speech made by one of the boys of the school. At the conclusion of the speech, "a barrel or hogshead of nappy ale standing close by the Barrs was broached and a glass offered to Mr. Mayor," who drank to the King's health, the "musketiers attending" firing a volley. The procession then went to the Fishergate Barrs, where another school-boy made

gentry, went to the Guild Hall where, after partaking of a sumptuous banquet, they are regaled with "store of pipes and Spanish tobacco."

During the eighteenth century the celebration of the Preston Guild grew more elaborate with each twenty years; but in 1822 the festivities reached their climax, lasting nearly a fortnight. It had become the fashion for all the neighbouring county families to repair to

THE MERCERS

a speech in Latin and another hogshead of ale was broached, with the same toasting and volleying as before. The ceremony was repeated at Friargate Barrs, after which the procession returned to the High Cross where the schoolmaster "entertains them with a learned speech." This time a hogshead of wine was broached; there were more toasts; and more volleys from the "musketiers." Then each trade went to its own hall and "nobly entertains each its own society," whilst the Mayor, accompanied by the nobility and

Preston for the Guild. The state of excitement in the town caused by the preparation for "the Guild" is humorously described in a rhyming letter, supposed to have been written by a commercial traveller to his employers at Norwich.

LETTER FROM MR. GILES RIDER TO MESSRS. BARKER & BOTHERUM, COCKEY LANE, NORWICH.

"*White Horse, Preston, Aug.* 20, 1822.

"Dear Sirs—You will wonder to hear that this town,

Like your own, my good friends, of reform-
ing renown,
Has at last got reform'd in a style rather
novel,
From the Mayor to the mob, from the hall
to the hovel.
Roam wherever you will, saws and hammers
resound,
As if Babel were rising once more from the
ground ;
And buildings spring up, or of bricks or of
boards,
For pictures and horses, for lions and lords.
Cross the street and a painter defiles your
new black,
Or the end of a beam lays you flat on your
back ;
Make a call, and your glove to the knocker
adheres,
While out walks your friend powder'd down
to the ears,
In a London-cut coat—then he speaks, *such*
a slang !
No more like your old friend than Ourang-
Outang !
'My dear Sir, what's the matter ? Sure
Preston is mad,
For naught as of yore can be seen or be had.
Every house is in mask from the Jail to the
Ribble,
Nay, the streets walk abroad in a new sort
of pebble.'
Your friend simpers and shrugs, as he hands
you a chair,
And replies with a smile, ' 'Tis the *Guild*,
my dear Sir.'
'The *Guild !* ' There's no action so rash or
absurd,
But will stand quite excused by the magical
word.
Should childhood be ruined, or dotage be
wed,
If 'tis done at ' The Guild,' there's no more
to be said.
Should you ask of a lawyer to seize or to sue
(A thing he is seldom unwilling to do),
Of a lady a kiss, or a doctor a pill,
Still the answer is one and the same—'tis
' The Guild.'
I call'd on my tailor, as honest a brother
As e'er measured one yard, and cabbag'd
another ;
He had shoulder'd his yard-wand by way of
a staff,
With his face pucker'd up, 'twixt a grin and
a laugh,
But not till I mutter'd some wish for my bill,

Could I wring from the snipper one word
but the Guild.
You will stare at this string, not of orders,
but rhymes,
But as folly's the rage, I comply with the
times.
I call'd on a friend—ask'd for orders—he
said,
' Just in time, my dear Sir, a front room and
good bed.'
So as nothing you see can at present be
done,
I've determined to see all this folly and fun.
When should orders be scant, and I find
nothing better,
With rhymes on the rout I may fill up my
letter.
" Your obedient servant,
" GILES RIDER."

The following was the order of the
procession arranged by the Marshal in
Fishergate :—
1. Tanners, Skinners, Curriers and
Glovers.
2. Cotton Spinners and Weavers.
3. Cordwainers.
4. Carpenters.
5. Butchers.
6. Vintners.
7. Tailors.
8. Plasterers.
9. Smiths.
10. Gardeners.
11. Lodge of Odd Fellows.
12. Printers and Bookbinders.
13. Lodge of Freemasons.
14. Corporation, Clergy and Gentlemen.

There was some trouble with the tailors,
who were dissatisfied with their place in
the procession. This they considered
derogatory to " their sacredly instituted
profession." Consequently they announced
that " they do not intend to favour the
Procession with their attendance, except
they are permitted to take that situation
which the high antiquity of their trade
demands—a trade first taught by instinct

THE BUTCHERS

and matured in the earliest age." Finally they gave this haughty ultimatum : " The only privilege they wish—the only right they require—is to be allowed to move in that situation which has always been assigned to them from the Creation of the World to the present time (the last Guild excepted), and they are resolved never to be disgraced by tamely acccepting any other."

The cotton spinners escorted a winding machine which was " worked by four interesting young females in white cotton dresses." There was likewise a loom upon which fourteen yards of linen was made during the two days' procession, half of this being presented to Lady Derby, and the other half to the Mayoress of Preston.

On the evening of the first day the Mayor gave a ball, at which we are told, " About nine o'clock the elegant and accomplished Mrs. Atkinson (the Mayoress), led off with the Earl of Wilton, in a country dance, followed by the Countess of Wilton and Mr. E. Grimshaw. The dresses of the Ladies were particularly splendid, uniting the very height of fashion with classical chasteness."

The second day was opened by the Mayoress's procession to church, when Mrs. Atkinson again roused the admiration of the somewhat fulsome chronicler :—

" Those who knew Mrs. Atkinson can picture to themselves the peculiar dignity with which she led the magnificent train up the central aisle of our venerable church. She was followed by the Countess of Derby, the Countess of Wilton, Lady Hoghton, Miss Hoghton, the Miss Stanleys (the lovely daughters of Lord Stanley), and a retinue of at least 160 ladies of the first distinction, the splendour of whose dress was only equalled by the attractive beauty of their personal charms."

Again there was a procession of the Guild through the streets, and in the evening the Mayor gave a banquet.

Races on Fulwood Moor were the chief

event of the third day, at which we are told—

"By two o'clock, the time when the horses started, there was a grand display of splendid equipages, all arrayed in new liveries, glittering in the sun like a birthday at St. James's."

In the evening the Mayor gave another ball, the description of which now verges upon the ludicrous by reason of its inflated style. When it was written it was taken quite seriously.

"THE MAYOR'S BALL

"This evening was attended by a most unprecedented display of fashion, particularly of the female world. The rooms were crowded to excess; to promenade was impossible. From a quarter-past nine till half-past ten, the Company poured in as fast as they could be set down from the carriages which brought them. . . . About 800 persons, of the very first rank and respectability, in the county and neighbourhood were present.

"A more enchanting spectacle it is not possible to conceive, a more agreeable and delightful society never, perhaps, met together; all was harmony, good humour, and condescension; a smile of pleasure dimpled every cheek, and the careworn countenance of age was refreshed and brightened in the participation of the joyous scene. The amusement of the evening commenced with country dances, led off by the same distinguished persons who opened the ball on Monday; and in the adjoining room some quadrille parties displayed their science in this elegant accomplishment, to the delight of the fashionable loungers who thronged the room, in their passage to and from the refectory. . . . The company began to thin about 2 o'clock, but the grey tint of streaky morn had spread her changing light on the horizon before the sons and daughters of Terpsichore had ceased to trip around the magic circle of her sphere."

Racing was again the chief occupation on the fourth, fifth, and sixth days, with a fancy dress ball on the evening of the fifth day.

THE WEAVERS

The second week of the Guild was opened with a balloon ascent which nearly resulted in a tragedy. The next day the balloon was descending at Preston when the aeronaut, a Mr. Livingstone, was thrown out, narrowly escaping being killed. The balloon shot up into the air assembled in the town. Oratorio and a masked ball on the evening of the eleventh day brought the Guild celebration to a close.

Apart from what may be termed the official entertainments, private hospitality was carried out on a large scale; there

THE PRESTON BELLMAN.

and disappeared. It was afterwards discovered near Selby.

Concerts were the attraction on the eighth day; oratorios and a charity ball on the ninth day. On the tenth the Mayoress gave a public breakfast, there was a concert in the theatre, and the stone of the New Church in the Fylde Road was laid with much ceremony, and in the presence of all the "quality" were feasting and music from one end of Preston to the other. For the townspeople and the hundreds of country folk who came to witness the celebrations, there was a circus in Woodcock's Timber Yard in Fishergate, Wombwell's Wild Beasts, and a Panorama of the Battle of Algiers, whilst Madame Hengler gave displays of fireworks at the Bowling Green,

The Mayor's Ball on Wednesday in the first week and the Mayoress's public breakfast, were given at the expense of the Corporation, tickets of admission being given to all who applied for them, the only qualification being that they should have been introduced to the Mayor and Mayoress. "His Worship," we are told, "also gave dinners in the Guild Hall by invitation, and was attended almost every day by about sixty gentlemen who on each occasion sat down to a repast which was provided on the most liberal and even sumptuous scale."

And in conclusion it is recorded with no little satisfaction that, "Not a single military person was ever in attendance at any of the entertainments or even in the town, as it was the anxious wish of the Mayor and authorities that the whole business should be conducted by the civil powers."

The illustrations are of the Guild Merchant procession in 1762.

ROCHDALE TOKENS

THE lack of small change after the death of Charles I. caused so much inconvenience to tradesmen that many of them issued metal tokens which represented the value of pennies, halfpennies and farthings. These they gave to their customers in change, and accepted them in payment for goods. Each token bore the name of the tradesman on the obverse side with perhaps a figure, and on the reverse the name of the place where the tradesman lived and the date, and sometimes their initials. The following were issued at Rochdale :—

Obverse. John Butterworth—Bust of the Queen of Bohemia crowned.

Reverse. Of Rathdell. 1662—I. B. (value of a farthing). John Butterworth was a mercer.

Obverse. James Hamar of—An eagle and child.

Reverse. Ratchdall 1655—I. H. (value of a farthing).

Obverse. Richard Kenion—His halfpeny.

Reverse. Of Rachdall 1666—R. K.

Obverse. Richard Kenion—His half-peny.

Reverse. Of Rachdall 1667—R. I. K.

Obverse. Robert Martlers—The Weavers Arms.

Reverse. In Rochdall 1666—His half-peny.

Obverse. Iosva Strengfellow—The Grocers Arms.

Reverse. In Rochdale I. S. (value of a farthing).

The different spellings of the word "Rochdale" upon these tokens is curious.

Milnrow is represented by one token—

Obverse. Richard Milne—An hour glass.

Reverse. Of Milnrow, 1671—His half-penny.

The issue of these tokens was prohibited by Act of Parliament in 1672 ; that they had been issued every year by tradesmen is shown by the two bearing the name of Richard Kenion, one in 1666, and the other in 1667.

The Leper's Inheritance

WHEN William the Conqueror made himself master of England, one of his relatives, Roger de Poictou, already held large possessions in the country—his estates embracing all the tract of country between the Mersey and the Ribble, and extending far into Yorkshire. It was this great lord of Lancaster who built the first castle at Clitheroe.

In the reign of the Conqueror's successor, William Rufus, Roger de Poictou granted the whole of Blackburnshire to Ilbert de Lacy, a Norman knight who had fought at the Battle of Hastings, and, together with this wide tract of country, the "great fee" of Pontefract. A "great fee" under the feudal system was a possession of the highest degree; Clitheroe was an "honour," or "seigniory," and came next in rank. By the grant of Pontefract and Clitheroe and the intervening lands, Ilbert de Lacy thus became one of the most powerful nobles in the North. He had power of life and death, and was overlord of many lords and knights who paid for the tenure of their lands by military service under his banner, which, in his turn, he carried wheresoever his sovereign had need of it.

The castle at Clitheroe had been built by Roger de Poictou on its limestone rock in the fertile plain between the Pendle and the Ribble, more as a temporary retreat, and a defence from the perpetual raids of the wild Borderers, than as a residence; and it was for the protection of the western confines of his vast possessions, as well as for the better maintenance of his dignity that Ilbert de Lacy raised the building, the ruins of which exist to-day. At Pontefract he likewise " builded himself a lordly castle." It was said that the Lacys could ride from their castle at Clitheroe to their castle at Pontefract, a distance of fifty miles, and rest in a house of their own at every stage of the journey.

For four generations the Lacys held these great estates with all the rights and powers of sovereign lords, keeping their state alternately at Pontefract and at Clitheroe. But Clitheroe Castle in their time dominated a very different view from that which may be seen from its ruined walls to-day. " Could a curious observer of the present day," says Dr. Whitaker, writing early in the nineteenth century, " carry himself nine or ten centuries back, and, ranging the summit of Pendle, survey the forked Calder on one side, and the bolder margin of Ribble and Hodder on the other, instead of populous towns and villages, the castle, the old tower-built house, the elegant modern mansion, the artificial plantation, the park and pleasure-ground ; or instead of uninterrupted enclosures, which have driven sterility almost to the summit of the fells ; how great must then have been the contrast, when ranging either at a distance or immediately beneath, his eye must have caught vast tracts of forest ground stagnating with bog or darkened by native woods, where the wild ox, the roe and stag, and the wolf had scarcely learned the supremacy of man—when, directing his view to the intermediate spaces, to the windings of the valleys, or the expanse of plains beneath, he could only have distinguished a few insulated patches of culture, each encircling a village of wretched cabins, among which could still be remarked one rude mansion of wood, scarcely equal in comfort to a modern cottage, yet then rising proudly eminent above the rest, where the Saxon lord, surrounded by his faithful cotari,[1] enjoyed a rude and solitary independence, owning no superior but his sovereign."

Twenty-eight of these Saxon lords had occupied the tract of country which Roger de Poictou granted to the first de Lacy.

In the year that saw Richard Cœur de Lion treacherously made prisoner by the Duke of Austria, whose hospitality he had sought after being shipwrecked on his return from the Holy Land, the family of de Lacy became extinct in the male line, Robert de Lacy, the last of his race, dying childless. His nearest relation was his half-sister Awbrey, the widow of Richard Fitz-Eustace of Halton and Constable of Chester, a nobleman of renown. Her eldest son, John, had been slain before the walls of Tyre in Syria, during the Crusade led by his king, Richard Cœur de Lion. Of John Fitz-Eustace's two sons, Richard was a leper, and the younger, Roger, had followed his father to Palestine, and as no tidings had been received from him since the close of the Crusade he was believed by his grandmother to be dead.

Leprosy, then, and for three hundred years afterwards, was one of the scourges of Europe. The infection of this deadly and loathsome disease was believed to have been brought into this country by the warriors returning from the First Crusade. This belief is supported by the fact that leprosy was unknown in the Roman Republic until Pompey the Great returned from his campaign in Asia. After that period the fell disease is constantly referred to by Roman writers. It is purely an Eastern disease, and as the great Roman Empire fell into decay and the intercourse with its former Asian and Syrian colonies grew less and less, leprosy gradually disap-

[1] Cotari were the tenants who owed personal service to their lord.

peared, and for many hundreds of years it had been unknown in Europe. Its outbreak in Europe after the First Crusade created a widespread horror. There was Biblical authority for the treatment of lepers as laid down in the enactments of Moses, and these, with various modifications, were most rigorously applied. Those whom it attacked, no matter how high a tunic and a large black cloak fastened round the waist by a girdle of leather. Then, kneeling before the altar, the unhappy wretch heard his own funeral service. All the larger towns had houses set apart for lepers, and to one of these the man was conducted by the priest, who, after exhorting him to patience and to suffer in penitence the heavy affliction laid upon

CLITHEROE CASTLE

or how lowly their birth and rank, were instantly cut off from their fellows : they became as if they were dead to their wives, their children, their parents and their family. The great nobleman in his castle, the merchant in his counting-house, the poor peasant in his hovel, each was reduced to the same level of dreadful equality. In some places the leper was taken to the parish church and after divesting himself of his ordinary garments, was clothed in the leper's garb—a shirt, him by the Almighty, cast earth upon his feet to indicate his final and complete severance from all human intercourse. When leprosy seized a man or a woman in remote districts they were driven forth to live where and how they could, but both in the towns and in the country the enactments were the same.

Whenever a leper appeared in public he was compelled to wear the black cloak, carefully concealing his face with the hood ; his feet were bare, and in his hand he carried a wooden clapper, which he sounded ceaselessly to warn people of his approach. He was forbidden to enter churches, mills or bakehouses, and when he went to the markets to buy provisions he could only indicate what he wanted by pointing to it with a long stick he carried, at the end of which was a cup. If he wished to buy ale or wine he could go no farther than the inn door. Lepers were forbidden also to pass through any narrow streets, to reply to any questions put to them by passers-by, and, above all things, not to touch children. Those lepers who were possessed of property when they were stricken, were permitted to use the income from it, but they had no rights over the property itself; they could neither dispose of it by sale, nor by legacy, nor could they inherit. The lepers were civilly dead and were not recognized by the law.

The poor leper depended entirely upon charity, and when his disease prevented him from wandering out into the highways, sounding his clapper as he went, and holding out his cup at the end of his long stick for the alms of the charitable, he died of starvation.

Notwithstanding the strict isolation of the lepers, the disease spread so rapidly that the single houses were abandoned and each town and locality, no matter how sparsely populated, had its lazar-house, where those stricken with the disease were segregated. Here they were supported at the public expense. The lazar-house of London occupied the site upon which now stands St. James's Palace.

Towards the close of the twelfth century, at about the time when Richard Fitz-Eustace was stricken with the malady, leprosy had increased so largely that the Church of Rome instituted a religious order, the Order of St. Lazarus, the members of which vowed themselves to the cure and nursing of lepers. Such vows were heroic, seeing the almost certain chance of infection and ultimate death.

Upon Richard Fitz-Eustace the leper's ban had fallen with all its horror, and in the flower of his age he had passed forth from his ancestral home at Halton in Cheshire, clad in the black robe, barefoot, and sounding the fatal clapper which sent men, women and children hurrying from his approach. Being a leper he could not succeed his father in the Cheshire estates, nor his grandmother Awbrey, Lady Fitz-Eustace, in the wide domains of the Lacys; his heritage consequently devolved upon his younger brother Roger, of whom, as we have seen, no tidings had been heard since he left Palestine.

An aged lady, feeble in health and borne down by the tragedy of her son's death in Palestine, the leprosy of one grandson and the uncertainty as to the fate of the other, therefore, was the heiress to the lordships, the manors, forests and castles of the Lacys on the death of her half-brother Robert de Lacy. Now the Dean of Whalley, a close friend and crony of the late lord of Clitheroe, had grown to believe that he would be left the vast domains upon the death of Robert de Lacy, to whom he was distantly related; and bitter was his disappointment when he found that the aged Lady Awbrey was the heiress.

The Deans of Whalley occupied a curious position which was a combination of the secular and ecclesiastical. The office was hereditary, and continued so until 1215, when priests of the Roman Catholic Church were forbidden to marry. Its holders were at once parson and lord of the manor, and, "like many other ancient and dignified ecclesiastics, they were mighty hunters, enjoying their privileges unmolested through a vast region of forest land then unenclosed, and were only inferior in jurisdiction to the feudal lords of these domains." Dr. Whitaker sums up the position of the Deans of Whalley thus : " On the whole, then, it appears that the Dean of Whalley was compounded of patron, incumbent, ordinary and lord of the manor ; an assemblage which may possibly have been met in later times, and in some places of exempt jurisdiction, but at that time was probably unique in the history of the English Church."

Robert de Lacy was borne to the Abbey of Kirkstall, built by his father, there to be laid in the family vault. The body was carried on a litter slung on a pole between two horses which were covered with a pall and trappings like a bier ; a sword of ceremony was borne, uplifted, in front of the litter ; the mournful procession, headed by the Dean of Whalley and a choir singing dirges, was closed by a priest bearing a cross and censer, and the late baron's servants.

The Dean of Whalley was as unscrupulous as he was ambitious, and even as he rode at the head of his friend's funeral procession he was revolving in his mind how the succession of the Fitz-Eustace family to Clitheroe and the de Lacy possessions might be prevented. Richard must of a necessity be passed over, Roger was either a captive, like the English King Richard Cœur de Lion, or was dead ; there only remained the aged Lady Fitz-Eustace, and in so remote and inaccessible a region, with the country distracted by the king's captivity in Austria, and the plottings of his brother John, a bold seizure of the de Lacy property might easily be effected.

On the steepest side of the hill upon which Clitheroe Castle stands, a hermit had made his dwelling, in a high narrow cell cut out of the solid stone. He was a saintly man known for many miles around as the "Holy Hermit of the Rock." He had dwelt for many years at Clitheroe, coming no one knew whence ; he never spoke of his past life or the reasons that led him to adopt so solitary and austere an existence.

The Holy Hermit of the Rock had enjoyed the full confidence of Robert de Lacy, who, when he felt the hand of death laid heavily upon him, gave into his charge the will which made Lady Fitz-Eustace heiress to the de Lacy domains. This fact was known to the Dean of Whalley, but before he could plan to secure possession of this all-important document from the Hermit, either by force or trickery, he was put to confusion by the arrival at Clitheroe of no less a person than Roger Fitz-Eustace, who was supposed to be dead in Palestine, or languishing in a foreign prison.

This bold Crusader had escaped the perils into which his royal master, Richard Cœur de Lion, had fallen, and arriving at Halton had learnt from his grandmother of the death of Robert de Lacy, and of her inheritance. Forthwith, he had sent out to Clitheroe to take possession of the castle and the de Lacy estates in his aged grandmother's name.

Roger Fitz-Eustace and his train made an imposing procession as they entered the old castle. The knight—who was called " Hell " by the Welsh because of his ferocious temper and the pitilessness with which he treated all prisoners taken in the constant warfare on the Welsh border—" was clothed in a light suit of armour, the hauberk, with the rings set edgewise, reaching down to the knees. His helmet was cylindrical, the *avantaille*, or face-guard, thrown up. He wore a coloured surcoat, a fashion that seems to have originated with the Crusaders, not only for the purpose of distinguishing the different leaders, but as a veil to protect the armour, so apt to heat excessively when exposed to the direct rays of the sun. It was of violet colour, without any distinctive mark or badge. His highly decorated shield was borne behind him . . . its shape was angular, and suspended from the neck by a strap called guige or gige, a Norman custom of great antiquity. A huge broadsword was carried by his armour-bearer, the person of the chief being without any further means of impediment or defence than a French stabbing-sword, fastened on one side of his pommel, and a stout battle-axe on the other. The horse was decorated with great and costly profusion. A small train of archers and crossbowmen brought up the rear of the escort, save the baggage and sumpter horses, laden not only with provisions but cooking utensils, and even with furniture for the household. In those days it was a matter both of economy and necessity for the occupants or lords of several castles to travel with accompaniments of this sort; though possessing many residences, most of them had the means and even conveniences only for the furnishing of one."

Although the unlooked-for appearance of Roger Fitz-Eustace made it impossible for the Dean of Whalley to carry out his project of forcibly entering into possession of Clitheroe Castle, he did not abandon hope of securing the prize he coveted. Shortly before the Fitz-Eustace's coming was announced he had attempted to obtain possession of Robert de Lacy's will from the Hermit of the Rock, but in this attempt he had been baffled by the holy man. The Hermit knew the contents of the will which was in his possession and which he would place in Roger Fitz-Eustace's hands. With diabolical ingenuity, therefore, the Dean conceived a plan which would at once rid him of the Her-

mit and his testimony, and make himself master of the castle and the property. He prepared a document purporting to be signed by Robert de Lacy, in which he, the Dean of Whalley, and his heirs for ever, were bequeathed the vast de Lacy possessions. Within a few hours of Fitz-Eustace's arrival at the castle, the Dean prepared the way by warning him that the Hermit was a traitor, and that although Robert de Lacy had given him his will for safe-keeping because of his holiness, it was the Hermit's intention to suppress the document, and, by fraud and subtlety, throw the de Lacy property into the treasury of the Church, and build a great abbey at Clitheroe.

Now the Hermit himself had caused a copy of Robert de Lacy's will to be sent to Lady Fitz-Eustace, and her grandson therefore knew the terms of the bequest, and, angered beyond measure by what appeared to be a deliberate usurpation of his rights, he commanded the Hermit to be brought before him, and confronted him with the Dean.

Immediately the holy man appeared the Dean besought Fitz-Eustace to have him bound, as he possessed magical powers, and unless held by main force would escape. At a sign from their lord the guards surrounded the Hermit, but, with a strength unbelievable in his emaciated figure, he seized their leader and hurled him to the ground.

Magic and the black arts were the only explanation of such a feat to the superstitious mind of the knight, and, moved by fear as much as by anger at this contempt for his authority, he commanded the guards, on pain of being hanged, to seize the Hermit. In the face of such a threat the men dared not hesitate and, rushing upon the Hermit in a body, they seized and pinioned him before he could make any resistance. At the same moment the Dean of Whalley snatched a roll of parchment, hidden in the folds of the Hermit's cloak, and hastily thrust it it at once to him, the Dean had concealed it in his own robe. With many apologies, and explaining that he acted thus for fear

"'I AM RICHARD FITZ-EUSTACE, THINE ELDER BROTHER!'"

within his own. There was no concealment in the action, and Fitz-Eustace, knowing that it was the will of Robert de Lacy the Dean had thus wrested from the Hermit, vented his displeasure in no measured terms, because, instead of handing the will should be spirited away by the magic and subtlety of the Hermit, the cunning Dean produced what appeared to be the parchment he had a moment before concealed. But it was the false will he handed to Fitz-Eustace, whose consternation as he read it knew no bounds : in place of Lady Fitz-Eustace and her heirs, the vast possessions of Robert de Lacy were left to the Dean of Whalley and his heirs for ever.

Vainly the Hermit protested the will was false, demanding that the Dean should be searched. Fitz-Eustace accepted the forged will as genuine and, taking advantage of this belief, the Dean immediately assumed all the rights of possession.

"Your ear and mine have been too long abused," he cried to Fitz-Eustace, "by this plotting wizard. He is now subject to my authority. Hereby I do assume my rights, and arraign the culprit before my tribunal ! "

He was about to take his place beside Fitz-Eustace on the dais in the great hall when the Hermit, with a sudden movement, broke free from the guards and threw himself upon the villainous churchman, and whilst with one hand he held him tightly by the throat, with the other he tore open his robe, disclosing a second parchment roll craftily hidden in its inner folds.

This parchment the Hermit gave to Fitz-Eustace, who, unrolling it, found it to be the original of the copy of Robert de Lacy's will which his grandmother had shown him at Halton.

With amazing effrontery and audacity the Dean had changed the two documents in Fitz-Eustace's own presence. The knight, beside himself with rage and fury at the base attempt to deprive him of the de Lacy bequest, commanded that the Dean should instantly be hanged. The guards were about to carry out his order when the Hermit interposed, saying that he had promised the Dean protection, and that his promise could not be foregone : the Dean should not be put to death.

Fitz-Eustace, scarcely able to credit so open a contempt for his authority, demanded by what right the Hermit imposed his will upon him. Thus the hermit made answer—

"I was an outcast, though heir to a vast heritage. I vowed that if He, whose prerogative it is, should cleanse me from my stains, my life should thenceforth be His, and consecrate to heaven. I was a leper, but my prayer was heard. I washed in yonder holy well which gushes from the rock, whose virtues had been reported to me. Washing daily, with faith and prayer, I was healed. I found, close by, a convenient hermitage ; and many caverns and secret chambers with hidden passages and communications, have been dug therefrom, by which I could pass to and fro, and thus visit the castle unseen. I was the confessor and companion of Robert de Lacy. At my desire he left the whole of his domains to the Fitz-Eustaces. But thou art not the eldest born of thy father."

The startled knight answered that his elder brother was dead, that he had been a leper, whereupon the Hermit, throwing off his cloak, showed himself clad in a complete suit of armour covered by a surcoat on which was emblazoned the crest of the Fitz-Eustaces.

"I am Richard Fitz-Eustace, thine elder brother," he cried. Then, saying that although healed he did not claim his birthright—the vows of heaven being upon him—one right only he demanded, and this was to free the trembling and terrified Dean, who, when he had first come to Clitheroe, sick of his terrible malady, had sheltered and fed him. "Moreover," the Hermit said, " he had some well-founded expectancy to these domains, by reason of kindred to the Lacys, had they not been devised by will to the Fitz-Eustace. His blood is noble as our own. He thinks there is injustice in the deed, but not to him shall the atonement come."

In order that the rankling wound might be healed, the Hermit urged that Roger de Fitz-Eustace's daughter and Geoffrey de Whalley, the Dean's son, should marry, and with this admonition, and repulsing all his brother's advances, he left the castle. He retired to his cell and died shortly afterwards, worn out by fasts and vigils.

The marriage between Geoffrey de Whalley, the Dean's son, and Maud Fitz-Eustace took place as the Hermit had advised—Fitz-Eustace giving his daughter the manors of Townley, Coldcoats and Snodworth as a marriage portion. From this union is descended the famous Lancashire family of the Townleys of Townley.

HAND=LOOM *v.* POWER=LOOM

The introduction of weaving by machinery was bitterly resented by the majority of the workers, and the following song had a great vogue at the time.

COME all you cotton-weavers, your
    looms you may pull down,
    You must get employed in factories,
    in country or in town,
For our cotton-masters have found out a
    wonderful new scheme,
Those calico goods now wove by hand,
    they're going to weave by steam.

In comes the gruff o'erlooker, or the master
    will attend ;
It's " You must find another shop, or quickly
    you must mend ;
For such work as this will never do ; so now
    I'll tell you plain,
We must have good pincop-spinning, or we
    ne'er can weave by steam."

There's sow-makers and drapers, and some
    are making warps ;
These poor pincop-spinners they must mind
    their flats and sharps ;
For if an end slips under, as sometimes
    perchance it may,
They'll daub you down in black and white,
    and you've a shilling to pay.

In comes the surly winder, her cops they
    are all marr'd ;
" They are all snarls, and soft, bad ends ;
    for I've roved off many a yard ;
I'm sure I'll tell the master, or the joss,
    when he comes in : "
They'll daub you down, and you must pay ;
    —so money comes rolling in.

The weavers' turn will next come on, for
    they must not escape,
To enlarge the master's fortunes they are
    fined in every shape.
For thin places, or bad edges, a go, or
    else a float,
They'll daub you down, and you must pay
    threepence or else a groat.

If you go into a loom-shop, where's three
    or four pairs of looms,
They are all standing empty, incumbrances
    of the rooms ;
And if you ask the reason why, the old
    mother will tell you plain,
My daughters have forsaken them, and gone
    to weave by steam.

So come all you cotton-weavers, you must
    rise up very soon,
For you must work in factories from morning
    until noon :
You mustn't walk in your garden for two or
    three hours a day,
For you must start at their command, and
    keep your shuttle in play.

A Manor for a Murder

DURING the troublous days when the Barons of England were fighting Henry III. for the liberties of the English people, and later, when the Houses of Lancaster and York were fighting each other for the English crown, there was nothing to prevent a man who had a grudge against his neighbour from satisfying that grudge by force. He could arm his servants and retainers, call up his friends, and attack his enemy's house with the knowledge that he would be safe from all pursuit by the law. His neighbour could retaliate with an equal certainty that he could not be called upon to answer for his aggression. The authorities were so busily occupied, either in defending their own positions and lives, or in ousting the rival faction, that they had no time to spare for the consideration of the grievances of private individuals, consequently might became right.

There are many instances of sanguinary affrays between Lancashire gentlemen in those days. Houses were pillaged, men were killed; yet no one was punished. Under the rule of Henry VII. such aggressions were punished with all the severity of the law. But this severity did not arise from Henry's sense of justice, or any regard to the safety of his subjects. The ruling passion of his life was avarice; the leading policy of his reign was to break the power of the nobility and the landed gentry. When they broke the law they were heavily fined, a large portion of the money going directly into the king's pocket. At one stroke, therefore, Henry satisfied his all-absorbing passion and carried out his policy, for the fines were so crushing that the transgressors were often compelled to sell their estates in order to pay them. His successor, Henry VIII., treated affrays and fights between the country gentry with the same severity, but from a different cause. The separation of England from the Church of Rome under this monarch introduced a religious significance into all party and private strife. Henry VIII. made it law that if a man—no matter how tried and loyal a subject—acknowledged the supremacy of the Pope—he was the king's enemy. Suspicious and supremely crafty, Henry was always ready to suspect danger to himself or defiance of his authority, and many a hot-blooded gentleman seeking to avenge an insult or a wrong according to the manners of the time, that is by force, found himself involved in a far more serious matter than a breach of the peace. If his answers with regard to the king's supremacy over the Pope were not considered satisfactory, his lands could be confiscated, and he himself executed as a traitor ; and, on the other hand, his assembling of an armed force, no matter how small, could be construed into a direct offence against the king, with whom alone was vested the right to call men to arms.

Bearing in mind the repression of private feuds by these two kings and the many salutary lessons that were given to county gentlemen who took the law into their own hands in the succeeding reigns, especially during that of Queen Elizabeth, a fatal affray which took place at Leigh, near Preston, in 1589, between Richard Hoghton, of Hoghton Tower, and Thomas Langton, baron of Newton, throws a vivid light upon the " good old days."

Richard Hoghton in 1589 was not living at his beautiful paternal home, Hoghton Tower, but at a smaller house called Leigh, near Preston. For some unknown reason there was a bitter quarrel between him and his neighbour Thomas Langton, baron of Newton, who lived at Boughton Tower. There is evidence to show that the quarrel was of long standing and that friends and neighbours were called upon to take sides. The passage of time, in place of softening the two men, only added to their mutual bitterness. No opportunity, however petty, was lost on either side to aggravate, to thwart or annoy. Both men were of ancient family, and of high position in the county ; opportunity, therefore, was not lacking for the expression of their antagonism. The quarrel involved most of the families in the neighbourhood—to be the friend of Hoghton meant being the enemy of Langton ; the friends of Langton scoffed openly at Hoghton. It was a grievous situation, and so bitter and incensed were both the men that neither would listen to the peace-making proposals of many of their friends. So violent a quarrel was bound to have a crisis, and

the crisis, with its tragic result, was brought about by a woman.

Mrs. Singleton, who was a daughter of Roger Anderton, the representative of an old Lancashire family, was a neighbour of the two enemies. She had been left a widow in August 1589, and Langton, an old friend of her husband, had taken her under his special protection, helping her in the management of her estate, and in the settlement of her husband's affairs. In the following November, Hoghton suddenly seized some of Mrs. Singleton's cattle and drove them away to his house at Leigh. Whether he had a claim upon the dead man's estate, or whether he was actuated by spite against Langton is not recorded ; all that is known is that he seized the cattle and impounded them in the courtyard of his house. Mrs. Singleton, who was clearly a woman of character and decision, as will be shown later, mounted her palfrey and sped to Boughton Tower. Her story of the theft roused her dead husband's friend to fury, and he instantly called his supporters together. These, to the number of eighty, assembled on Preston Marsh at 11 o'clock on the night of November 21, 1589, armed with pikes, guns, hedging bills fixed to long staves, swords and daggers. Langton gave his small army a watchword, " The crow is black," and dividing it into two companies, set out for Leigh, Mrs. Singleton leading one company, he himself the other. No secret was apparently made of the reason for this gathering together of armed men, for early in the evening news reached Hoghton that an attack was intended upon his house. He therefore hastily armed his servants, some thirty in all, with all the weapons at his disposal— a curious collection. Besides staves, there was, " 1 pike, 1 gun charged with haile-shotte, 2 pistols, 1 bow and arrow, swords and daggers."

When the attacking party reached Leigh the company led by Langton broke down the entrance gate, whilst the other, under immediately sallied forth with his thirty men. In a moment the two armed bands were in the midst of a fierce and bloody

" HOGHTON DID NOT SUBMIT QUIETLY "

the intrepid Mrs. Singleton's direction, broke down a paling and a hedge and endeavoured to drive off the stolen cattle. Hoghton did not submit quietly to this breaking down of his gate and hedges, but encounter. There was no light save that given by the horn lanterns carried by some of Langton's people, and these were speedily extinguished in the fray, but they cut and slashed at one another in the dark, Langton and Mrs. Singleton's men incessantly calling out their watchword, "The crow is black!" to which the Hoghton men replied, "No, it is white!" So bitter was the rancour between the two parties that neither side would give way, and the shooting, hacking and stabbing went on, accompanied by the wild shouts of men and the screams of women, until Hoghton and one of his servants lay dead upon the ground, and Langton was so severely wounded that he had to be carried to his home. Others of the combatants also suffered, and it was said that some of the servants bore marks of the encounter to the day of their death.

In the thirty-second year of Elizabeth's reign so flagrant a transgression of the law, and its fatal results, could not pass unnoticed. Langton was arrested in his bed at Boughton Tower, and although suffering from his wounds, was carried off to prison, Mrs. Singleton and others concerned sharing the same fate. One would expect to hear that an exemplary sentence for manslaughter and aggression was the conclusion of the story, but the case could not be tried because no jury could be impanelled. Thomas Langton was evidently a man of wide influence, and one whose vengeance was feared, for a jury could not be got together. There was considerable correspondence between the authorities in London and the authorities in Lancashire, but the fact remained that Langton and his accomplices could not be tried for lack of a jury. This unusual situation, after continuing for some time, was finally settled in a manner that is amazing to the modern mind. Langton offered the rich manor of Walton, "one of his best estates," to the Hoghton family, and the offer was accepted!

It is probable that the aggressive Langton realized that sooner or later the authorities would succeed in impanelling a jury, in which case Mrs. Hoghton and her son would appear as prosecutors. If they did not appear there would be no trial: it was therefore wiser to lose the manor of Walton than "abide the uncertain issue of a verdict." The Hoghtons, on their side, may have justly agreed that, seeing the number of times the authorities had failed to impanel a jury, there was every prospect of Langton going unpunished, and that the addition of a rich manor to their property was more satisfactory to them than any punishment meted out to Langton by the law.

THE SCULLION KING

THE Peel of Fouldrey, the now ruined castle upon the Isle of Walney, once sheltered within its walls a baker's son who, for a month, bore the title of King of England.

When Henry VII. defeated Richard III. drowned in the Tower in a butt of Malmsey wine, it was believed, at the instigation of Richard III., and his son was the next male heir of the Yorkist line. His claim was so clear and so paramount that for safety's sake Henry shut the boy up

THE PEEL OF FOULDREY

at the Battle of Bosworth, and Sir William Stanley placed the crown taken from the dead Richard's helmet upon his head, there was a child living (the Earl of Warwick, son of the Duke of Clarence, brother of Edward IV., and Richard III.), who, by many, was considered to have a juster claim to the throne than the Tudor Henry.

The Duke of Clarence had been in the Tower of London. Although the mysterious disappearance of the two sons of Edward IV.—the Prince of Wales and the Duke of York—had enabled Richard III., to usurp the throne, there was a widespread belief that they had not been murdered, and that both were still alive. It was upon this belief that an ambitious and unscrupulous priest named Richard Simon founded a consummately skilful plan to drive Henry from the throne, and gain great honours and rewards for himself. In carrying out this plan he used as his tool a youth called Lambert Simnel. The parentage of this youth is unknown, but "Simnel" is supposed to be a nickname because of his father's trade as a baker; other accounts fix the father's trade as that of a carpenter, but whatever his occupation he was a man of humble position. His son was described as a "comely youth and well favoured, not without some extraordinary dignity and grace of aspect." The priest Simon conceived the idea of passing off Lambert Simnel as one of the sons of Edward IV., believed to have been murdered in the Tower by their uncle Richard, "and thereby securing an archbishopric for himself." But so gigantic an imposture could not be carried out without money, and Simon undoubtedly received the support of Queen Elizabeth Woodville, the mother of the murdered princes, and now mother-in-law to Henry VII.; the Earl of Lincoln, who was the cousin of the dead boys; and Lord Lovell, one of the foremost of the Yorkist leaders.

Simon was so astute that he knew his imposture would be instantly detected if he produced this workman's son as either the Prince of Wales or the Duke of York, therefore, in order to fit him for the part of a royal prince, he took Lambert Simnel to Oxford to be educated. Great care was devoted to his manners and deportment as well as to his education, with the result that, as we have seen, the chronicler remarked upon his " extraordinary dignity and grace of aspect."

Apparently Simon and his fellow plotters had not decided which of the two princes Simnel should personate, for late in 1486, when a report ran through the country that the Duke of Clarence's son,

the Earl of Warwick, had escaped from his close confinement in the Tower of London, Simon entirely altered his plans and took Lambert Simnel to Ireland, where he publicly declared him to be the Earl of Warwick, whose life he had saved by effecting his escape.

Ireland was a stronghold of the Yorkists, and so complete was Simon's tale, and so fully was it borne out by Lambert Simnel, whose appearance and manner deeply impressed the Irish, that Gerald Fitzgerald, the Earl of Kildare, the King's Deputy for Ireland, was persuaded of the genuineness of his claim. Sir Thomas Fitzgerald, the Lord Chancellor of Ireland, the Archbishop of Dublin and all the other prelates, high officials and great noblemen, followed his example, and believing Simnel to be the rightful Earl of Warwick and the nephew of Edward IV. and Richard III., declared themselves in his favour. There was only one dissentient voice, that of the Archbishop of Armagh.

The great news was instantly communicated to the adherents of the Yorkist cause, both in England and abroad. Edward IV.'s sister, " Margaret the Bold," Duchess of Burgundy, openly acknowledged the impostor as her nephew, and persuaded her son-in-law, Maximilian, the King of the Romans, to send fifteen hundred German soldiers under a noted leader, called Martin Schwarz, to Ireland to support his claim to the English throne.

Yorkists flocked to Dublin from all parts of England and Ireland, and Simon's hopes must have run high as he saw the instant success of his imposture.

Meanwhile, word of the proclamation of the supposed Earl of Warwick in Dublin, of his public recognition by the Duchess of Burgundy, and the armed force that was gathering to his standard, reached London. By taking the real Earl of Warwick from the Tower and parading him on horseback through the streets, Henry VII. thought the imposture would be exposed, but Simon accused the King of showing a false Earl of Warwick to the people, and consummated his audacity by causing Lambert Simnel to be crowned at the Cathedral at Dublin as Edward VI., with a diadem taken from an image of the Virgin. Coins were struck bearing the effigy of the new king, and proclamations were made in his name.

Enthusiasm ran high throughout Ireland, " the countenance thus unexpectedly given to the rebellion by persons of the highest rank, and the great accession of military force from abroad, raised the courage and exultation of the Irish to such a pitch that they threatened to overrun England, nothing doubting but their restless and disaffected spirit would be fully met by a similar disposition on the part of those whom they invaded." With this hope Lambert Simnel and his army set sail on June 4, 1487, for Lancashire, landing on the Isle of Walney and taking possession of the Peel of Fouldrey, which then belonged to the Abbey of Furness. Here the mock king installed himself, Simon and the leaders of the expedition believing that the Lancashire gentlemen would flock to his standard. But they were doomed to disappointment.

Built in the reign of Edward III. by the monks of Furness Abbey for a place of safe retreat against the ravages and attacks of the Scots, the Peel of Fouldrey has never before or since witnessed such a scene as that which marked Lambert Simnel's residence within its walls.

"The narrow bay by the island was glittering with gallant streamers. Ships of war, in all their pride and panoply, majestically reposed on its bosom. All was bustle and impatience. The trumpet note of war brayed fiercely from the battlements. Incessant was the march of troops in various directions. Tents were pitched before the castle. Guards were appointed ; and this hitherto peaceful and solitary spot resounded with the din of arms and the hoarse clang of preparation for the approaching strife. Messengers were constantly passing to and fro from the mainland. The insignia of royalty were ostentatiously displayed, and the captains and leaders within the fortress fulfilled the duties of this mimic and motley court in honour of their anticipated sovereign."

Lambert Simnel was treated with all the honours of a king, even by the Earl of Lincoln, another nephew of Edward IV. and Richard III., and whom the latter had chosen as his heir. Every royal ceremony was duly observed, although the baker's boy's kingdom consisted of only a few acres, and his palace was " an ugly, ill-contrived castle."

The mock king is described as possessing considerable self-possession, and wearing his regal honours with great assurance, but he was entirely under the domination of the priest Simon.

In landing in Lancashire, however, the Earl of Kildare and the other leaders had made a great mistake. They had supposed that the inhabitants of the north of England, and especially of the great county palatine, would immediately join them, but Lancashire was heart and soul against the Yorkist cause, as had been proved throughout the Wars of the Roses. Henry VII., by crushing out the power of the hated Yorkist party, had made himself popular in Lancashire, nor was it likely that, after giving hundreds of lives and spending enormous treasure in support of the House of Lancaster, the nobility and gentlemen of the county would join a rebellion the object of which was to place a member of the hated House of York upon the throne.

Messengers were dispatched in all directions, but their journeys were fruitless. Lambert Simnel, with his German mercenaries and wild Irish soldiers, remained at Fouldrey waiting in vain. The Abbot of Furness, who owned large tracts of country and could call many men to arms, was approached, but his only answer was to demand by what right his castle of Fouldrey had been forcibly occupied; and out of all Lancashire only one knight, Sir Thomas Broughton, a man of some position in Furness, joined the rebel standard. Thus disappointed in their hopes of Lancashire support, the leaders decided to evacuate the Peel of Fouldrey, and, marching to Swartz Moor, close to Ulverstone, encamped there to await the hoped-for reinforcements from Yorkshire.

But again their hopes were vain, and finally, finding that unless they moved southward their men would be without means of subsistence, the rebel leaders took their German and Irish soldiers southwards, plundering the country-folk on the way, until they reached Newark, where they encountered the army sent against them by Henry.

Simon, and the Earls of Kildare and Lincoln, knowing the fate that would befall them in the event of defeat, were resolved to conquer or to die, and animated their followers with the same spirit. For over three hours the battle waged furiously, the grim obstinacy of Martin Schwarz and his German soldiers again and again checking the onrush of the royal troops. At times it seemed as if the rebels must be the victors, but they were outnumbered. One by one the Earl of Lincoln, Martin Schwarz, Sir Thomas Broughton, and their other leaders were slain, and finally, after a horrible carnage in which four thousand of the rebel soldiers and nearly as many of the royal troops were killed, Lambert Simnel's imposture was for ever swept away.

Both he and the priest Simon were taken prisoners and carried to London. Henry seems to have realized that so young a man could have only been a tool in the hands of others, and whilst Simon was condemned to imprisonment for life, Lambert Simnel was made a scullion in the King's kitchen, in order to show, so it was said, the Duchess of Burgundy that Henry was so securely placed on her brother's throne that he could treat all attempts to displace him with contempt.

One cannot help conjecturing upon the life led by Lambert Simnel as a scullion in the royal kitchen. He must have been made a butt for the coarse wit of the many servants and retainers that in those days thronged a royal household. Since he had aspired to the royal throne and had only succeeded in reaching the royal kitchen, it is scarcely possible, human nature being the same in every age, that he would be left to bear his ignominy in silence. But freed from the domination of the priest Simon, Lambert Simnel appears to have taken his fate philosophically, and to have performed his menial duties so well that in course of time he was removed from the kitchen and given the post of falconer to the King. From the royal service Simnel passed into that of Sir Thomas Lovell, a person of consequence about the Court, and apparently reached a higher degree by the change, for amongst those who attended Sir Thomas's funeral in 1525 was "Lambert Symnell, yeoman."

Such was the ending of an imposture of which the Peel of Fouldrey saw the beginning. One wonders if Lambert Simnel ever married, and if in his old age he recounted the marvellous adventures of his youth to his children—how he, the baker's son, had for a brief space been acknowledged Earl of Warwick, and King of England; how coinage had been struck in Ireland bearing his image, the first time in history that the features of a baker's son have appeared as those of a reigning sovereign. Whether he kept silence concerning the imposture of his youth or related the story of his royal state at Dublin and at Fouldrey, Lambert Simnel must have congratulated himself on the contempt that made him a royal scullion when, a few years after the exposure of his own imposture, Perkin Warbeck, who declared that he was the Duke of York, and led an army against Henry, was captured in the New Forest and ignominiously hanged at Tyburn.

DURING a visit to a parish in the district of Oldham a bishop was shown over the parish school. In one of the rooms a scripture lesson was being given, the subject being Jacob's dream of the ladder and the angels. The bishop was much interested, and taking the Bible from the teacher himself continued the lesson. When the chapter was finished he asked if the children would like to ask him any questions on what they had been reading.

Up went a little boy's hand. "Please, sir, have angels wings?"

"Yes, all angels have wings," the bishop answered.

"Then why did they go up t' ladder?" the boy asked. "Why didn't they fly?"

The bishop, utterly at a loss for an answer, could only say that stories in the Bible must always be accepted as they were written. His answer clearly did not satisfy the children, for one little girl said, "I know, sir, why them angels didn't fly. They must ha' be i't mowt (moult)!"

THE Battle of PRESTON

THE BATTLE OF PRESTON

WHEN the Revolution of 1688 drove James II. from the English throne, and his daughter Mary, with her husband, William, Prince of Orange, were made joint sovereigns in his stead, there were many people who regarded them as usurpers. James had been dispossessed of the Crown because of his tyranny, and because he had tried to force Roman Catholicism—to which he had become a convert in the lifetime of his brother Charles II.—upon the nation. Mary was his eldest daughter, and both she and her husband were Protestants, hence their selection as King and Queen in place of James's son, born of his second marriage, and who, like his father and mother, was a Roman Catholic.

James II., although he fled to France on hearing of the landing of his son-in-law at Torbay in Devonshire, did not relinquish his crown without a struggle, and both in Scotland and Ireland a desperate fight was made for the Stuart cause. James himself crossed from France, where he had been given shelter by Louis XIV., and landed in Ireland, but the failure of the siege of Derry, which withstood his army for one hundred and five days, the garrison during that time being reduced from seven thousand to three thousand, and his utter rout and defeat at the Battle of the Boyne, only served to place his daughter and her husband more securely on the throne.

Queen Mary II. died of smallpox in 1694, and William III. then reigned alone until his death in 1702. Throughout all these years James II. intrigued ceaselessly, and gradually the Jacobites, as his supporters were called, increased in numbers. James's agents were continually passing to and fro between France and England bearing letters and instructions from the dethroned monarch to his adherents, especially in Lancashire, where the old Roman Catholic families were Jacobite to a man. The endless plots and schemes for the restoration of the ex-king received a strong impetus by the indignation, which ran like wild-fire through the ranks of the Jacobites, when the succession to the throne was arranged in 1701 by an Act of Parliament, called the Act of Settlement.

William and Mary were childless, and it had therefore been decided that upon the death of the survivor the Princess Anne, Mary's younger sister, who was also a Protestant, should succeed. Anne was married to Prince George of Denmark, and had many children. But one after another these children died — a Divine punishment the Jacobites declared for Anne's "unfilial" behaviour to her father—and in 1701 it became evident that upon her death there would be no direct heir to the throne, the heir in point of birth, James II.'s son and Anne's half-brother, being debarred because of his religion. The next heir in blood relationship was Anne's cousin the Duchess of Savoy, the daughter of Henrietta, Duchess of Orleans, who was the sister of Charles II. and James II. But here again the fact that the Duchess of Savoy was a Roman Catholic made her succession to the Crown of England illegal, and Parliament therefore had to go back to an earlier generation of the Stuart family in order to find a Protestant heir. That most unfortunate Princess, Elizabeth, daughter of James I., and sister to Charles I., had married the Elector Palatine of the Rhine, who for a short space of time had been King of Bohemia. In England Elizabeth had always been extremely popular and was known as the "Winter Queen," because of her husband's brief reign at Prague. One of her daughters, Sophia, had married the Elector of Hanover, and being a firm Protestant, as was her mother before her, she and her heirs were declared the successors to the throne of England by the Act of Settlement.

James II. died in the same year, and Louis XIV. of France immediately recognized his son as James III. of England, contemptuously disregarding the Act of the English Parliament. In the following year Anne became Queen.

It was always believed that she favoured the succession of her half-brother James, and regarded her second cousin, the Electress Sophia, with no favourable eye, and that but for the Act of Settlement she would have declared James to be her heir. When she lay dying, in 1714, a plot was set on foot to proclaim the young man as king, but it failed, and the Electress Sophia of Hanover being dead, her son George became King George I. of England, and the Protestant succession was assured.

It was now that the plots, and schemes, and intrigues, which had been spreading like a net all over England and Scotland during the reigns of William and Mary and of Anne, took definite shape. Misled by the strong feeling for the Stuart cause in Scotland and the north of England, the leading Jacobites were convinced that only a signal was needed and the whole country would rise and drive the Hanoverians back to Germany. There was certainly some reason for the mistake they made. Even careful people openly expressed Jacobite sympathies, and the practice amongst the nobility and upper classes of passing the wine-glass over a finger-bowl full of water before the toast of "The King" was drunk, to signify that it was not the ·Hanoverian George who was being toasted, but the "King over the Water," the Stuart James, became so prevalent, that it was actually done in King George's own presence. From this insult arose the custom which is still observed to-day, of finger-bowls only being provided for the King and Queen, or any member of the Royal family, at any meal at which they may be present, and for none of the other guests.

Night after night King George must have heard the ballad singers under the very walls of St. James's Palace itself, singing songs in favour of the young Stuart exile, and, if he could have understood their words, would scarcely have echoed such sentiments as this—

"The man in the moon may wear out his shoon
    By running after King Charles's Wain ;
But all to no end, for the times will not mend
    Till the King enjoys his own again."

But the women were the strongest ad-herents to the Stuart cause. The romance of their exiled life, the contrast between the personality of King James III., as the Jacobites styled him (the Hanoverians called him the Old Pretender), and that of the phlegmatic George I., who did not speak or understand the language of the people he had been called upon to reign over, appealed most strongly to the feminine imagination, and there were many men whose judgment was entirely overcome by the enthusiasm of their womenkind for the Stuarts and their cause. One old Scotch lady declared that she would drink the health of James III. of England and Eighth of Scotland in the presence of a number of devoted Hanoverians. Her friends did their utmost to dissuade her, as the consequences of an open avowal were serious and she ran the risk of being haled before the justices. But she was not to be deterred, and, rising, gave this text of Scripture, and the reference to it—

"'The tongue no man can tame,' James iii. and 8 "; then she drained her glass.

George I. was crowned in October 1714, but although there was no disturbance in London, there were serious riots at Bristol, and in other towns of importance, which incited the Jacobites to further efforts and to make definite plans for a rising. The Earl of Mar, who had been Secretary of State to Queen Anne, believing the statements of the Jacobite leaders, hastened to Braemar, his Scottish property, and called together the Chieftains of the Clans. With fervid eloquence he urged them to rise against the Hanoverian King and restore the banished Stuarts. Wild enthusiasm was roused by his appeal, and forthwith the Earl raised the Stuart standard and sent forth the fiery cross—a summons to war that no Highlander dared disregard, for refusal to obey meant death by the sword and the burning of his home.

Meanwhile, Lord Widdrington, a Roman Catholic nobleman of Northumberland, who was closely related by marriage with the Towneleys of Lancashire, had gone to Manchester in order to gain adherents to the Stuart cause. At that time there were scores of the younger sons of the Lancashire gentry in Manchester, "apprentices" to the trade of cotton-spinning. Their fathers and grandfathers had fought for King Charles I. in his war with the Lancashire there would be a general insurrection of at least twenty thousand men."

At the same time that the Earl of Mar was raising the Stuart standard in Scotland, preparations for a rising were being made in Northumberland, and on October 6, 1715, the Earl of Derwentwater, Lord Widdrington and Mr. Thomas Foster, the member of Parliament for the county, collected their adherents and

THE NORTH EAST PROS- - PECT OF LANCASTER.

Parliament, and as a result estates and fortunes were so much reduced that no provision could be made for cadet members of the county families, and they were therefore compelled to seek a livelihood in commerce. But these young men brought with them to Manchester from the ancestral halls of their families an inherited loyalty to the House of Stuart. The righteousness of the Stuart claim to the throne was an inheritance of their blood. Lord Widdrington, therefore, met with an enthusiastic welcome and was assured "that immediately upon the Scottish force making its appearance in marched to Kelso, where they joined a detachment of Lord Mar's army. Foster was chosen General of the Jacobite forces, not because of his military capacity, but because both Lord Derwentwater and Lord Widdrington were Roman Catholics, and it was feared that if either were appointed the leader, Protestant susceptibilities might be hurt, especially as George I. had issued the following proclamation—

"The endeavouring to persuade my people that the Church of England is in danger under my government, has been the main cause of the artifice employed in carrying this wicked and traitorous design (the insurrection). This insinuation after the solemn assurances I have given, and my having laid hold on all opportunities to do everything that may tend to the advantage of the Church of England, is both unjust and ungrateful ; nor can I believe so groundless and malicious a calumny can make any impression upon the minds of my faithful subjects, as that they can be so far misled, as to think the Church of England is to be secured by setting a Popish Pretender on the throne."

By way of Penrith, Appleby, Kendal and Kirby Londsdale, the Jacobite army marched to Lancaster which they entered on November 7, with swords drawn, drums beating, banners flying and the bagpipes screaming forth wild music of triumph. Before he reached the county town, General Foster had been informed that the majority of the inhabitants, notwithstanding the fact that the Mayor and Corporation five months previously had sent King George an address of loyalty to the throne and to the Hanoverian succession, were only anxious to be on the side of the stronger, but their difficulty was to know which of the two— Jacobite or Hanoverian—would prove the stronger. On the other hand many of the leading families outside the town were ardent supporters of James III. This proved to be correct.

When the news came of the advance of the Jacobite army upon Lancaster, Sir Henry Hoghton, of Hoghton Tower, who was a strong Hanoverian and was in command of the forces in North Lancashire, hastily collected five or six hundred of the militia and placed them in the town ; he was joined by Colonel Charteris of Hornby Castle, a man of evil repute, whose story

will be found elsewhere in these pages. Sir Henry and Charteris, together with the chief inhabitants, held a Council of War. Their chief concern was a ship, then lying [in the Lune, belonging to a Quaker merchant of Lancaster, called Lawson, and upon board of which were six cannon and some small arms. Since these weapons would form a rich booty for the Jacobites, Sir Henry Hoghton offered to buy them, but Mr. Lawson declined to sell unless he received a bond for ten thousand pounds to cover him against any damage that might be sustained by the ship, in case the Jacobites heard he had sold the cannon to be used against them. Sir Henry refused to give the bond, and called another Council of War, at which he, Colonel Charteris, and a third magistrate, issued a warrant and seized not only the guns but the cargo of the vessel. Urgent messages had been sent to Preston for soldiers to help the militia in the defence of the town, and each day Sir Henry expected their arrival. But the Jacobite army approached nearer and nearer, and no dragoons appearing, Sir Henry was obliged to abandon both Lancaster and commandeered guns, and retire with his militia from the town. Before he left, however, he ordered Mr. Lawson to moor his ship out of the reach of the Jacobites—an order that was not obeyed.

Colonel Charteris and another officer suggested that the bridge should be blown up before the militia retired, in order to prevent the Jacobites from entering the town. The pavement on the north side had already been torn up, when it was pointed out that the trouble was useless, for the river could easily be forded a little below the bridge at low water. So the bridge was left undemolished.

Immediately the Jacobite Army had

entered Lancaster the leaders proceeded by way of Bridge Lane and China Lane to the Market Square where King James III. was proclaimed as "the lawful Sovereign of these realms." When the fanfare of trumpets and the acclamations of the troops had ended, General Foster ordered the arrest of a stationer called Christopher Hopkins, who had been seen numbering the Jacobite Army as it defiled past his shop. But Hopkins had had time to communicate with a friend of his, one Ralph Farebrother, and when he was arrested, Farebrother was already on his way to Newcastle carrying the total number of the Jacobite forces to the Hanoverian general, Carpenter.

Then came the reception of the Jacobite gentlemen who had hastened to Lancaster to place their swords at General Foster's disposal. Albert Hodgson came from Leighton Hall, the old home of the Middleton family, the last heir of which had fought for Charles I. Leighton Hall had descended through his daughter to his grand-daughter, who had married Albert Hodgson. From Borwick Hall, the old home of the Bindlosses, came Ralph Standish. By a singular coincidence both the last male representatives of the Middleton and Bindloss families had received a baronetcy for their services to Stuart sovereigns, the former from Charles I. and the latter from Charles II., and both had died without a male heir. Sir Robert Bindloss had entertained Charles II. at Borwick Hall when he was making his way southward to give battle to Oliver Cromwell at Worcester, and in 1665 was Mayor of Lancaster. Borwick had descended to his daughter upon his death, and she had married Ralph Standish of Standish, as hot a Jacobite as her father. John Dalton came from Thurnham Hall. He was one of the largest landed proprietors in North Lancashire, owning the

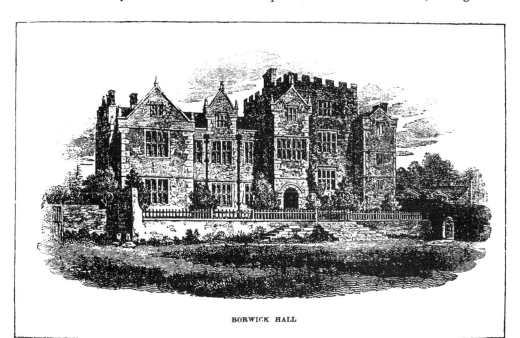

BORWICK HALL

43

ASHTON HALL

whole of the township of Bulk, the Friar-age lands in Lancaster, the hall and lands at Aldcliffe, the estates of Thurnham, and the land which had belonged to the monks at Cockersand. His great-grandfather had died fighting for King Charles I. at the battle of Newbury. Ashton Hall, too, would have sent support to the Jacobite cause, if its owner, the Duke of Hamilton, had still been alive, such support indeed as would have caused a very different history to be written of the Jacobite rising.

The Duke of Hamilton was one of the leaders of the Jacobite party, and there is little doubt that had he been living he would have taken over the command of the forces from the incompetent hands of General Foster. But the Duke had been killed in a duel in London three years previously. A bitter political quarrel had broken out between him and Lord Mohun, and a duel took place in

Hyde Park. Both men fought furiously. The Duke lunging heavily, his sword passed through his adversary up to the hilt, whereupon Lord Mohun shortened his weapon and plunged it into the Duke's breast. The Duke's second caught him in his arms, but at that instant Lord Mohun's second, Colonel Macartney, stepped behind the Duke's second and leaning on his shoulder deliberately stabbed the Duke to the heart. Never was there a more deliberate murder, and the Jacobites declared that the Duke of Hamilton was slain because of his adherence to the Stuart cause.

Albert Hodgson, John Dalton, Edward Tyldesley, Richard Butler of Rawcliffe, and one of the Waltons of Cartmel, were all made captains in the Jacobite Army.

Six Highlanders were then appointed to search the town for arms, and forcing the unwilling Mayor, Mr. Parkinson, to go with them, by threats, they went from house to house. "At every house they demanded armes, which if the owner of them did not deliver, Jack the Highlander was to plunder him. They got very few small armes here, but those as they took they did not pay for." Nor were they more successful in their search for gunpowder; there was very little supply in the town, only one shopkeeper, called Samuel Satterwhaite, having any quantity—a barrel, and this he "thought it properer" to throw into the town well! This extraordinary proceeding was said to have been suggested by Colonel Charteris with the idea of poisoning the water.

On the following day a notice was posted up in the Market Place offering a reward of thirty pounds for the apprehension of Ralph Farebrother, who had gone post-haste to Newcastle on the previous day with the numbers of the Jacobite army carefully noted down by Christopher Hopkins before his arrest. In the course of the same morning the Jacobite Commissioners proceeded to examine the books of the Custom House, but there was nothing due to the Crown save a quantity of brandy which had been seized from some Isle of Man smugglers a few days previously. This brandy, and a little claret, the Commissioners took in the name of King James III. General Foster having been informed of the six cannon on board Mr. Lawson's vessel in the Lune, a detachment of men was sent to take them, which they did without any opposition, and mounted them on new carriages, the wheels of which were taken from Sir Henry Hoghton's coaches!

At ten o'clock the little Sanctus bell at the east end of the south aisle of St. Mary's Church was rung vigorously by Mr. Paul, a minister of the Church of England, who had joined the Earl of Derwentwater, and officers, soldiers and townspeople all trooped to the church.

Those who were early in their places were afforded the historical spectacle of a certain Mr. Ginn skilfully erasing the name of King George from the prayer for the King, and substituting for it the name of King James. In the place of "George, Prince of Wales," he put "The King's Mother," the words being "writ with such a nicety that many takes them to have been printed." The Vicar of Lancaster had been asked to take this memorable service, being supposed to be friendly towards the Jacobite cause, but "it seems that he was not so averse to it, any more than some of his brethren, but he wanted to see how far the scales would turn before he would think of venturing so far." The Jacobite minister, Paul, therefore took the service.

"Abundance of persons went this day to this church," says Peter Clarke, who kept a daily diary of the events during the Jacobite march through Lancashire, "and the said Mr. Paul read the usuall prayers only instead of praying for King George, pray'd for his new master by the name of King James, and instead of George, Prince of Wales, he prayed thus: To bless the King's Mother and all the Royall Ffamily." In the afternoon the officers were entertained by the townsfolk, Peter Clarke saying with some asperity: "This afternoon the Gentlemen soldiers dressed and trimmed themselves up in their best cloaths for to drink a dish of tea with the Ladyes of this town. The Ladyes also here appeared in their best riging, and had their tea-tables richly furnished for to entertain their new suitors." The evening was occupied in a very different fashion—"This evening a discourse about religion happened between the Minister of this towne and two Romish priests."

The Jacobite forces only occupied Lancaster for two days, leaving on the 9th for Preston, thus committing the last of the many mistakes which brought disaster upon them. They should have made Lancaster their headquarters. The town was not only easy of defence, but it had communication with the sea by which help could have reached them from France and Ireland, and it stood in the midst of a district sympathetic to the Stuart cause. Foster seems to have been lured southward by the promise made to Lord Widdrington that twenty thousand men from Manchester, and the surrounding neighbourhood, would flock to the Jacobite banner directly it was raised, and was therefore anxious to reach Manchester. Accordingly on the 9th November, 1715, "both Horse and Footmen marched out of this towne carrying along with them the said six ship guns, and some of the brandy, and their prisoner Christopher Hopkins. Him they took about two miles, and so dismissed him. The Horse came to Preston this night, but the Foot lodged at Garstang and other country houses."

The good people of Lancaster had expected every kind of evil treatment from the rebels, but to their credit, Clarke states : " During the continuance of the Earl of Derwentwater's men in this towne no inhabitant received any bodily damage. The gentlemen paid of their commons (board) here, but very sorrowfull to part with their new Loves. The commonalty (*i. e.* the soldiers) paid little or nothing here." A Quaker, called William Stout,

did not fare so well in regard to his pocket as some of his neighbours, as he dolefully states : " It was a time of tryall, and in fear that the Scotts and Northern rebels would have plundered us, but they were civill, and to most paid for what they had ; but I had five of the Mackintosh officers quartered on me two days but took nothing with them."

Foster's plan was to gain possession of Warrington Bridge and then march to Manchester, where he expected the promised twenty thousand men would join his standard. By securing Warrington Bridge it was intended that Liverpool should be cut off from any relief from the south, and thus could be easily captured. But Liverpool was in no way sympathetic to the Jacobites, and when the news arrived that the rebels had reached Preston seventy guns were placed in positions most convenient for the defence of the town, the streets were flooded, and where the water could not reach, barriers were erected.

In those times of slow communication rumour played a part we cannot realize in these days of telegrams and quick communication by rail and motor-car. The wildest stories ran from one end of Lancashire to the other. It was declared that if the Jacobites were successful they would introduce the Inquisition into England, that they would torture such of King George's officers and privates who would not be Papists, and that they would even put women and children to

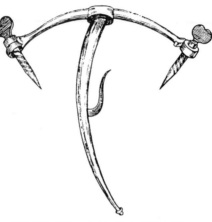

THE GAG SUPPOSED TO BE CARRIED BY THE HIGHLANDERS

death if they persisted in remaining Protestants.

One of the means of torture was said to be a murderous iron gag, with screws at either end to fasten it into the jaws, and a long prong to be thrust down the throat, the tongue being pierced by a sharp hook in its centre. Such a gag, it was solemnly affirmed, had been taken from one of the rebels at Preston, and a picture of it was afterwards displayed in up the next day, being Thursday the 10th of November, they marched straight to the Cross, and were there drawn up as usual, while the Pretender was proclaimed. Here they were also joined by a great many gentlemen, with their tenants, servants and attendants, and some of very good figure in the county ; but still all Papists." Amongst these was Richard Townley of Townley, but even with this addition General Foster's forces only numbered

PRESTON MARKET PLACE

all the print shops in London and in Lancashire. This story was a deliberate calumny. If such an instrument was actually found in the possession of the rebels, and this is openly doubted, it was in all probability part of the Highland accoutrement.

It was stories such as these that nerved Liverpool to the utmost resistance.

The foot-soldiers arrived at Preston on the following morning, " The foot coming four thousand men. In order to distinguish the Scottish soldiers from the English recruits, the Scots used blue-and-white cockades, the English red-and-white ones.

A curious inertness and indolence fell upon General Foster and the whole of his army at Preston. He knew that General Carpenter, at the head of a Hanoverian force, was hastening after him from Newcastle, and Patten, his chaplain, records that he "depended upon the assurances of the Lancashire gentlemen that no force could come near them by forty miles, but they could inform him thereof." Yet at the same time General Wills was only twelve miles off at Wigan. One of the Jacobite officers, in a journal he kept of the march of the rebels, says that on November 10th, "We received certain notice of General Wills' being in Wigan, twelve miles distant from us, with two regiments of dragoons, who lay night and day at their horses' heads in order to fly if we should march towards Manchester or Chester. Though we had an opportunity of cutting off the enemy, yet General Foster would not allow us, nor suffer us to march toward Manchester." In place of two regiments General Wills was actually concentrating all his available forces at Wigan, but Foster made no attempt to break through to Manchester, or even to protect his position at Preston.

Nor did General Wills rely solely on the regular troops at his command. He called upon the gentlemen in sympathy with the Hanoverian cause to raise men amongst their tenantry, as is shown by a letter written by Sir Henry Hoghton of Hoghton Tower to the Reverend James Woods, a Presbyterian minister at Chowbent. The letter was written under the authority of General Wills, who countersigned the superscription. This is the letter which was in existence in the year 1793, and was fortunately copied.

"To the Rev. Mr. Woods in Chowbent for His Majesty's Service.

Charles Wills

"The officers here design to march at break of day for Preston, they have desired me to raise what men I can to meet us at Preston to-morrow, so desire you to raise all the force you can, I mean lusty young fellows to draw up on Cuerden Green, to be there by 10 o'clock, to bring with them what armes they have fitt for service, and scythes put in streight polls, and such as have not, to bring spades and billhooks for pioneering with. Pray go immediately all amongst your neighbours and give this notice.

"I am your very faithful servant
"H. Hoghton"
"Wigan, 11th Nov. 1715."

A very significant reason for the Jacobite lethargy is given by Peter Clarke in his *Journall* of the insurrection. "The Ladys in this toune, Preston," he says, "are so very beautyfull and so richly atired, that the gentlemen soldiers from Wednesday to Saturday minded nothing but courting and ffeasting."

At that time Preston, because of its mild climate and beautiful situation, was the winter residence of the leading gentry of Lancashire, who went there for the "season," as their descendants now go to London. Many county families had houses in Preston, and the winter was one long gaiety, with balls, routs, concerts and plays. Suddenly plunged into this atmosphere of pleasure and amusement after their long marches from Scotland and all the wearing anxieties attendant upon such an enterprise, the Jacobite officers gave themselves up to the delights of Preston — and with the most fatal result to their cause. The direction of the movements of the Government troops had been placed in the hands of that great soldier, the Duke of Marlborough, who was well versed in human nature. The Duke, "while he was aware that the Insurgent force would suffer some detention at Preston, then considered as the district where the Roman Catholics most abounded, must also have calculated upon the allurements incidental to a town long regarded as the metropolis of Lancashire. In directing therefore the general operations of the Government forces, the experienced veteran did not overlook the enervating effect liable to result from and the "courting and ffeasting" were the undoing of the Jacobites.

On Friday night Lord Derwentwater received a letter stating that at twelve o'clock that day General Wills had been joined by seven more regiments and was about to march upon Preston. With

JACOBITE OFFICERS GIVING UP THEIR SWORDS TO GENERAL WILLS AT PRESTON

such gay quarters as the Lancashire Capua was likely to afford. He adverted to Preston as the net of the fowler, in preparation for the wild birds of prey who were to be gathered therein: 'It is here,' said the Duke, with prophetic discrimination, 'that we shall find them!'" The "very beautyfull" ladies of Preston others of the Jacobite leaders, he immediately sought General Foster, whom he found in bed. But this letter did not shake the general's belief that he had only to consider the possibility of an attack from General Carpenter, who was forty miles behind him. A council was hastily summoned, and orders were given to send a party of the horse towards Wigan as an advanced guard, and another party of the foot to Darwen and Ribble bridge; the whole army also had orders to be in readiness to take the field. Yet, for some reason that has never been explained, Foster countermanded all these orders, still from his bed.

On the Saturday morning he had a rude awakening. The vanguard of General Wills was seen approaching from the direction of Walton-le-Dale. Then, and then only, would Foster believe the danger that threatened him. A council was hastily summoned, at which Brigadier Mackintosh was asked to suggest the best course to pursue. He advised that the Jacobites should draw the Hanoverians into the streets of the town, where, from behind barricades, and from the windows of the houses a destructive fire could be poured upon them whilst the Jacobites themselves remained under cover. This advice was instantly followed, and when General Wills arrived he found four barriers had been hastily erected to oppose his entry. One barrier was below the church, another at the end of a lane leading to the fields, a third was across the Lancaster road, and a fourth across Fishergate. General Wills immediately attacked the barrier below the church, which was defended by General Mackintosh, the Earl of Derwentwater, Viscount Kenmure, and the Earls of Wintoun and Nithsdale. The attack was met by a murderous fire from the Jacobites. Two of the six ship's guns which had been brought from Lancaster were placed upon this barricade under the charge of a seaman. But owing it was said to this seaman's heavy potations, in the excitement of the moment, his first shot went wide and hit the top of a chimney, to the great amusement of the Government forces. The second shot, however, turned their laughter to dismay, for it wrought such havoc amongst them that they were obliged to halt, and finally to retire beyond the range of fire, leaving many dead and wounded behind them. Meanwhile the other three barriers had been hotly attacked and defended with no less success; and as night fell the Government forces retired, worsted in this, their first attack. "That night," says the Jacobite officer whose diary has been quoted, "both armies lay upon their arms, but General Foster went to bed." On the previous night, when he was informed of the near approach of General Wills, it was said that Foster "had received some little damage in the course of a convivial entertainment, so as to render it necessary that, instead of studying military despatches, he should retire to bed." The day's hard fighting would appear not to have driven away the effects of the "convivial entertainment."

Great was the rejoicing in Preston that Saturday night. Elated by the withdrawal of the Government troops the Jacobites saw themselves marching in triumph to London; but in the morning their bright hopes were dashed away. During the night General Carpenter had arrived, and joining forces with General Wills, together they had completely invested the town. So securely were the Jacobite forces hemmed in, that the Highlanders, finding all escape impossible, wished to sally forth, sword in hand, and try to cut their way through. But Foster, however, discouraged their bravery and sent Colonel Oxburgh secretly to General Wills to know what terms would be given if his force surrendered. The reply was, "They have killed several of the king's subjects and they must expect the same fate."

All that day the secret negotiations went on, General Wills finally saying that if the Jacobites laid down their arms and surrendered at discretion he would prevent his soldiers cutting them to pieces, and give them their lives until he received further orders. dignation knew no bounds. They declared they would not surrender, but would die fighting, and the whole Jacobite army was consequently thrown into the greatest confusion. General Foster had no longer

A JACOBITE REBEL GOING TO EXECUTION AT LANCASTER

The passing of messengers to and from the Government camp at length aroused the suspicions of the Scottish leaders, and when they found that negotiations were actually being carried on their in- any authority over the raging High-landers; they had no responsible leader, and in the midst of the confusion and recriminations, he accepted General Wills' terms and agreed to surrender at discretion. On the following morning General Carpenter entered Preston, and in the old Market Place where the Pretender had been proclaimed King of England only four days before amid a scene of delirious enthusiasm, the Jacobite soldiers laid down their arms and were taken prisoners. The Scottish officers and gentlemen were divided into three parties and sent to the Mitre, the White Bull and the Windmill Inns, whilst a great number of the Northumberland and Lancashire gentlemen were confined in the house of a Mr. Wingleby. The Highlanders and the other soldiers were placed under a strong guard in Preston church, the town being compelled to give them bread and water. " It was an unseasonable time of the year for imprisonment within the cold and cheerless aisles of a church," says the chronicler, " which caused the hapless captives to seek for additional protection from the inclemencies of a November month by ripping the linings from the seats, or pews, for additional clothing. To what melancholy reflections must this scene have given rise, when contrasted with the thoughtless gaiety of the few days' sojourn in Preston which preceded the insurgent capitulation !—a capitulation in which all the fearful results of unsuccessful rebellion would scarcely fail to be seen in perspective ! To such noblemen as had instigated the rebellion, forfeiture of title and dignities ; and to all titled or untitled landed proprietors, forfeiture of estate ; to less dignified insurgents, if they escaped a capital sentence, colonial slavery ; and to all ranks indiscriminately the dungeon and the contingency of the scaffold."

Owing to the neglect of General Wills to place troops on the side of Preston leading to Liverpool, numbers of the insurgents made their escape during the surrender in the Market Place. The prisoners in Preston Church were eventually distributed between the gaols of Lancaster, Liverpool and Chester. About four hundred were taken to Lancaster Castle, a regiment of dragoons being quartered in the town to guard them. Their fate is thus laconically described : " The King allowed them 4^d a day for maintenance, viz. 2^d in bread, 1^d in cheese, and 1^d in small beer, and they lay in straw in the stables most of them, and in about a month's time about 100 of them were conveyed to Liverpool to be tried, and about 200 of them continued about a year, and about 50 of them died, and the rest were transported to America."

" Truly a plain narrative of fact," says the late William Oliver Roper, " the details are left to be filled in—the degradation and the misery of the four hundred prisoners crammed into those castle stables, their wretchedly insufficient allowance of fourpence a day, their bed of what straw they could get, none knowing from day to day whether he might not be tried for his life, the transportation of half the number to endure the fever heats of the West Indies, the deaths occurring week after week—under these circumstances is it to be wondered at that one man in every eight who entered that Castle never lived to come out ? "

Of the many scenes of horror witnessed within the walls of Lancaster Castle none ever exceeded this herding together of four hundred half-starved men. Those who were condemned to be executed suffered all the barbarities then meted out for high treason, being hanged, drawn and quartered. Their heads were stuck upon posts on the top of the Castle Gate. The hangman's bill for eight of these executions reads : " February 16th and 18th, charge at Garstang and Lancaster on executing four at either place, £22 0s. 8d."

The officers and leaders of the Jacobite

army were sent from Preston to London, amongst them being General Foster, the Earl of Derwentwater, the Reverend Robert Patten (Foster's chaplain), Ralph Standish of Borwick, Albert Hodgson of Leighton, John Tyldesley, Richard Butler of Rawcliffe, and John Dalton of Thurnham, as well as the Scottish lords the Earls of Nithsdale and Wintour, Viscount Kenmure and Lords Widdrington, Carn-

our horses being led by troopers, with halters upon our horses' heads." But at St. Albans Foster became so ill, from having had to sleep upon damp ground, that he could not sit his horse, and therefore made his entry into London in a coach. It was given out that he had taken poison, and he passed amidst the yells and execrations of the mob. Patten, the chaplain, wore his canonicals on this

THURNHAM HALL

wath and Nairn. On the 9th of December they arrived in the capital, the road from Highgate being crowded " with multitudes of spectators on foot, on horseback, or in coaches, exclaiming, 'No Popish Pretender!' 'Down with the Rebels!' 'Long live King George!'"

General Foster was the object of the crowd's special derision. " Whilst the other prisoners were conducted loose and untied on horseback," says Patten, " he and I were distinguished from the rest by

march through London, which a rabid Hanoverian described as " bating some circumstances of pomp and magnificence, it revived the idea of the triumph of ancient Rome." A Quaker spying out Patten said to him, " Verily Friend, thou hast been the trumpeter of Rebellion to these men. Thou must now answer for them!" According to Patten's account, the grenadier who was guarding him, indignant at this insult to misfortune, applied the butt end of his musket, and "shoved the spirit in the ditch;" whereupon the Quaker said to the soldier, "Thou hast not used me civilly! I doubt thou art not a real friend to King George!"

To Patten's lasting infamy he turned King's evidence. He, who had ceaselessly quoted Scripture in support of the Jacobite cause, made statements and confessions which led to seven of the peers who had joined the rising being tried for high treason. "Great many scruples offered themselves to my consideration," wrote this clerical traitor, "in consequence of which I made it my request to Lord Townshend that he would be pleased to allow a Clergyman to converse with me. The request was granted, and his learning and solid reason prevailed upon me. From thence I began to think it incumbent on me to make all the reparation I could for the injury I had done to Government, and as the first thing in that way I became an evidence for the King, which I am far from being ashamed of, let what calumnies will follow." Very different was the conduct of the Rev. William Paul, who had joined the Jacobites at Lancaster. He was condemned to death, and appeared on the scaffold in cassock and gown. He met his terrible death with the utmost fortitude and bravery, saying that he wished he had quarters enough to send to every part of the kingdom, in order that they might show that a clergyman of the Church of England had been martyred for being loyal to his king.

Of the seven peers against whom Patten testified, the Earls of Nithsdale and Derwentwater, and Viscount Kenmure were sentenced to death; Lords Widdrington, Carnwath and Nairn were also sentenced, but afterwards were reprieved. The Earl of Wintoun escaped from the Tower of London, as did also the Earl of Nithsdale disguised as a woman. The Countess of Derwentwater went to Kensington Palace, and, throwing herself on her knees before George I., pleaded passionately for her husband's life. "The King listened civilly, and quite as civilly dismissed her in tears and despair." Lord Derwentwater and Lord Kenmure were both beheaded on Tower Hill.

The trial which aroused the greatest interest, however, was that of General Foster, which was fixed for April 18, 1716, but a week before that date the news ran through London, "Tom Foster is off and away!" His servant by some means or another had taken the impression of the master-key belonging to the Governor of Newgate Prison; a duplicate key was made from this wax impression and given to Foster. The Governor was a gentleman who liked good food and good wine, and Foster frequently asked him to dine with him. One night the Governor, who was more drunk than usual, finished all the wine on the table and roared out for more. Foster ordered his servant to bring another bottle, but the man did not return, and Foster, on the excuse of going to see what delayed him, slipped out of the room, locked the door upon the Governor, and with the aid of the master-key quietly walked out of the prison, and with the help of friends escaped to France.

During the trials of the Lancashire gentlemen the court was crowded. First came Edward Tyldesley, who was sworn to have raised a troop of men, to have been seen marching with his sword drawn, to have dined with the Jacobite officers at Preston, and to have drunk the health of James III. In Tyldesley's defence, Sir George Warrender swore that he was an inoffensive person, not given to speaking against King George, whilst his housekeeper deposed that he was carried away from his house by the Jacobites. It was further shown that arrangements had been made for his escape from the Jacobites, upon which the Judge remarked that doubtless many Jacobites would be ready to take that course when the fall of Preston seemed imminent. The summing up was dead against Tyldesley, but the jury acquitted him, whereupon the judge discharged them, protesting against their verdict on the ground that men who had followed Tyldesley into the war had been hanged, yet he, their leader, was allowed to escape.

John Dalton, of Thurnham Hall, also pleaded that he had been forced into the Rebellion. The Vicar of Cockerham came all the way from Lancashire to testify in his behalf. He said he had never heard Mr. Dalton speak against the Government, and that several times he had expressed scruples regarding the Romish religion. Upon this he was asked by the judge why he, a clergyman of the Church of England, " had not endeavoured to improve, towards a conviction in the Protestant faith, the doubts which he had thus uttered regarding the validity of Popish tenets. To this it was replied by the Vicar that he had made some essay in that way, but that he had subsequently found Mr. Dalton fixed upon these questions, and altered in his judgment." The Vicar further added that Mr. Dalton was a peaceable Roman Catholic, and that he had seen him drink King George's health on several occasions. This evidence was of no avail, the facts were too strong, and he was found guilty. Dalton then craved the King's pardon,

and desired the Court to interfere for an exercise of the royal clemency. The Lord Chief Justice held out few hopes of a pardon, saying he regretted that he had not better reasons than the case afforded for recommending the interposition of the King's mercy.

Sir Francis Anderton, of Lostock, was also found guilty, but was afterwards pardoned. " He was wont to say very cheerfully that he had lost a good estate for being out with the rebels but one day." Albert Hodgson, of Leighton, and Ralph Standish, of Borwick, were likewise condemned to death, but after lying with John Dalton for a long time in the unhealthy cells of Newgate they were all three released on the payment of enormous fines. Richard Butler, of Rawcliffe, died in prison. The payment of the fine left John Dalton so destitute that he was obliged to walk all the way from London to Cockerham. He found his home, Thurnham Hall, practically deserted, and his wife in the woods behind the house gathering sticks to light her fire, there being no servants left to perform even the most menial offices. For generations afterwards the descendants of these Lancashire gentlemen, who bought their lives by the payment of heavy fines, were impoverished, and in some cases they had to sell their estates in order to meet the fines.

Thus ended the Jacobite Rebellion of 1715 in Lancashire, ignominious death or total ruin coming upon all those who had taken part in it.

THE SIEGE OF LATHOM HOUSE

THE name of Lathom House will ever be associated with a woman's courage in the face of overwhelming odds.

When Charles I. and the Parliament decided upon that appeal to arms which

the King bade him remain in Lancashire, where, " with naked or thinly-armed men, he sustained the fury of the rebels and kept the field against them for seven months together, storming several of their towns, and defeating them in sundry

CHARLOTTE DE LA TRÉMOUILLE, COUNTESS OF DERBY

is known in history as the Great Rebellion, James Stanley, the seventh Earl of Derby, raised a force of three thousand men, with which he was about to hurry to the King's support when Charles raised his standard at Nottingham in 1642. But

battles." However, notwithstanding the bravery of the Royalists, by the summer of 1643, " all the fortified towns and houses in Lancashire, except Lathom, were in the hands of the Parliamentarians." At the same time news reached Queen

Henrietta Maria, who was at York, that the Scotch were about to invade England to support the cause of the Parliament, and it was their intention to send an army to the Isle of Man, and thence to some convenient landing-place in Lancashire, thus avoiding the danger of being intercepted by the Royalist forces in the North of England. She therefore commanded Lord Derby, to whom the Isle of Man belonged, to repair thither instantly and prevent the landing of the Scottish forces. Lord Derby obeyed the command, and in June, 1643, left Lathom House in charge of his intrepid wife, Charlotte de la Trémouille.

The Countess of Derby was a daughter of a great French nobleman, the Duc de la Trémouille, who was of such high birth that he had the right not only to sit in the presence of royalty, but to marry into a royal family. His wife was a daughter of William the Silent, Prince of Orange, and ruler of Holland, and therefore if Lady Derby had lived twenty-four years longer (she died in 1664) she would have seen a close kinsman of her own, William III., who was Prince of Orange, upon the throne of England.

Seeing that Lathom House was the only Royalist stronghold left in the whole county, it was clear that its attack could only be a matter of time, and both before and after Lord Derby's departure for the Isle of Man it is more than probable that the fortifications of the house were strengthened and ammunition and stores collected together. The successful resistance of the siege can only be accounted for by this supposition.

Lathom House of Charles I.'s time was a very different building from the Lathom House of to-day, and happily an accurate description of it, written by one who passed many happy years within its walls, has been preserved. This account was written by Samuel Rutter, the favourite companion and the chaplain of the Earl of Derby, who made him the tutor of his eldest son. He was also Archdeacon of Man, and "governed the Church with great prudence during the late unhappy civil wars." When Charles II. was restored to the throne, Rutter's pupil—then become Earl of Derby by the execution of his father—who had the rights of a sovereign in the island, made him Bishop of Man. This is his description of old Lathom House—

"Lathom House stands upon a flat, upon a moorish, springy, and spumous ground, and was encompassed with a strong wall of two yards thick; upon the walls were nine towers, flanking each other, and in every tower were six pieces of ordnance, that played three one way, and three the other; without the wall was a moat eight yards wide, and two yards deep, upon the back of the moat between the wall and the graff, was a strong row of palisades around. Besides all these there was a high, strong tower, called the Eagle Tower, in the midst of the house, surmounting all the rest; and the gate-house had also two high and strong buildings with a strong tower on each side of it. . . . Besides all that has hitherto been said of the walls, towers, moat, etc., there is something so particular and romantic in the general situation of this house as if Nature herself had formed it for a stronghold, or place of security; for before the house to the south and south-west is a rising ground so near it as to overlook the top of it, from which it falls so quick, that nothing planted against it on those sides can touch it farther than the front wall; and on the north and east side there is another rising ground even to the edge of the moat, and then falls away so quick that you can scarce at the distance of a carbine shot, see the house over that height, so that batteries placed there are so far below it as to be of little service against it: and let us observe, by the way, that the uncommon situation of it may be compared to the palm of a man's hand, flat in the middle and covered with a rising ground round about it, and so near to it that the enemy, during the siege, were never able to raise a battery against it, so as to make a breach in the way practicable to enter the house by way of storm."

Speedily after Lord Derby's departure the Parliamentarian Governor of Manchester — Holland — called upon Lady Derby either to submit to the propositions of the Parliament or yield up Lathom House. Her answer was that she would "neither tamely give up her house or purchase her peace with the loss of her honour," but not then being in a position to resist a sudden attack, she temporised by placing all Lord Derby's estates at their disposal on the consideration that she might have a " peaceable abode in her own house," and keep as many men-at-arms as were necessary to defend her house and her person from the outrages of the common soldiers of the Parliament. To this proposition the Governor agreed, but Lady Derby was not permitted to go beyond the gardens of Lathom ; the estate was sequestrated, and she was subjected to " daily afronts and indignities from unworthy persons." In order to avoid giving the Parliament any cause for reprisal, she restrained her small garrison from " all provocation and annoyance of the enemy," and thus succeeded in staving off the siege for seven months. But that most zealous of the Puritans in Lancashire, Alexander Rigby, a Preston lawyer become a Colonel in the Parliamentary Army, had a personal grudge against Lord Derby, and " restless

in his malice sought all occasions to disturb her quiet." One method he pursued was to send troops to plunder the houses of Lady Derby's neighbours, hoping to provoke her into going to their assistance. In the beginning of February, 1644, Rigby was successful. A troop of his horse had taken some of her friends prisoners, and the garrison of Lathom sallying out to their rescue, a skirmish took place, which resulted in the prisoners being freed and one of the Parliamentary officers being wounded. Rigby instantly made complaint to Sir Thomas Fairfax, who had then come into Lancashire after defeating the Royalists at the battle of Nantwich, and at a Council of the " holy states," as the Parliamentary leaders called themselves, held at Manchester, it was decided that Lathom must be surrendered, and failing that, be taken by force. Word of this determination instantly spread abroad, and the Puritan minister at Wigan, one of the Bradshaws, preached a sermon against Lady Derby upon a text from Jeremiah—

" Put yourselves in array against Babylon round about : all ye that bend the bow shoot at her ; spare no arrows ; for she hath sinned against the Lord." (Chap. 50. v. 14.)

The reverend gentleman did not mince matters. According to him Lady Derby was Babylon, and he described her in terms which, although drawn from the Scriptures, are not in use in polite society. When he concluded he announced that he reserved the verse following for the text of a sermon to be preached after the downfall of Lathom—

" Shoot against her round about : she hath given her hand ; her foundations are fallen ; her walls are thrown down.".

Three thousand men, commanded by Sir Thomas Fairfax, under whom were Colonel Rigby, Colonel Ashton of Middleton, Colonel Egerton and Colonel Holcroft, marched upon Lathom, and, when they were at some two miles distance, an officer, Captain Markland, was sent with a letter from Fairfax to the Countess, in which, after offering the mercy of the Parliament to Lord Derby if he would submit, the General, in the most courteous terms, asked for the surrender of Lathom upon conditions to be made known afterwards. Lady Derby, anxious to gain time to collect more provisions, replied, "She much wondered that Sir Thomas Fairfax should require her to give up her Lord's house without any offence on her part done to the parliament, desiring that, in a business of such weight, which struck both at her religion and her life, and that so nearly concerned her Sovereign, her Lord, and her whole posterity, she might have a week's consideration, both to resolve doubts of conscience, and to have advice in matters of law and honour."

The capital letters used by the brave lady in referring to her King and to her husband, and the small " p " she contemptuously accords to the Parliament, are significant of her attitude.

Fairfax, rightly suspecting the reason of Lady Derby's desire for a week's consideration, refused her request and desired that she should go to New Park—a house of Lord Derby's a quarter of a mile from Lathom—to see him and his colonels. "She was to come thither in her coach," says Captain Hansall, who was at Lathom during the siege; and he adds sarcastically, "no mean favour, believe it. This," he continues, "her ladyship flatly refused, with scorn and anger, as an ignoble and uncivil motion." She replied : " Say to Sir Thomas Fairfax that, notwithstanding my present condition, I do not forget either the honour of my Lord, or of my own birth, and that I conceive it more knightly that Sir Thomas Fairfax should wait upon me, than I upon him."

During the next two days letters and messages passed to and fro, and, finally, Fairfax asked the Countess to receive Colonels Ashton and Rigby, "unto which her ladyship condescended." Her reception of the two officers shows Lady Derby to have been a clever woman as well as a brave one. Everything was done to impress them with the strength of the garrison and her means of defence. The ramparts were manned, the cannon in the towers were trained ready for action, with the gunners beside them, and the two officers passed through a double line of soldiers on their way to the great hall, where, seated upon a dais with a daughter standing on either side, and surrounded by her ladies and her women, the Countess received them with queenly dignity.

When Rigby and Ashton approached, Lady Derby motioned them to be seated. They laid before her Fairfax's proposals, which were that Lathom with all the arms and ammunition of war it contained should be surrendered, that the Countess and all the people in the house should be allowed to go where they pleased, and that the Countess and her menial servants should be allowed to inhabit Knowsley House, and have twenty muskets for her defence, or else join her husband in the Isle of Man. The last proposal was : "That the Countess for the present, until the Parliament be acquainted with it, shall have allowed for her maintenance all the lands and revenues of the Earl, her husband, within the Hundred of Derby, and that the Parliament shall be moved to continue this allowance."

Lady Derby answered the two men with quiet scorn, refusing to consider the proposals, "as being in part dishonourable and in part uncertain." " I know not how to treat with those who have not power to perform their own offers till they have first moved the Parliament," she said.

"It were a more sober course first to acquaint yourselves with the pleasure of the Parliament, and then to move accordingly." Then she added haughtily : "For my part I will not trouble you, good gentlemen, to petition for me. I shall esteem it a greater favour to be permitted to continue in my present humble condition."

ways and those of my house. You would do well to do as much for your ministers and agents of religion who go about sowing discord and trouble in families, whose unbridled tongues do not spare even the sacred person of his Majesty."

Negotiations went on uninterruptedly during the next ten days, the terms of surrender being again and again altered.

COLONEL ALEXANDER RIGBY

The two colonels apparently had nothing to say in answer to Lady Derby's spirited rejection of their terms, but remonstrated with her upon the errors of her ways and of those of her friends and servants, but she silenced them with—

"I shall know how to take care of my

Fairfax seems to have been honestly anxious not to proceed to extremities with Lady Derby. He was a gentleman in spirit—which is more than even the most impartial historian can say for others of the Parliamentarian leaders, who, like himself, were gentlemen by birth —and her undaunted courage, her unswerving fidelity both to her husband and King Charles must naturally have appealed to that spirit. He persuaded six of her neighbours of the " best rank " to send her a petition, " That, in duty to her ladyship and love to their country, they must humbly beseech her to prevent her own personal dangers, and the impoverishing of the country, which she might do if she pleased to slacken of her severe resolution ; and to condescend in part to the offers of the gentlemen." This petition failing to shake the indomitable lady in her resolution, Fairfax sent her a letter he had received from Lord Derby, begging him to allow the Countess and her children to leave Lathom, "considering the roughness and inhumanity of the enemy," not knowing, by reason of his long absence, either how his house was provided with victuals and ammunition, or strengthened for resistance. He was therefore desirous to leave " only the hardy soldiers for the brunt, if it seems good to my wife." Lady Derby thanked Sir Thomas Fairfax for his courtesy, and informed him that she would willingly submit to her Lord's commands, and therefore willed the General to treat with him ; but till she was assured that such was his Lordship's pleasure she would neither yield up the house nor desert it herself, but wait for the event according to God.

Even in the face of this refusal Fairfax sent another set of proposals, the first of which was : " That all former conditions be waived." He offered that Lady Derby and every person in the house, with all arms, ordnance and goods, should have liberty to go where they would, provided Lathom was yielded up to him. To this Lady Derby made her final answer. She " refused all their articles," she said, " and was truly happy that they had refused hers, which she would rather offer her life than hazard the like again. That, though a woman and a stranger, divorced from her friends and robbed of her estate, she was ready to receive their utmost violence, trusting in God both for protection and deliverance."

Next morning Lady Derby and her small garrison of three hundred men found that the siege had begun, the enemy during the night having commenced to dig trenches and pile up earthworks. At this juncture Sir Thomas Fairfax, to his great relief, was sent to Yorkshire, leaving the command of the two thousand besiegers to his cousin Sir William Fairfax, but Alexander Rigby was virtually the commander. Whatever Rigby's merits, he was clearly biassed by a personal feeling against Lord Derby and his Countess, and his prosecution of the siege was at once malignant and barbaric. An indication of the man's character is given in *A Discourse of the Warr in Lancashire*, which has been reprinted by the Chetham Society of Manchester. " Although admired by many, he was esteemed by few, loved by none. Some very bad things are said of him, which, I fear, are true ; but the worst is so bad that I hope it is not true, although the evidence against him is very strong. He is said to have contrived a scheme and bargain by which the Royalist masters of three Cambridge Colleges, St. John's, Queens' and Jesus, were to be sold for slaves to the Algerians." A man who could devise so fiendish a fate for those who differed from him in their opinion as to the form of government of the country, was capable of any malignity. Slavery under the pirate days of Algiers was one of the terrors which beset all those who ventured into the Mediterranean in the seventeenth century, and it lasted until the eighteenth century, when Lord Exmouth, commanding an English fleet, bombarded

Algiers, and destroyed that stronghold of piracy and misery.

Rigby had procured a large mortar-piece from London upon which he relied for the speedy destruction of the Lathom defences ; besides this he had " demi-cannon, culverins, and perriers," mounted upon the earthworks outside the walls. The large mortar cast great stone balls as well as bomb shells, and one of these, " falling near the place where the Lady and her children with all the commanders were seated at dinner, shivered all the room, but hurt nobody." From the very outset, however, the Parliamentary forces were perpetually harassed by the Countess's soldiers. Suddenly a postern gate would open and out would rush a body of men who, with one of the six Lancashire gentlemen aiding the Countess in the defence, would storm the trenches and earthworks, and drive the assailants away with the loss of many killed and wounded. Before the besiegers could rally, the sortie-party would be safely back within the walls of the Castle. " These sallies and frequent alarms," says young Hassall, " so diseased the enemy that their works went slowly on, they having been there three weeks, and not having cast up one mount for ordnance." Rigby and the other colonels, finding they could make no headway during the day, had their guns set up at night, but here again they were subject to frequent alarms, clay balls in which lighted matches were stuck being thrown amongst the men from the walls. The Parliamentary soldiers, believing these were lighted bombs, fled in terror. And so the siege proceeded, the advantage lying wholly with Lady Derby, whose conduct of the defence was masterly. To such desperation were the leaders of the besieging party reduced that they issued the following notice—

" *To all Ministers and Persons in Lancashire, well-wishers in our successe against Lathom House, theise :*

" Forasmuch as more than ordinary obstructions have been from the beginning of this present service agaynst Lathom House interposed against our proceedings, and yet still remaine, which cannot otherwise be removed, nor our successe furthered, but onely by divine assistance ; it is therefore our desires to the ministers, and other well-affected persons of this county of Lancaster, in public manner, as they shall please, to commend our case to God, that as wee are appoynted to the said employment, soe much tending to the settleing of our present peace in theise parts, soe the Almighty would crowne our weake endeavours with speedy successe in the said designe."

This was dated April 5, 1644, and signed by John Ashton and Ralph Moor; " the four following days," says Hassall, " were on their parts slept out in this pious exercise." " On Wednesday," he adds, " our men resolved to waken them." The account he then gives is descriptive of the constant sallies which took place.

" About eleven o'clock Captain Farmer and Captain Molineux Radcliffe, Lieutenant Penketh, Lieutenant Worrill and 140 soldiers, sallied out at a postern gate, beat the enemy from all their works and batteries, which were now cast up round the house, nailed all their cannon, killed about fifty men, took sixty arms, one set of colours and three drums. In this action Captain Radcliffe deserves this remembrance, that with three soldiers, the rest of his squadron being scattered with the execution of the enemy, he cleared two sconces, and slew seven men with his own hand. Lieutenant Worrill, engaging himself in another work among fifty of the enemy, bore the fury of them all, till Captain Farmer relieved him, who, to the wonder of us all, came off without any dangerous wound. The sally port was this day warded by Captain Chisenhall, who with fresh men stood ready to succour our men had they been put to any extremity ; but they marched bravely round the works and came in at the great gates where Captain Ogle, with a party of musketeers, kept open the passage. Captain Rawstorne had the charge of the musketeers upon the walls, whom he placed to the best advantage to vex the enemy in their flight. Captain Fox, with colours in the Eagle Tower, gave signals when to march and when to retreat, according to the motions of the enemy, which he observed at a distance. In all this service we had but one man mortally wounded, and we took only one prisoner, an officer, for the sake of intelligence. In former sallies some prisoners had been taken and were released by exchange. Colonels Ashton and Rigby had promised to set at liberty as many of the King's friends who were then prisoners in Lancaster, Manchester, and Preston, and other places as her ladyship proposed ; but they most unworthily broke their conditions, it suiting well their religion neither to observe faith with God nor with men, and this occasioned a greater slaughter than either her ladyship or the captains desired, because we were in no condition to keep many prisoners, and knew their commanders would never release them but upon base and dishonourable terms. The same night they played a saker twice, to tell us they had cannon that would speak, though our men had endeavoured to stick up their lips. This whole night was one continued alarm with them, there being nothing but shouts and cries amongst them, as if the cavaliers had still been upon them."

It was on the 24th April that Rigby took command, and " having wearied his soldiers, wasted his powder, and emptied himself of a good part of his exacted and plundered moneys, finding her ladyship inclined to yield nothing to his great guns, but daily to beat and baffle his soldiers, is now for present fire and ruin." He had procured a new stock of grenados and also fire-balls which he was going to pour into the house the whole of one afternoon from his great mortar, until the place was yielded up or burnt to the ground. Before proceeding to this extremity, however, he sent a messenger to Lady Derby, summoning her to surrender Lathom House and all that it contained, and submit to the mercy of the Parliament ; she was commanded to return her final answer before two o'clock on the following day. The Countess received the messenger in the court-yard, surrounded by her officers. She read the message, then said to the messenger—

" A due reward for your pains is to be hanged up at my gates, but thou art but the foolish instrument of a traitor's pride. Carry this answer back to Rigby (with a noble scorn tearing the paper in his sight), and tell that insolent rebel, he shall neither have persons, goods, nor house ; when our strength and provisions are spent, we shall find a fire more merciful than Rigby's, and then, if the providence of God prevent it not, my goods and house shall burn in his sight ; and myself, children, and soldiers, rather than fall into his hands, will seal our religion and loyalty in the same flame ! "

The soldiers standing round heard these brave words ; they broke out into shouts and cheering, " all closing with this general voice, ' We will die for his Majesty and your honour—God save the King ! ' "

It is abundantly clear from the history of the siege that Lady Derby would have carried out her threat ; she would have herself set Lathom House on fire and perished in the flames rather than yield it up. The mortar-piece was the greatest danger she had to face, for, as Hassall says, " The little ladies (Lady Derby's daughters) had stomachs to digest cannon, but the stoutest soldier had no heart for

messenger ; at which the most hazardous sally of the whole siege was decided upon. Nothing could save Lathom from destruction except the silencing of the mortar. At four o'clock therefore on the following morning, with similar arrangements as in the sally, the description of which is quoted above, the little garrison

CAPTAIN KAY

grenados." These grenados exploded when they struck, and being filled with pieces of iron and large nails caused more wounds and deaths than the cannon-balls of iron and stone. A serious conference took place between Lady Derby and her captains after the departure of Rigby's

issued forth, and in an hour the enemy were driven from their earthworks. Whilst one party of soldiers prevented their return, another party, helped by some of the house servants, levelled the ditch, and getting the mortar-piece on to a low drag pulled it with ropes into the house. They tried to capture the big guns in the same manner, but their weight and their distance from the house made this an impossibility. The terrible mortar was drawn into the courtyard, and the delighted Countess, showering praises upon her brave defenders, immediately ordered her chaplain to be called, "and gathered her household together in the chapel to return thanks to God."

A further triumph over her enemy Rigby was reserved for Lady Derby: "The days on which our men gave Rigby that shameful defeat, he had destined for the execution of his utmost cruelty. He had invited, as is now generally confessed, all his friends, the holy abettors of this mischief, to come and see the house either yielded or burned, he having proposed to use his mortar-gun with fire-balls or grenados all the afternoon; but her ladyship, before two o'clock (his own time) gave him such a very scurvy satisfying answer, that his friends came opportunely to comfort him, who was sick of shame and dishonour, in being routed by a lady and a handful of men."

From this time forward the besiegers lost heart. Desertions occurred every day, whilst the energy of the besieged seemed to increase. On May 1, Rigby, writing to the Deputy-Lieutenant of Lancashire asking for aid, thus describes his situation : "We are obliged to drive them (the garrison) back as often as five or six times in the same night. These constant alarms, the strength of the garrison, and the numerous losses we have had oblige the soldiers to guard the trenches sometimes two nights running, and always the whole of the two nights; my son does this duty as well as the younger officers. And for my own part I am ready to sink under the weight, having worked beyond my strength." This appeal brought him some small addition

to his forces, and, finding all attack upon the house useless, Rigby then began to dig trenches in what he believed was the direction of the source of the Lathom water-supply ; but he overlooked the fact that the springs which fed the deep well in the house rose on the higher ground to the south-east, and therefore could not be tapped. Heavy rain came on, causing the side of the trench to give way, which killed three of his men.

On May 23 a proposition of surrender was once more laid before Lady Derby. She was called upon to yield up the house and all that was in it, and submit herself to the mercy of the Parliament. Lady Derby smiled when the paper was read to her, and "in a troubled passion challenged the captain with a mistake in the paper, saying *mercy* instead of *cruelty*."

"No," says he, "the mercy of the Parliament."

"The mercies of the wicked are cruel," cried Lady Derby. "Not that I mean a wicked Parliament, of which body I have an honourable and reverend esteem, but wicked factors and agents such as Moor and Rigby, who, for the advantage of their own interests, labour to turn kingdoms into blood and ruin. Unless they treat with my lord, they shall never have me, nor any of my friends alive."

The captain, finding Lady Derby immovable in her resolution, and doubtless acting on instructions from his colonels, then intimated that her own conditions for surrender would be accepted. She replied that she would never treat without commands from her lord, and dismissed the man with—

"Let that insolent fellow, Rigby, send me no more propositions, or his messenger shall be hanged at my gates ! "

But relief was at hand for the brave woman and her faithful men. Lord

Derby had arrived at Chester in March, 1644, and throughout the siege had been making desperate but ineffectual attempts to raise men and march to his wife's rescue. He appealed to Prince Rupert, the nephew of Charles I. and a close kinsman of the Countess of Derby, for assistance, and after many delays the Prince arrived in Cheshire. He, with Lord Derby, and eight thousand men entered Lancashire by Stockport Bridge on May 25, driving

Blackburn or Lancaster to the relief of York, where the Marquis of Newcastle was being besieged by Oliver Cromwell and Sir Thomas Fairfax, he decided upon Bolton as being out of the Prince's way. But scarcely had the Parliamentary forces entered the town than the Prince's army appeared upon the moors. In trying to avoid Lady Derby's avengers, Rigby had marched straight to their first objective. A bloody encounter took place, the

LATHOM HOUSE, REBUILT AFTER THE SIEGE

back a Parliamentary force sent to bar his passage. News of the relief coming to the beleaguered Countess speedily reached her enemies, and as he ran the risk of being hemmed in between the garrison and Prince Rupert's army, Rigby, in the dead of the night of the 26th, marched his men to Eccleston Green. He seems to have been undecided which road to take, but having reason to believe that Prince Rupert would march either through

Puritans fighting with the utmost desperation, and Lord Derby, burning with resentment for all that his wife had suffered, himself led the attack upon the town. With his own hand he killed an ensign-bearer, and captured his colours, the first taken that day. "On his first pressing into the town, closely following the foot at their entrance, his lordship met with Captain Bortle, formerly one of his own servants, but now the most virulent enemy against his lady in the siege. Him he did the honour of too brave a death of dying by his lord's hand, with some others of his good countrymen, who had for three months thirsted for his lady's and his children's blood."

The battle between the Royalists and Puritans at Bolton was called "The Bolton Massacre"; some years later Lord Derby paid for his gallantry that day with his head.

The same night Lord Derby and Prince Rupert entered Lathom in triumph, leaving sixteen hundred dead and seventy prisoners behind them at Bolton. One can imagine the joy of the meeting between husband and wife after a whole year's separation and all the misery they had undergone. Prince Rupert presented Lady Derby with "twenty-two of those colours, which three days before were proudly flourished before her house," taken at Bolton.

Shortly afterwards Lady Derby and her children went to the Isle of Man. Neither she nor Lord Derby were present at the second siege of Lathom House in the winter of 1645, but the small garrison and their servants resisted bravely until all their provisions were exhausted, and they were ordered to capitulate by King Charles himself. Lathom was then gutted and its contents destroyed by the Puritans.

Throughout all that time of anxiety and ceaseless fighting when Lady Derby proved herself such a heroine she was in constant communication with her husband, although to all appearances every channel by which letters could pass was closed to them. Writing to Prince Rupert from Chester, Lord Derby said: "I hourly receive little letters from her;" and of his methods in replying he says: "When Lathom was besieged in the year 1644, my wife, some children and good friends in it, I did write letters to them in cipher as much in as little compass as I could. I rolled the same in lead, sometimes in wax, hardly as big as a musket-bullet, that if the bearer suspected danger of discovery he might swallow it, and physic would soon find it again. I have writ in fine linen with a small pen, which hath been sewed in the bearer's clothes, as part of the linings. I have put a letter in a green wound, in a stick, pen, etc."

Even darker days were in store for the heroic Countess of Derby, as we shall see in the story of her husband's life.

THE BOWBEARERS OF BOWLAND

THE Forest of Bowland was famous so long ago as the days of the Saxons for the skill of its inhabitants in archery. It formed part of the great estate given in Lancashire by William the Conqueror to Roger de

A survey was made in 1652, during the Commonwealth, of the "Chace of Bolland part of the possessions of Charles Stewart, the late king, of which he was seized as in right of the Duchy of Lancaster; but now settled on trustees, for

EDMUND PARKER IN THE COSTUME OF BOWBEARER OF BOWLAND ABOUT THE YEAR 1790

Poictou, which ultimately passed into the possession of the Lacies. From this great family it went to swell the domains of the Duchy of Lancaster, and when the son of John of Gaunt became King Henry IV., together with all the other property belonging to the Duchy, it passed into the possession of the Crown. And so it remained until the reign of James I.

the use of the Commonwealth of England." From this survey we learn that the Forest was held from the Crown by several tenants on leases, "but now, for moste part, the said landes are held in fee-farme, being sold to the respective tenants by King James and King Charles as appears by diverse letters patent." Thus, in 1652 there were only fifteen lease-holders left,

68

and of these Robert Parker of Browsholme, held 929 acres, and Robert Sherburne of Mitton 3,693 acres. These leases did not include woods, underwoods, mines and quarries, which were strictly kept for the benefit of the Crown.

The principal officers of the Forest were a Bowbearer and a Steward, the latter of whom held courts at which any of the inhabitants of Bowland who had felled timber without licence, or killed any of the deer were fined. All the tenants, whether they were lease-holders or fee-farmers, were obliged to allow the deer to go "unmolested into their several grounds," and if they kept any dog, bigger than would go through a stirrup, to hunt the deer out of the corn they were fined by the Steward's Court. In 1652 there were "of redd deere of all sortes, viz. staggs, hyndes and calves, 20; which wee value to be worth £20; and of fallow deere 40; which wee value to be worth £20." For these 60 deer there were twelve keepers, a sure sign that the stock had sadly wasted during the war of the Great Rebellion.

The Bowbearer, who represented the King, was appointed by letters patent. One of these documents is still in existence. It is dated in the second year of the reign of Richard III., and appoints James Harrington to the office.

It is in Latin, of which the following is the translation:—

"Richard the Third by the grace of God, King of England and France, Lord of Ireland, to whom all these presents shall come, health in the Lord. Know ye that in consideration of the true and faithful service which the well-beloved knight of our body, James Harrington, has formerly performed and intends to perform in the future, we have granted and confirm unto him the office of Master Forester of the stewards, bailiffs, foresters and the drivers of our Forest of Bowland in the counties of York and Lancaster, to have and to hold and enjoy the aforesaid office of the said James for himself or his deputy, or his deputies; being duly qualified from the feast of St. Michael the Archangel last occurring, during his life, receiving in and for the holding of the said office a sum of £21 and 10d. as an equivalent for certain rights of *putura*[1] which belonged to the said office in the time of our ancestors, and were of custom held and received from various of our tenants and dependants within the said country and forest by way of fees over and above the 10 marks annually due by ancient custom for the fee of the said Master Forester.

"Given under the Seal of the Duchy at London. 16 February in the second year of our reign."

Later, the position became practically vested in the family of the Parkers of Browsholme, who were Bowbearers of Bowland from father to son. Our illustration shows Edward Parker, who was Bowbearer in the reign of Charles II., with the insignia of his office, a staff tipped with a buck's horn, and a bugle at his girdle. That the office was held by this family as early as 1591, is shown by a letter from Sir Anthony Mildmay, the Chancellor of the Duchy of Lancaster, to whom a "fee-stag" was to be given each year in virtue of his office. In modern English it runs thus: "After my hearty commendations. These shall be to will and require you to deliver, or cause to be delivered, to my very good Lord William, Bishop of Chester, or to the bearer hereof in his name, my fee stag of the season to be had within her Majesty's forest of Bowland; and this my letter shall be your sufficient warrant and discharge.

[1] Putura was a right claimed by foresters and bailiffs to take meat for their own hounds and dogs gratis, from the tenants within the forest boundaries.

"Great Bartholemew, the XXVIIth of June 1591.

"Ant' Mildmay

"To the Master of her Majesty's game within the forest of Bowland; and to his Deputy or Deputies there."

During the war between Charles I. and the Parliament, the Edward Parker of that day seems to have enjoyed the protection of both sides. In 1644, this letter mit some insolence without command from their superiors is the cause of my writing at this time; hoping hereby, through your care, to prevent a future evill, in all thankfullness I shall acknowledge (besides the great obligation you putt on Mr. Parker) myself to bee,

"Your much obliged

"RIC. SHUTTLEWORTH.

"Gawthrop, 13 February, 1644."

I pray God bless the life of Master Edmund Parker. His Wife and all the Children that with him wonnes, His five Daughters and Seven Sonnes.

Anno. Dom. 1450.

NEC FLUCTU MOVETUR.

NEC FLATU

ANCIENT SAMPLER AT BROWSHOLME HALL

was written "For the Colonels and Lieut-Colonels within Craven," by a fanatical Parliamentarian and sequestrator of Royal estates :—

"Noble Gentlemen. I could desire to move you in behalfe of Mr. Edward Parker of Broosome, that you would be pleased to take notice of his house, and give order to the officers and souldiers of your regiments, that they plunder not, nor violently take away, any of his goods, without your privities; for truly the proneness of souldiers sometimes to com-

Four years later it was the turn of the Royalists.

"These are to intreat all officers and souldiers of the Scottish armie, and to require all officers and souldiers of the English armie under my command, that they for bear to take or trouble the person of Edward Parker, of Brousholme, esquire, or to plunder his goods, or anie other hurt or damage to doe unto him in his estate.

"THO. TYLDESLEY.

"This 8th day of August

"*Anno Dom* 1648."

In 1818 Thomas Lister Parker was Bowbearer of Bowland, but the office had become only a titular honour, for in 1805, a fine herd of wild deer which had been carefully raised by his ancestors from the sixty red and fallow deer noted in the Commonwealth survey of 1652, was destroyed.

The forest of Bowland ran into Yorkshire as well as into Lancashire. Whitaker

thus describes it in 1818 : " The beautiful river Hodder, famous for its umber, rising near the cross of Grete, and passing through the parish of Sladeburn, intersects the forest and forms the only ornamental scenery of a tract otherwise bleak and barren, by its deep and fringed banks. On one of these is the little chapel of Whitewell, together with an inn, the court-house of Bowland, and, undoubtedly, a very ancient resting-place for travellers journeying from Lancaster to Clitheroe or Whalley. The landscape here is charming. The Hodder, brawling at a

great depth beneath the chapel, washes the foot of a tall conical knoll, covered with oaks at its top, and is soon lost in overshadowing woods beneath. But it is for the pencil and not the pen, to do justice to the scene. On the opposite hill, and near the keeper's house, are the remains of a small encampment, which have been supposed to be Roman, but they are too inconsiderable to justify any conjecture about them. At no great distance a cairn of stones was opened, and found to contain a sort of kist vaen and a skeleton. . . . On an adjoining height was discovered a quarry and manufactory of querns, or portable millstones, of which, though probably introduced by the Roman soldiers into Britain, the use appears to have continued among us till after the Norman Conquest."

The home of the Parkers was Browsholme Hall, in the Yorkshire portion of the Forest of Bowland. It was rebuilt in 1604, and nearly two hundred years later was " improved " and " modernised." But a store of ancient manuscripts and relics were most carefully preserved. Amongst these was a skull which was said to have been used by a former Parker during his prayers as a reminder of death. But the most valuable relic is the original seal of the Commonwealth, used upon the documents giving Puritan ministers licence to preach. The seal was of heavy silver,

ANCIENT DOGGANGE (A STIRRUP) OF THE FOREST OF BOWLAND

and bore the inscription, "The Seale for the approbation of Public Preachers." In the centre were two palm branches, and within them an open book, upon which was inscribed "The Word of God." There was also the remains of an ancient sampler, upon which the "modernising" spirit of the early nineteenth century had evidently been at work. As shown in the illustration, the pattern of the needle-work round the edges and the quarterings of the coat of arms, have almost disappeared, and the ancient lettering has been replaced by type.

Another relic of the past was the stirrup through which every dog belonging to the tenants in the Forest of Bowland had to pass. Heavy fines were inflicted upon those who kept dogs of such a size that they could not go through the stirrup.

SOME LANCASHIRE PROVERBS

LANCASHIRE proverbs are very numerous, and always to the point. In many counties the use of proverbs is slowly dying out, but this is not the case in Lancashire. For example, you will hear a cautious Lancashire man holding back a too eager friend from passing in front of a moving waggon or omnibus, say, "Nay, howd on! *There's as mich room behint as before!*" To one who is exaggerating in telling a story you will hear it said, "Come! Tha's said enough, thou'st overdoin' it, owd lad. *There's a difference between scrattin' yor head and pullin' th' hair off!*"

By getting married a man *larns what mayl is a pound*, and when he is choosing a wife he is warned that *Fine faces fill no butteries, an' fou uns rob no cubbarts.*

When an argument at a club or the ale-house waxes warm, and the disputants begin to lose their temper, some humourist of the party will say, "Come, come lads! No wranglin'. Let us go in for a bit o' peace and quietness, as Billy Butterworth said when he put his mother-in-law behint the fire."

The person who is bright and amusing in other people's houses, but gloomy and ill-tempered in his own home, is well described in, *He hangs th' fiddle at th' dur sneck.* On the other hand, *Th' quiet sow eats a' t' chaff*, most accurately describes the man who speaks little, but who is very observant and takes in all he hears. This proverb is in use in other places besides Lancashire; the form is slightly different—*The silent sow gets most of the wash*; but its meaning and application to quiet people are the same.

But a purely Lancashire proverb is, *There's most thrutching where there's least room*, and from this perhaps arose the story of how when the flea and the elephant were passing into the Ark together, the flea said to the elephant, "Now then, maister! no thrutching!"

QUEEN ELIZABETH AND THE LANCASHIRE DIVINE

WHEN Queen Elizabeth succeeded her sister, Queen Mary Tudor, the "Bloody Mary" of unhappy memory, she immediately proceeded to re-establish the Protestant religion in England. But the changes in the State religion, following upon the break between Henry VIII. and the Pope, from Roman Catholicism to Protestantism under that monarch and his son Edward VI., to Roman Catholicism under his daughter, Mary Tudor, had left the bulk of the people in a state of bewilderment.

Under Henry and Edward the Roman Catholic priests had been driven from the parish churches to make room for ministers of the Reformed religion. The services and their ceremonial had been entirely changed, the rood screens had been torn down ; and the saying of the Mass was forbidden by law. Under Mary the ministers of the Reformed faith were in their turn driven out, the Roman Catholic priests were restored, and with them the ancient ceremonial, the rood screens and the saying of the Mass. To the convinced Protestant and Roman Catholic these changes made no difference. Both followed the practice and the worship of their faith regardless of the edicts of kings and queens. Under Henry VIII., and Edward VI., the Roman Catholics suffered for their belief ; under Mary Tudor it was the turn of the Protestants, and under Elizabeth Roman Catholics again fell beneath the ban of the law.

Notwithstanding the re-establishment of Roman Catholicism under Mary Tudor the great mass of the English people were in sympathy with the principles of Protestantism, yet it behoved Queen Elizabeth to move with circumspection in the chaos of religious thought which distracted the country upon her accession. She herself was a firm Protestant, but she was a wise woman, and seeing the danger of drastic measures, she not only hesitated to take the title her father, Henry VIII., had assumed as Supreme Head of the Church of England, but as a further concession to the feelings of her Roman Catholic subjects, the Mass was said at her Coronation. This was the last time the Mass was said at the crowning of an English sovereign. But at the same time Elizabeth ordered that the Gospel of the day should be read in English as well as in Latin, and one of her earliest proclamations was to order the daily lesson, the Ten Commandments, the Litany, the Lord's Prayer, and the Creed to be read in the churches in the native tongue until Parliament should decide upon the religious services of the people.

The first Act of her Parliament was to invest Elizabeth with the Supreme Headship of the Church, both spiritually and temporally. Her hesitation in assuming this title was due, it is said, to Thomas Lever, a Lancashire minister and an advanced Puritan. So much confusion of opinion, however, existed, that fourteen Bishops refused to take the oath acknowledging the Queen's supremacy and were deprived of their sees in consequence. This was followed by another Act of Parliament called the Act of Uniformity, in which the proper services and ordinances were fully set out, but so little was it regarded that Elizabeth's most trusted counsellor, Cecil—the ancestor of the present Marquis of Salisbury—wrote of the Reformed ministers : "Some perform divine service in the chancel, some in the body of the church, some in a seat made in the church, some in the pulpit with their faces to the people. Some say with a surplice and others without one. In some places the table stands in the body of the church, in others it stands in the chancel; in some places the table stands altarwise, distant from the wall a yard, in others in the middle of the chancel, north and south; in some places the table is joined, in others it stands upon trestles; in some has a carpet, in others none. Some administer the communion with surplice and cope; others with surplice alone; others with none. Some with a chalice; others with a communion cup; others with a common cup; some with unleavened bread, some with leavened. Some receive kneeling, others standing, others sitting. Some sign with a cross, others sign not. Some minister with a surplice, others without; some with a square cap; some with a round cap; some a buttoned cap; some with a hat; some in scholar's clothes; some in others."

Queen Elizabeth herself, although a staunch Protestant, had a leaning towards a ceremonial service, due to her natural love of pageantry, and there is little doubt

that had she consulted her own inclinations the services of the Reformed Church would have received much of the splendour which has ever distinguished those of the Church of Rome. But there was a powerful body of men, amongst them three notable Lancashire clergymen — Alexander Nowell, Edwin Sandys and Thomas Lever—who, having imbibed the theories and tenets of Calvin during an exile in Switzerland in the reign of Mary Tudor, were bent upon reforming the Reformed Church. They were in consequence known as Puritans. Each of these three Lancashire divines represented a different school of Puritan thought. On the accession of Elizabeth, Nowell had been made Dean of St. Paul's Cathedral, London; Sandys, Bishop of Worcester; and Lever, Archdeacon of Coventry, and when, in 1562, the Queen summoned a convocation to prepare "the articles of faith and offices of religion," these three men were appointed members. The difficulties that faced Elizabeth in this momentous settlement of the services of the Church of England

PISCATOR HOMINUM

Alexander Nowell

are exemplified by the opinions of these three Lancashire prelates—" Nowell had no personal objection to the ceremonies, but wished to conciliate the Puritans by dispensing with many of them ; Sandys had very strong objections to the ceremonies, but wished to conciliate nobody, and therefore strove to reject them, although he would rigorously enforce them until they were legally abolished ; Lever regarded the ceremonies as utterly unchristian, and would on no account conform if they were legally established." Nowell was chosen as the spokesman of the convocation, and it was owing to his anxiety to conciliate all parties that the services of the Church of England were settled upon the lines in which they are still preserved, the Puritans being beaten by one vote only.

Alexander Nowell was the second son of John Nowell of Read, an ancient family long settled in the parish of Whalley, and was closely related to the Towneleys, the Hopwoods and Heskeths, and other old Lancashire families. He was educated at the grammar school at Middleton, and at thirteen went to Brazenose College, Oxford — the college of nearly all Lancastrians. Very early in his career he became an ardent supporter of the Reformation, and after taking orders was appointed a Prebendary at Westminster Cathedral, where, learning that he was to be arrested by Bishop Bonner as a " heretic," he fled abroad and took refuge with other exiles for their faith's sake at Strasburg. During his exile and ever afterwards, Nowell was noted for his broad-mindedness and liberality of thought. " He always endeavoured to mediate in the troubles between the contending parties, and to concede his own opinion to either side for the sake of preserving unity and peace." His moderation, his high reputation as a

scholar and as a man of business, the sacrifices he had made for the Reformed Church, and, above all, his lack of all puritanical scruples either for or against ceremonies, and his earnest wish to bring " all true Protestants into harmonious action within the established Church," marked him out for the highest preferment ; some thought for the Archbishopric of Canterbury itself.   But for some reason, which has not come down to us, Queen Elizabeth cordially disliked him. When he was proposed as Provost of Eton she refused to have him anywhere so near Windsor, and struck his name from the list of clergymen selected by the Archbishop of Canterbury to preach before her.   When she attended St. Paul's Cathedral, as was then the custom of the sovereign, Queen Elizabeth could not escape Dean Nowell's ministrations.   But the poor Dean could not please her, and on two occasions, at least, felt all the weight of the royal wrath.

One New Year's morning the Queen found a Prayer Book, illustrated with pictures of saints and angels, provided for her use at St. Paul's.   Closing it angrily, she commanded the verger to bring her " a plain book."   When the service was over, she proceeded directly to the vestry and demanded of Dean Nowell,

" How came it to pass that a new Prayer Book was placed upon my cushion ? " speaking with that haughty anger she had inherited from her father, Henry VIII.

" May it please your Majesty, I caused it to be placed there," answered the Dean.

" Wherefore did you do so ? "

" To present your Majesty with a New Year's gift."

" You never could present me with a worse," cried the angry Queen.   " You know I have an aversion to idolatry.

The cuts resemble angels, saints, nay, grosser absurdities, pictures of the Blessed Trinity."

you read our proclamation against images, pictures and Romish relics in churches? Was it not read in your deanery? You

"'RETIRE FROM THAT UNGODLY DIGRESSION! TO YOUR TEXT, MR. DEAN!'"

"I meant no harm," protested the Dean, "nor did I think to offend your Majesty."

"You must needs be ignorant, then," the Queen said contemptuously. "Have

must needs be very ignorant to do this after our proclamation!"

The poor Dean was overwhelmed. "It being my ignorance, your Majesty may the better pardon it," he murmured.

But Queen Elizabeth was in no way mollified. "I am glad to hear it was your ignorance, rather than your opinion," she replied in the same tone of anger and contempt.

"Be your Majesty assured it was my ignorance," cried the trembling Dean, entirely overcome by the royal anger. "Be your Majesty assured it was my ignorance!"

"If so, Mr. Dean, God grant you His Spirit and more wisdom for the future. Pray let no more of these mistakes be committed in the churches of our realm;" and so saying the Queen left the cathedral, vouchsafing the unhappy Nowell no leave-taking or any sign of recognition.

Although Nowell won the admiration of all his contemporaries, and although Elizabeth was urged again and again by the Archbishop of Canterbury and others to give him preferment in which his great talents might have a wider scope, and so more greatly benefit the Church, she invariably turned a deaf ear, her feminine prejudice against the man outweighing, for once, her foresight and wisdom as a Queen. If her unceasing rancour had been directed against Nowell's friend Edwin Sandys, also a Lancashire man from Hawkshead-in-Furness, Elizabeth might have pleaded some justification, for when he was Master of Catharine Hall and Vice-Chancellor of Cambridge, Sandys had preached a sermon, after the death of Edward VI., in honour of the proclamation of Lady Jane Grey as Queen of England in place of Queen Mary Tudor. Support of Lady Jane Grey was as traitorous to Queen Elizabeth as to her half-sister Mary Tudor, since Jane Grey's accession to the throne would have likewise dispossessed Elizabeth, but she seems to have borne no grudge against Sandys, and made him Bishop of Worcester and afterwards Archbishop of York.

Once more Dean Nowell fell under Elizabeth's keen displeasure, and this time the censure was public, and of a nature even more crushing than the rebuke over the "idolatrous" Prayer Book.

The Dean was preaching a Lenten sermon at St. Paul's Cathedral, before the Queen, and, probably with the unpleasant episode of the Prayer Book strong in his mind, hoping to show Elizabeth his strong feelings against any symbol that smacked of "popery," he spoke slightingly of the crucifix. But the poor Dean could not do right.

Elizabeth was seated in the royal closet which was occupied by the sovereign during divine service in old St. Paul's Cathedral, near the pulpit. It was observed that an expression of anger swept across the royal features when the Dean mentioned this subject, but as he set out to expatiate upon his reasons against the use of the crucifix, the Queen rapped her fan handle sharply upon the window ledge of the closet, and in a loud voice that was heard distinctly from one end of the building to the other, called out—

"Retire from that ungodly digression! To your text, Mr. Dean—leave that! We have heard enough of that."

The Dean was so dismayed that he could not go on. For a few moments he stood staring in speechless amazement at the angry monarch, then, with a vain effort to collect his thoughts, stammered a few broken words. But it was useless, and after a painful silence he left the pulpit. He was so overcome that the Archbishop of Canterbury "took him home with him and comforted him." Nowell was too strongly imbued with the fighting Lancastrian spirit to accept the Queen's censure without protest, and the next day wrote a letter to the Lord Treasurer Cecil in which he defended his sermon.

Dean Nowell was a great fisherman, as well as a great divine, and under his portrait in the hall of Brazenose College is an inscription, "piscator hominum" (fisher of men), which punningly alludes to his hobby and his qualities. Through his love of fishing this Lancashire Dean was accidentally the inventor of bottled ale. In addition to the deanery of St. Paul's, he held the rectory of Great discovery arose the great industry of bottling ale.

As a divine, Dean Nowell's name is for ever associated with the Catechism in the Book of Common Prayer. He was its author.

He did not forget his native county in the days of his prosperity, for he endowed a school at Middleton, in which place he himself was educated, which was called

READ HALL, THE BIRTHPLACE OF DEAN NOWELL

Hadham in Hertfordshire, and whilst in residence there fished continually in the River Ash. One day he placed a bottle containing some ale, which he had taken to drink with his frugal meal, in the grass by the riverside in order to keep it cool. In the excitement of the sport he forgot both his meal and the beer. A few days later he chanced to find the bottle, and on opening it found that the beer was in an effervescent state, making much froth when poured out. From this accidental

Queen Elizabeth's School, and was under the government of the Principal and Fellows of his old college at Oxford, Brazenose. Besides this endowment, he founded thirteen scholarships at Brazenose, to be held by scholars from Queen Elizabeth's School at Middleton, or from the schools at Whalley and Burnley.

Dean Nowell lived to the great age of ninety-five, and was buried in the Mary Chapel behind the high altar in old St. Paul's Cathedral.

THE "WARRINGTON ADVERTISER"

FROM the famous printing press of Thomas and William Eyres at Warrington there was issued on March 23, 1756, *Eyres' Weekly Journal, or Warrington Advertiser*, which was supposed to have been one of the earliest newspapers published in Lancashire. But it had its forerunners, both in Liverpool and Manchester. It was a small sheet of four pages, with three columns to the page. On the front page was a wood-cut of a post-boy of the period, riding out of the town over the old stone bridge leading to the south. This is probably the only illustration extant, in which the watch-house, upon the first pier of the bridge, is shown. A copy of this, the first Warrington newspaper, is most carefully treasured at the Free Library there, the date being " From Tuesday April 27 to Tuesday May 4, 1756." Curiously enough there is not a single item of local or county news. First there is a letter, dated Dublin, March 17, 1744, "supposed to have been wrote by a gentleman upon his travels in Ireland to a noble lord in England," and to which the Editor, disregarding the fact that the letter is twelve years old, prefaces, " We doubt not the Justness of his Sentiments, and the Genteel Manner in which they are express'd will afford an agreeable entertainment to our readers."

The editor relied upon the posts from London for his material, giving items of news under the heading of each day's post. Thus all the news on Thursday, the 29th March, 1756, was extracts from private letters as to an impending war, followed by three notices, each set out under a large heading, concerning Ireland, Scotland, and Country News. Under the heading of Ireland there is a notice that eleven rioters who were under sentence of transportation had been sent on board a tender in Dublin Bay, " at which they were much pleased in hopes of fighting the French." They evidently preferred fighting to prison. For Scotland, the news was that a ship, laden with meal and barley bread for the Clyde, had been cast away at Stornoway ; whilst under the heading of " Country News," there is the notice of the theft of the Communion cloth and a velvet cushion from Norwich Cathedral.

The news from London was not exciting, although we were at war with France. After various items concerning the movements of troops, comes this : " On Saturday in St. James Park, the serjeants and corporals of the first regiment of Foot Guards performed for the first time, the manual exercises of the Prussians, and we hear all the regiments of the Crown are to be instructed in the same exercises." The London news ends with an extract from a letter from Bawtrey, in Yorkshire, dated 20th inst., dealing solely with the weather. " The season or climate, which you will," it says, " has a regular kind of intermission — to-day has been its bad day ('tis a kind of tertian you must know) and a sore fit it has had ; it has rained fourteen or fifteen hours incessantly, and is extremely cold ; Friday last was just such another. The adjacent country makes the finest Dutch landscape imaginable. After all 'tis no jesting matter ; it puts a stop to all husbandry, great part of our barley is yet unsown, and as that is the staple commodity of this part of the country, it is well if many of our farmers do not find themselves more affected by the inclemency of the season than they are aware of."

The only items of Lancashire interest are the "Imports at Liverpoll," which afford a singular contrast with the imports of to-day.

Manchester : Ronald M'Donald, Londonderry, with 156½ trusses linen yarn.

Batchelor : Ralph Gill, Londonderry, with 2 bundles linen cloth, 22 cowhides, 153 trusses linen yarn.

Vread · Mich. Somme, Rotterdam, with 493 bags oats.

Nancy : Thos. Wilkinson, Wexford, with a parcel of oats and oatmeal.

Boyne : Pat Martin, Drogheda, with 118 trusses linen yarn, 4 bundles linen cloth, 68 cowhides, 1 bag feathers.

Young Theodore : Frank Vroesam, Rot-

There are only four advertisements in the paper. One states that a milliner's shop at Warrington opposite the Red Lion, and belonging to Mrs. Byron, had been broken into on " The night between the 7th and 8th." The most important things stolen were, "two light full chintzes, one of them runs with two remarkable flower'd stripes, the other runs with a large flower partly in a stripe and the other part in sprigs, partly in a stripe."

EYRES' WARRINGTON PRESS

terdam, with 682 wainscot boards, 6 logs oak, 29 malts flax, 15 bundles steel, 2 Hogsheads Geneva.

Duke : Peter Collier, Drogheda, with a parcel of oats and oatmeal.

Catherine from Youghal, *Margaret* from Wexford, and *Mary* from Wexford, with parcels of oat and oatmeal.

Of seven remaining entries of ships all came from Ireland with oats and oatmeal, except the *Hannah,* from South Carolina, which brought "20 Barrels, 40 Half-barrels of rice, 79 barrels of pitch, 4 tons of logwood, 3 casks indigo, and 6 barrels rice."

In addition pieces of lawn, handkerchiefs, " foreign plain lawns from four shillings to ten shillings a yard," a box of ribbons, cotton gloves and one pair of worked thread mitts, had been taken.

Another theft is also advertised, this being " an old bay gelding with a large star on face, short and strong, and full of flesh," which was stolen from the stable of the Red Lion, opposite to Mrs. Byron's millinery establishment.

The other two advertisements are of books. One is a " Description of Three Hundred Animals," being very proper presents for Youth ; the other is of " A

New and Compendious system of Practical Arithmetic."

There were no leading articles in these first numbers of the *Warrington Advertiser*, no expression of opinion on the momentous events then happening in Europe, nothing but a bare recital of stale news gathered from the *London Gazette*. And beyond the notice of Liverpool imports and the two advertisements of the robbery at the Red Lion and the milliner's shop there was no local or county reference. But in those days of meagre news, the brief accounts of the day's posts and the quotations from the *London Gazette* were doubtless read by the good folk of Warrington with eager curiosity.

The printing press of the Eyres Brothers was famous far beyond the confines of Lancashire. John Howard, the philanthropist and prison reformer, came to Warrington especially that they should print his book upon the state of prisons in England and on the Continent; they also printed the early poems of a local poetess, Mrs. Barbauld.[1] The Eyres Brothers turned out beautiful work. One wishes that the type of the *Warrington Advertiser* could be used for our newspapers to-day.

[1] See "A Lancashire Poetess."

THE OLD MANOR COURT-ROOM, WARRINGTON, WHERE THE LORD OF THE MANOR DISPENSED JUSTICE

PRINCE RUPERT OF THE RHINE

A STORY OF WINDLESHAW ABBEY

O F all the generals who fought for King Charles I. in the Great Rebellion none aroused so much enthusiasm amongst the Cavaliers, or so much detestation amongst the Roundheads, as the King's own nephew, Prince Rupert of the Rhine.

Prince Rupert was the third son of that hapless sister of Charles I. who was known as the " Winter Queen." Married to Frederick, Elector Palatine of the Rhine, her husband's ambition, and perhaps her own, brought a speedy end to her happiness, for the Elector by accepting the invitation of the Bohemians to become King of that country, raised up enemies who not only drove him from the city of Prague within a year of his coronation, but also laid waste his hereditary possessions of the Palatine in Germany, putting thousands of its inhabitants to the sword. Prince Rupert was born some six weeks after his father's coronation as King of Bohemia in October 1619. He thus came into the world at the very height of his parents' fortunes when the new King, handsome and debonair, and the new Queen, who had ever been especially beloved in England, were beginning to reign over the enthusiastic and Protestant Bohemians. Eleven months later Prince Rupert was

borne in his mother's arms across the bridge at Prague in her panic-stricken flight from the Palace, into which the Austrian troops were already pouring. He had been given a golden cradle by the ladies of Prague, but never was a gift less emblematical of the Prince's future life.

From the moment of their flight from Prague, his parents were King and Queen without a throne, Elector and Electress without a country, and for many years lived at the Hague, pensioners upon the bounty of Holland, and upon such supplies as the Winter Queen could, by prayers and entreaties, extract from her father James I. of England. Her husband never saw his native land again, but died in exile at the Hague. Prince Rupert therefore was brought up in Holland, and in a home where the means were so straitened, that the Queen, his mother, often had no money to pay the tradesmen or the wages of her servants. He early showed his strong inclination for a military life, and at the age of fifteen served as a volunteer in the life guards of the Prince of Orange, the ruler of Holland under whom he received his military training. Two years later Prince Rupert paid his first visit to England with his brother, the Prince Elector (their father, the King of Bohemia, had died five years previously), where they were warmly welcomed for their mother's sake, and where Prince Rupert made a deep impression upon his uncle Charles I.

Sir Thomas Rowe, who was one of the most devoted adherents of the Queen of Bohemia, thus wrote to that unfortunate lady of her third son ; " I have observed him of a rare condition full of spirit and action, full of observation and judgment. Certainly he will *réussir un grand homme*, for whatever he wills he wills vehemently : so that to what he bends he will be in it excellent—His Majesty (Charles I.) takes great pleasure in his unrestfulness, for he is never idle, and in his sports serious, in his conversation retired, but sharp and witty when occasion provokes him." In a second letter he added : " It is an infinite pity he is not employed according to his genius, for whatever he undertakes he doth it vigorously and seriously. His nature is active and spriteful, and may be compared to steel, which is the commanding metal if it be rightly tempered and disposed."

An amazing scheme was proposed about this time for the founding of an English colony in Madagascar, of which it was suggested that Prince Rupert should be the Governor, a striking proof of the impression he had made at the English Court of his powers of leadership and resource. Charles I. considered the project quite seriously, and went so far as to ask the assistance of the East India Company in the proposed expedition, and the poet Davenant addressed a laudatory ode to the seventeen-year-old Prince Rupert, celebrating his future conquests in the far-away island. Prince Rupert himself seems to have responded to, the suggestion with all the enthusiasm of adventurous youth, but his mother took a wiser view than her brother or her son : " As for Rupert's conquest in Mada-

gascar," she wrote, " it sounds like one of Don Quixote's conquests, where he promised his trusty Squire to make him King of an island." She told her son that such a scheme was " neither feasible, safe, nor honourable for him," and apparently fearing that he might be led into some disastrous adventure at the English Court, she urged his return to Holland, saying, " Though it be a great honour and happiness to him to wait upon his uncle, yet, his youth considered, he will be better employed to see the wars." Thereupon Rupert, of whom his mother once said, " he never did disobey me though to others he was stubborn and wilful," returned to Holland. Shortly afterwards he joined his brother, the Elector, in an attempt to regain their hereditary possession, the Palatine. They were defeated by the Austrians, and Rupert, after performing prodigies of valour, was taken prisoner, and for three years was held in close captivity, being ultimately released through the good offices of Charles I.

Prince Rupert's career really began with the outbreak of the Civil War, for when Charles I. raised his standard at Nottingham in 1642, his nephew instantly joined him and was made general of the horse. During the next two years Prince Rupert was at once the hope and the despair of the Royalist party ; the hope by reason of his valour, his brilliancy of attack, and the indomitable energy he displayed in marches and countermarches ; their despair because of his rash impetuousness and his over-riding of all counsels. In the story of the Siege of Lathom House it is recorded how Prince Rupert raised the siege in 1644, after the bloody massacre at Bolton : this massacre caused his name to be execrated amongst the Parliamentarians in Lancashire.

From Latham the Prince marched to

York, which was then being defended by the Marquis of Newcastle for the King against the Earl of Manchester and Sir Thomas Fairfax for the Parliament. On put to flight: this battle of Marston Moor was one of the most disastrous to his uncle's cause. The following extract from the *Perfect Diurnall*, a London news

PRINCE RUPERT

hearing of the approach of the Prince, the two generals raised the siege, and marching their forces to Marston Moor offered him battle. Flushed with his victories in Lancashire and Cheshire, the Prince imprudently accepted the challenge. His force was utterly routed and he himself sheet, of the 9th July, 1644, shows the extent of the disaster—

"This day Captain Stewart came from the Leaguer at York with a letter of the whole state of the late fight and routing of Prince Rupert, sent by the three generals to the Parliament. The effect whereof was this : That understanding Prince Rupert was marching against them with 20,000 men, horse and foot, the whole army arose from the siege, and marched to Long Marston Moor, four or five miles from York ; and the Prince, having notice of it, passed with his army the byway of Burrow Bridge ; that they could not hinder his passage to York, whereupon our army marched to Todcaster to prevent his going southwards ; but before the van was within a mile of Todcaster, it was advertised that the Prince was in the rear in Marston Moor, with an addition of 6000 of the Earl of Newcastle's forces, and was possessed of the best place of advantage both for ground and wind. The right wing of our horse was commanded by Sir Thomas Fairfax, which consisted of his whole cavalry and three regiments of the Scots horse ; next unto them was drawn up the right wing of the foot, consisting of the Lord Fairfax and his foot, and two brigades of the Scots foot for a reserve : and so the whole armies put into a battalia. The battle being begun, at the first some of our horse were put into disorder ; but, rallying again, we fell on with our whole body, killed and took their chief officers, and took most part of their standards and colours, 25 pieces of ordnance, near 130 barrels of powder, 10,000 arms, two waggons of carbines and pistols ; killed 30,000 and 1500 prisoners taken."

After hiding in a beanfield, Prince Rupert succeeded in reaching Lancashire, attended only by Captain Chisenhall, who had been one of the heroic defenders of Lathom House. The Prince's object was to get to Knowsley, where he believed he would be in security until he could escape to the coast, and cross to Waterford to levy more forces. But he was closely pursued, a thousand men being sent after him by Fairfax, to join with the Parliamentary forces in Lancashire, to prevent his escape. So hot were the soldiers on his track that the Prince was forced to take refuge in a small inn close to the ruins of Windleshaw Abbey near St. Helen's, passing himself and Chisenhall off as ordinary wayfarers.

Mr. Barrett, an antiquary of Manchester, who made a drawing of the ruins in 1780, thus describes them as they then appeared : " This ruinated Chapell at Windleshaw near St. Helen's in Lancashire is nearly levell'd with the ground, except a few stones left at the north side of the east end, and these last now grown over with bushes ; most of the steeple is yet standing, the upper part quite surrounded with ivy, whose friendly care seems resolv'd to preserve the remains of this venerable fabrick to the last extremity, yet what is it the corrosive teeth of time doth not destroy ? Of late an unknown ruffian hand, arm'd with axe or bill, hath nearly separated the root of ivy from the branch, so of course this verdant monument of antiquity which hath long preserved the steeple from wind and weather must now most likely in a little time die itself. The Chapell and ground adjoining is now made use of as burying ground for the Roman Catholicks in the neighbourhood. The priests lye buried within the now fallen Chapell walls, under handsome gravestones, and agreeable to their order with their heads to the east. The layity bury near the Chapell, and fix stones at the head, on all which is a cross and name of the dead. On the south side is a stone cross with three steps. The whole burying ground lay waste in open field till within these two years it hath been inclos'd with a new wall. The place, though in ruins is still had in great veneration by the neighbourhood. When this place was founded, or by whom, or to what saint dedicated, I have not learn'd, but suspect the patron saint to be St. Thomas, for near here is a well which goes by his name, and bath'd in oft in summer in regard of extraordinary virtues being ascrib'd to the water. The chapell is but small, about twelve yards long and three wide, the steeple about eight yards high; the place said to be demolish'd during the wars of Charles the First."

This chapel, or abbey as it was called, was founded by Sir Thomas Gerard of Bryn in 1435, and was dedicated to St. Thomas, and, at the time when Prince Rupert took refuge near by, had only lately been ruined by the Puritans.

A curious legend clung for many generations about this old ruin, a legend which Roby expanded into one of the most dramatic of his "Traditions." It is known that Rupert and his companion were hardly pressed when in the neighbourhood of Knowsley, and that their project of reaching the coast and so gaining Ireland having been frustrated, they made their way southwards to Oxford where Rupert joined his uncle, King Charles. Roby introduces into his story, Marian, the beautiful daughter of the innkeeper, a Puritan parson called Gilgal Snape, and Steenie Ellison, a half-insane gravedigger.

Prince Rupert and Chisenhall set off from the inn in spite of the warnings of the beautiful Marian, who had already received some intimation as to the identity of the Prince and the danger he was running. They had proceeded about a mile or two on the road through a dense fog when they became aware they were being pursued, and taking advantage of the obscurity they leapt their horses through a gap in the hedge, behind which they concealed themselves. In a few moments two horsemen passed slowly by and they heard the following conversation—

"I say again, heed it as we may, this mist will be the salvation of our runaways.

After having dogged them to such good purpose from Lathom, it will be a sorry deed should they escape under this unlucky envelope."

"Tush, faint heart—thinkest thou these enemies of the faith shall triumph and our own devices come to nought? Nay, verily, for the wicked are as stubble, and the ungodly as they whom the fire devoureth."

"But I would rather have a brisk wind than all thy vapours, thy quiddities and quotations. Yet am I glad they have not ta'en the turn to Knowsley!"

"Which way soever they turn, either to the right hand or to the left, we have them in the net, and snares and pitfalls shall devour them."

The voices of the speakers died away in the mist, and Chisenhall asked the Prince what should be done. Rupert answered him—

"Why of a surety, friend, there be many reasons why we may pray for a safe passport from this unhappy land, but it seemeth as though our purposes were to be for ever crossed. Towards Knowsley, now, it doth appear we must proceed, our haven and hiding-place; these rogues having got wind that we did not intend to pass by thither, we must countermine the enemy, or rather double upon their route."

Judging that they were then about two miles from Knowsley, Rupert and his companion turned their horses in what they believed was the direction across country, but, after wandering for over an hour in the fog, to their rage and vexation, they found themselves close to the ruins from which they had started. Scarcely had they realised that they had been moving in a circle when the Prince's bridle was seized by Steenie, who, with demoniacal laughter, cried out—

"Back again so soon?—Wi' the de'il at your crupper too?"

Prince Rupert drew his pistol, but before he could fire it his horse made a sudden spring and, stumbling, fell, bringing its rider heavily to the ground. Chisenhall at once went to his master's assistance and found him lying unconscious. All his efforts to restore the Prince being fruitless, he galloped off to the inn to procure assistance, deeming it wiser to

Chisenhall could do nothing. Marian suspected Steenie had some hand in the Prince's removal, and after some persuasion and with the promise that she would get tidings of his friend on the following day, induced him to hide in an upper chamber above one of the outhouses.

"Keep snug here in thy quarters, friend," she said, "for since you left there

WINDLESHAW ABBEY IN THE EIGHTEENTH CENTURY

run the risk of captivity for them both, than allow the Prince perhaps to die.

The innkeeper, his wife, and the beautiful Marian were much surprised at Chisenhall's return, but immediately they heard his news, set out with such simple restoratives as they possessed to the spot where he had left the Prince. To Chisenhall's horror and dismay the Prince was no longer there. His horse was quietly grazing, but of Rupert there was no sign.

came divers of the people to inquire, and as He would have it, from me only. Ye be sons of Belial, they said, and Cavaliers. But ye have eaten and drunken in our dwelling, and though red with the blood of the saints, I cannot deliver you into the hands of your pursuers."

With the idea of discovering whether the Prince had been found lying unconscious by his pursuers and taken away, or whether he was the victim of one of

Steenie Ellison's impish tricks, Marian went to see Gilgal Snape, a Puritan minister who lived near by. By adroit questioning she discovered that although Gilgal knew of the presence of the two strangers at her father's inn and the quality of one of them, he was so well informed in all matters concerning the preparations made for their capture that if the Prince had fallen into his enemies' hands, he would have had word of it. She next questioned Gilgal as to Steenie and his whereabouts, the half-witted sexton being a black sheep whom the Puritans from time to time had persuaded to enter the fold, from which as often Steenie had slipped with terrible backslidings.

" Knowest thou where he abideth ? " asked Marian, " or if he doth attend the outpouring of the word hereabout ? "

Gilgal's answer is typical of the language used by the Puritan ministers of the day, and shows the belief that the mental crises from which the half-witted, such as Steenie Ellison, suffer from time to time, were direct possession by the devil.

" Verily nay," he said, " but I have heard that he hath been seen in the house of ungodly self-seekers, and notorious Papists and malignants, even with our enemies of Garswood. He hath likewise been found resorting unto that high place of Papistry, Windleshaw, of late ; despising—yea, reviling—the warnings and godly exhortations of the Reverend Master Haydock, who did purpose within himself to win, peradventure. it might be to afflict with stripes, this lost one from the fold, that he might bring him back. But he hath sorely buffeted and evil entreated this diligent shepherd with many grievous indignities, such as tying him unto a gate, and vexing him with sundry of Satan's devices. Yet we would fain hope that he is a chosen vessel, though now defiled by the adversary. He will

return peradventure, as heretofore, when the day of his visitation is past."

In the dead of that same night Marian found Steenie digging a grave near the ruined chapel. Although almost overcome by horror she forced herself to speak to him, and from his half insane babbling discovered that the grave was intended for Prince Rupert who was securely bolted in the tower. Marian further discovered that whilst Steenie had no intention of killing the Prince or harming him, yet so firmly was the idea fixed in his clouded brain that the grave he was digging must be for the Prince and the Prince only, that he was determined to keep him so that he should not escape being buried in the grave. With quick woman wit, Marian pointed out that the prisoner in the tower would not be likely to occupy the grave unless Steenie starved him to death. " I thought not of that before, Marian," he said, " he will want some food. Ay! Ay! bless thy little heart, I did not think on't, but for thee Marian I should ha' kept him there and he might have starved outright." Marian sped back to the inn and returning to the tower with a basket filled with provisions, was taken by Steenie to a small chamber which was lighted only by a grating and where she found the Prince, who was sadly in need of the food she brought.

The pursuit upon him being so close, Marian suggested that he should stay where he was whilst Chisenhall remained in equally safe hiding at the inn. In thanking her for her timely succour Rupert said that he had not the means to reward her kindness as he would wish. From his words Marian realized the difficulty attending his flight without sufficient money to meet the expenses of the way, and at once boldly asked Steenie, who was notoriously a miser, to lend her what he could. She seems to have had some subtle influence over this madman, for without much ado he handed her his little treasure which she immediately gave to Rupert. Suddenly Steenie burst out in a paroxysm of fear and distress, declaring that he had bought the grave which he had dug for Rupert. He explained to his dismayed hearers that he had sold his own grave to the devil for a gold piece, and that so long as he kept the piece, he would never die. . Inadvertently he had handed this price of his grave to Marian amongst the other coins, and as Rupert now held it, Steenie cried that he had sold his grave to him. In vain they endeavoured to calm him, but his clouded wits prevented him seeing the logic of any argument. With increasing terror he protested again and again that his death was imminent, and that he himself would speedily occupy the grave he had intended for Prince Rupert.

Rupert offered to restore the coin but Steenie replied : " 'Tis needless ; the token once from my grasp and in the fingers of another whose grave I have digged, would never change my doom by its return. Keep what thou hast and may it serve thee more faithfully than it hath served me ! But remember—let me say it while my senses hold together, for I feel the blast coming that shall scatter them to the four winds—remember, if thou part therefrom, as I have done, to some doomed one, thou shalt go to the grave in his stead. But a charmed life is thine as long as it is in thy possession. Away— leave me—the master will be here presently for his own ! Leave me, I say ; for when the fiend cometh, he'll not tarry. But be sure you make fast the door, lest I escape, and mischief happen should I get abroad."

It was only too evident that a paroxysm of madness was about to assail the unhappy Steenie. Prince Rupert and

Marian therefore hastened from the tower, bolting the door on the outside. Marian hid Rupert with Chisenhall, and at the break of day hastened to Gilgal Snape, begging him to go at once to Windleshaw chapel and exercise the gift in "binding the strong man armed" for which he was famous throughout the countryside, or in other words the casting out of devils from those who were possessed.

Gilgal accompanied her at once to the tower from which rang the cries and shrieks of the wretched Steenie, who believed that he was being tormented by the devil. Dismissing Marian, the Puritan divine mounted to the encounter with the evil one alone.

In the evening he sought the girl at the inn. All day he had wrestled with the evil spirit, which he had finally conquered, but he told Marian that, shortly after it had been driven forth from his body, Steenie Ellison had died. He likewise told her that the evil spirit, before it was cast out, had uttered many strange divinations and prophecies. It had told him that Marian was harbouring two sons of Belial, one " even the chief captain of the King's host" and furthermore that this man wooed her for his bride. He bade her to take him instantly to " this Joab the son of Zeruiah, this captain of the King's host." Trembling and afraid Marian took him to the loft where the two fugitives were hiding.

" I am one of few words," said Gilgal, " and so much the rather as that I now stand in the presence of mine enemies. What sayest thou, Prince Rupert, the persecutor of God's heritage who didst not stay thine hand from the slaughter even of them that were taken captive ? What sayest thou that the word should not go forth to kill and to slay, even as thou didst smite and not spare, but didst destroy utterly them who, when beleaguered by thine armies in Bolton, were delivered into thine hand!"

The surprised Prince Rupert accused Marian of betraying him, but to this Gilgal replied that all had been revealed to him by the prophecy of the evil spirit, who, besides discovering the identity of the Prince, and that he had wooed Marian to be his wife, had said that if Prince Rupert should wed, a son of his would sit upon the throne of the unhappy realm of England.

"And what if I should not wed?" said Prince Rupert.

"'To this point too was the prophecy accordant," answered Gilgal, " the sceptre nevertheless shall be given to one of thy race; thy sister's son shall carry down the line of kings to this people; and the Lord's work shall still prosper. Now," he said to Marian, "daughter of many prayers—for I have yearned over thee with more than a father's love—choose thee without constraint this day. Thou hearest the words of this prophecy; wilt thou be the mother of kings, or the lowly and despised follower of God's heritage?"

Marian chose " to suffer affliction with the people of God than obtain all the treasures of Egypt." This answer saved the Prince, according to Roby. " Thou hast come forth as gold from the furnace," said Gilgal to Marian; " thou hast kept the faith and held fast thy profession." And when she asked whither the Prince could go, Gilgal said—

"Take no thought for their safety; thy constancy hath earned their deliverance. My safe conduct will carry them unharmed beyond the reach of their enemies; but let them not return—it is at their own peril if they be found again harboured in this vicinage, and their blood be on their own heads!"

And so Prince Rupert joined King Charles at Oxford to continue his daring and brilliant feats of valour throughout the rest of that unhappy war. Rupert never married, but the son of his sister, the Electress Sophia of Hanover, succeeded to the English throne, thus fulfilling the prophecy given by the demoniac at Windleshaw Abbey.

"COCKS" AND "CATCHPENNIES"

BEFORE the days of cheap newspapers the sellers of broadsheets, which were known as "cocks," or "catchpennies," did a roaring trade, especially after the execution of murderers whose crimes had attracted much popular attention. These broadsheets varied, but as a rule were much the same size as a page of one of our modern magazines ; they told their story sometimes in prose, but more often in verse, and were generally decorated with an illustration at the top. The same illustration did service for countless broadsheets ; the account of executions, no matter what the circumstances or the locality, being headed by the same rough drawing of a gallows with a man hanging dead. The paper was bad, the printing and illustrations worse, whilst grammar was not the strong point of the stories told upon these broadsheets. Poetry was more popular than prose because the sellers advertised their wares by reading the contents aloud in the streets, little crowds of people gathering round to hear the "patter," as it was called. A clever "patterer" was certain of a ready sale.

The centre or manufactory of this street literature was in Seven Dials, in London, a curious character called Jemmy Catnach, having the monopoly of its production, after having driven a rival—a retired bumboat woman from Portsmouth—from the field ; and it was through Catnach that the name "catchpenny" came to be applied to this form of publication. Two men, Weare and Thurnell, had committed a murder which excited public interest. They were tried, convicted, sentenced to death and hanged. A fortnight after the execution Catnach brought out a broadsheet headed, "We are alive again," but the space between the "we" and the "are" was so small that at first sight it read, "Weare alive again." Thousands of copies were bought by the astonished crowds in the streets, with the result that Catnach netted over £500 by the trick. The broadsheet itself contained nothing about the murderer, and thus the fraud led to the sheets being called "catchpennies." "Cocks" was the older term, and was supposed to have come from the fact that many of the stories related on the sheets were "cooked" stories, but the more probable explanation is that the story of the Cock Lane Ghost in London first appeared on one of these sheets, and was for many years one of the most favourite with the street-sellers and buyers.

Although the "cocks" and "catchpennies" were printed and published in London, their biggest sale was in the North of England, and especially in Lancashire. From time to time, therefore, concession was made to local feeling, and in a collection of these sheets there are several relating to Lancashire. One, "Th' Owdham Chap's Visit to th' Queen," relates in dialect how the writer went up to London, soon after the birth of the Prince of Wales (the late King Edward VII.), and saw Queen Victoria, the Prince Consort and the infant Prince at Buckingham Palace. The writer's imagination was stronger than his respect for Royalty. Another, written at the time of the establishment of the police force in Manchester is called, "Manchester's an Altered Town," and gives an interesting account of the changes in the city. It is also a good example of the quality of the verse of these "catchpennies"—

"Once upon a time this good old town was
    nothing but a village,
Of husbandry and farmers too, whose time
    was spent in tillage ;

But things are altered very much, such
  building now allotted is,
It rivals far, and soon will leave behind,
  the great Metropolis.
     O dear O !
       Manchester's an altered town,
          O dear O !

Once on a time, were you inclined your
  weary limbs to lave, sir,
In summer's scorching heat, in the Irwell's
  cooling wave, sir,
You had only to go to the Old Church for
  the shore, sir ;
But since those days the fish have died,
  and now they are no more, sir.

When things do change, you ne'er do
  know what next is sure to follow ;
For, mark the change in Broughton now,
  of late 'twas but a hollow ;
For they have found it so snug, and
  changed its etymology,
They have clapt in it a wild beasts' show,
  now called the Garden of Zoology.

A market on Shudehill there was, and it
  remains there still, sir :
The Salford old bridge is taken away, and
  clapt a new one in, sir ;
There's Newton Lane, I now shall name,
  has had an alteration,
They've knocked a great part of it down
  to make a railway station.

There's Bolton Railway Station in Salford,
  give attention,
Besides many more too numerous to
  mention ;
Besides a new police to put the old ones
  down, sir,
A Mayor and Corporation to govern this
  old town, sir.

There's Manchester and Salford old bridge
  that long has stood the weather,
Because it was so very old they drowned
  it altogether ;
And Brown-street Market too, it forms
  part of this sonnet,
Down it must come they say, to build a
  borough gaol upon it.

Not long ago, if you had taken a walk
  through Stevenson Square, sir,
You might have seen, if you look'd, a
  kind of chapel there, sir :

And yet this place, some people thought,
  had better to come down, sir ;
And in the parson's place they put a
  pantaloon and clown, sir.

In former times our cotton swells were
  not half so mighty found, sir,
But in these modern times they every-
  where abound, sir,
With new police and watchmen, to break
  the peace there's none dare,
And at every step the ladies go, the
  policemen cry, 'Move on, there.'

In former days this good old town was
  guarded from the prigs, sir,
By day by Constables, by night by watchmen with Welsh wigs, sir ;
But things are altered very much, for all
  those who're scholars
May tell the new policemen by their
  numbers on their collars."

A ballad upon another sheet which is
entitled, "Miles Weatherhill, the Young
Weaver, and his sweetheart, Sarah Bell,"
set forth the story of a young man who
was executed at Manchester for the murder of his sweetheart. The girl was a
servant at Todmorden Parsonage, and
because he was refused permission to see
her, Weatherhill made an attack upon the
inmates of the house, killing two of them.
The writer of the following doggerel was
clearly in sympathy with the murderer,
for he says—

" Three innocent lives has been sacrificed,
    And one serious injured all through
      true love.
  If they'd not been parted, made broken-
      hearted,
    Those in the grave would be living
      now ;
  And Miles would not have died on the
      gallows
    For slaying the maiden and Parson
      Plow.

And all good people, oh, pray consider,
    Where true love is planted, there let it
      dwell ;
And recollect the Todmorden murder,
    Young Miles the weaver, and Sarah
      Bell."

In the "Wigan Murder" is related the "examination and confession of John Healey, who sums up a particularly revolting and cruel murder thus—

"John Healey is my name,
    It was strong whisky did my head inflame,
    With four companions at their desire,
    At Button Pit, near Wigan,
    To thrust poor James Barton in the
        furnace flames of fire."

A very popular form of the "cocks" was that in which gossiping tales, sometimes

1839, a comparatively rich man, and although the "Seven Dials Literature;" as it was called, continued to be issued by another firm, it gradually languished, and is now only represented by the sheets of ballads which hawkers sell at fairs, and which may also be seen in stationers' shops in the poorer quarters. There was a knack in writing these effusions of the street, literary quality being the last consideration, and one of the last of the authors is said to have written many

ROBERT GREEN,
THE CELEBRATED BALLAD SINGER IN BURNLEY

distinctly scurrilous, were told of Mr. and Mrs. ——, or Mr. and Miss ——. They generally began, "Near this street," or "In this neighbourhood," and guileless folk would be induced by the hawkers to buy them in the firm belief that they actually referred to happenings in their own district. The task of filling in the names was a pleasing one for those of evil minds or malicious intentions.

Jemmy Catnach retired from the business of publishing "catchpennies" in

hundreds. The growth of newspapers gradually drove the "patterer" and the ballad-singer, with their illiterate and crudely printed "catchpennies," from the streets, since they provided fuller and more vivid details of "last moments on the scaffold" and "dying confessions." The general spread of education likewise caused them to be regarded with contempt.

Of the Lancashire ballad-singers, or "patterers," Robert Green of Burnley was the most famous.

THE ROMANCE OF RADCLIFFE TOWER

RADCLIFFE TOWER AS IT WAS MANY YEARS AGO

THE ruins of Radcliffe Tower, now surrounded by mills, manufactories and bleaching-works, are all that is left of the glories of an ancient family. William Camden, the great Elizabethan chronicler, visiting Lancashire in 1582, said no county in England abounded with so many old families bearing the same name as the place in which they lived, as the county palatine. In Anglo-Saxon times the red sandstone rock by which the Irwell runs at Radcliffe, was called the Rate-clive, or the Red Cliff. The Normans dubbed it Rougemont, but the older form prevailed, and when a little village sprang into existence near by, it was called Radcliffe, which in turn gave its name to one of the most powerful families not only in Lancashire, but in the kingdom—the Radcliffes.

The family owned the Tower for nearly five hundred years, and during that period founded many branches, such as the Radcliffes of Ordsall, the Radcliffes of Smithells, the Radcliffes of Todmorden, the Radcliffes of Chadderton, of Wymersley, of Milnesbridge, and the Radcliffes of Dilston in Northumberland.

History does not tell us the beginnings of the first Radcliff, or how he came to the place, but that the family was already settled there in the twelfth century is proved by the charter for the foundation of Burscough Priory, granted by Robert Fitz Henry de Lathom early in the reign of Richard Cœur de Lion. Amongst the witnesses to the founder's signatures appears the name of Henry de Radeclive.

It is in the time of this Henry's son, William de Radcliffe, that we find the spelling of the name as it is to-day and the first mention of Radcliffe Tower. This William was a knight, and was described as "William Radcliffe of the Tower" on being summoned to the Grand Inquest of the County of Lancaster in 1211. During the next two hundred years Radcliffe Tower passed from father to son—except on one occasion, when an uncle succeeded a nephew who died without issue—until the year 1403, when a great change came in the family fortune. The then reigning Radcliffe, James, married a rich Yorkshire heiress, the daughter of Sir John Tempest of Bracewell, and set about re-building his own home. Although nothing remains to give any size or indication of the ancient dwelling of the Radcliffes it may be safely assumed from the name by which it was known— "The Tower"—that the building resembled one of the peels on the Border. This was replaced by James de Radcliffe by a fortress. In those days "men built less against the elements than their next neighbours." For this reason no man could fortify his house without a special licence from the King, and Henry IV. being at Pontefract Castle, in the August of 1403, a petition was laid before him by Radcliffe. Permission to embattle and fortify a house was only given to men of proved loyalty, a necessary precaution in times when might was right. Henry IV. was Duke of Lancaster, in succession to his father John of Gaunt ; and James de Radcliffe, therefore, held his house and lands directly from the King as Duke, in return for military service. His loyalty naturally would be undisputed, since the King was not only his sovereign, but his over-lord as well. The licence was immediately granted by letters patent. The original is in Latin, but its translation gives a description of the stronghold, of which nothing now remains except the ruined tower—

"Know ye that of our special grace we have granted and licensed, for us and our heirs, as much as in us is to our beloved esquire, James de Radcliffe, that he his manor-house of Radcliffe (which is held of us as of the House of Lancaster *in capite*, as it is said) with walls of stone and lime [1] to enclose anew, and within these walls a certain hall, with two towers, of stone and lime in like manner to make anew ; and those walls, hall, and towers, so made, to kernel [2] and embattle. And the manor-house so enclosed, with the hall and towers aforesaid so kernelled and embattled, for a certain fortalice he may hold to him and his heirs for ever, without any accusation or impediment of us or our heirs, or our officers, or those of our said heirs whatsoever. In testimony whereof, we have caused these our letters to be made patent—Witness the King at the Castle of Pontefract on the 15th day of August, by the King himself."

The "certain hall" mentioned in the royal letters patent, which was forty-two feet in length and twenty-six feet in width, and adjoined the Tower, saw many a scene of revelry and feasting and also of tragedy. It was there, according to the old ballad "Fair Ellen of Radcliffe," that the wicked stepmother caused the beautiful and beloved Ellen of Radcliffe to be killed and cooked in a pie, which was set before her father when he came back from hunting.

"Then all in black this lord did mourne,
    And for his daughter's sake,
He judged her cruell stepmother
    To be burnt at a stake.

" Likewise he judged the master-cook
    In boiling lead to stand ;
And made the simple scullion-boy
    The heir of all his land."

[1] Mortar was then called lime.
[2] Kernel, to crenellate.

The terrible crime of the ballad and its terrible punishment, are not borne out by the history of the Radcliffes, there being no instance of the estates being left to anybody outside the family. After the death of the builder of the Tower, James Radcliffe, in 1410, five Radcliffes succeeded from father to son until 1518, when, John Radcliffe dying unmarried, family traditions, which had always been Lancastrian, and joined the Yorkists in the Wars of the Roses, for he was slain on that terrible Palm Sunday in 1461, when 33,000 English men were killed at the Battle of Towton—one of the bloodiest of the battles in the Wars of the Roses. He also was a Sir John, and was cut down whilst guarding the passage of the river

THE HALL, RADCLIFFE TOWER

the direct male line ceased and the estate passed to Robert Radcliffe, Lord Fitzwalter, who was descended from the second son of the builder of the Tower. This younger branch of the family had been both more distinguished and more unfortunate than the elder. Its founder, Sir John Radcliffe, of Attilborough, was known as the "good Sir John." His grandson appears to have forsaken the Aire at Ferrybridge. It was his son who became the first Lord Fitzwalter, but after enjoying the favour of Henry VII., and being the steward of his household, he was suspected of complicity in Perkin Warbeck's attempt upon the throne. Suspicion lead to trial; he was found guilty of high treason and beheaded at Calais, a fate that was shared by his uncle for the same offence. The Radcliffes did not trim their sails in those changing times with the cleverness and dexterity that characterized their great neighbour in Lancashire, Thomas Stanley, Earl of Derby.

A Radcliffe was a favourite of Richard III., but with the careless and variable spelling of the time he was called Ratcliff, and as such he appears in Shakespeare. A bitter rhyme, which cost its writer his life, was warmly greeted by Richard's opponents—

"The Catte, the Ratte and Lovel our dog,
Rulyth all England under a Hogge."

The Rat stood for Ratcliff, the Cat for Catesby, another royal favourite, and the dog for Lord Lovel, that being his crest. The Hog was Richard III.'s cognizance.

It was to Ratcliff that Shakespeare made Richard relate the awful dream in which all his victims had passed before him, on the night before the Battle of Bosworth, in *King Richard the Third*. In the morning Ratcliff enters the King's tent to awake him for the coming battle.

Ratcliff. My lord !
King Richard. Who's there ?
Ratcliff. Ratcliff, my lord ; 'tis I. The early village cock
Hath twice done salutation to the morn ;
Your friends are up, and buckle on their armour.
King Richard. O Ratcliff ! I have dream'd a fearful dream—
What thinkest thou ? Will our friends prove all true ?
Ratcliff. No doubt, my lord.
King Richard. O Ratcliff ! I fear, I fear.
Ratcliff. Nay, good my lord, be not afraid of shadows.
King Richard. By the apostle Paul, shadows to-night
Have struck more terror to the soul of Richard,
Than can the substance of ten thousand soldiers,
Armed in proof, or led by shallow Richmond.
It is not yet near day. Come, go with me ;
Under our tents I'll play the eaves-dropper,
To hear if any mean to shrink from me.

Ratcliff shared the fate of his royal master at the Battle of Bosworth, being killed upon the field. Richard lost the battle and his life by the desertion of the Stanleys. Thus Lancashire played an all-important part in a day that swept the House of York for ever from the throne of England.

It was Robert Radcliffe, the second Lord Fitzwalter, who succeeded his kinsman, John Radcliffe, in 1518, in possession of the Tower, and the other estates belonging to the direct line of the family. With him the fortunes of the Radcliffes soared to heights undreamt of by the Sir Johns and Sir Jameses who had reigned at Attilborough and Radcliffe. The second Lord Fitzwalter became one of the most prominent courtiers of King Henry VIII., and for many years enjoyed the confidence of that unstable and fiery monarch. Taking the King's side in his divorce from Queen Catherine of Aragon, Lord Fitzwalter, who had already been created a Viscount, was rewarded with the Earldom of Sussex. Marriage played a great part in the fortunes of Tudor courtiers. The first Earl of Sussex married three times. His first marriage paved the way to his future position. Whilst still suffering under the attainder and loss of title and estate, which were part of his father's sentence when he was beheaded at Calais, Robert Radcliffe married a daughter of the Duke of Buckingham. A year later he was restored to his father's barony of Fitzwalter and his paternal estates. Twenty-seven years later he became a widower, and then allied himself with Lady Margaret Stanley, daughter of the second Earl of Derby ; his third wife was the daughter of a Cornish knight.

With the Earl of Sussex's second marriage the fate of Radcliffe Tower is closely interwoven. By Lady Margaret Stanley he had a daughter called Anne, and when she married Lord Wharton, the only means of providing the stipulated dowry was by the sale of Radcliffe Tower and the other

SIGNATURE OF ROBERT RADCLIFFE, FIRST EARL OF SUSSEX

Radcliffe estates in Lancashire. Some chroniclers state that the third Earl of Sussex, grandson of the first earl, sold the cradle of his race in 1583, the year of his death, but documents prove that it was the first earl.

Despite the brilliance of their position, the Earls of Sussex seem to have been in a chronic state of impecuniosity. Execution for debt against the second earl, son of the first earl, was stayed only by the personal intervention of Queen Mary Tudor. The third earl, who was a great personage at the Court of Queen Elizabeth, and Deputy and Viceroy of Ireland, incurred such a heavy debt to the Crown that he could not pay it, and his estate was in consequence ordered to pay five hundred pounds a year, a considerable sum in those times. His brother Henry, who succeeded him as fourth earl in 1583, wrote a most piteous letter to Queen Elizabeth six years later, saying he was hopelessly bankrupt, as the estate he had inherited from his distinguished brother only brought in four hundred and fifty pounds a year, and there was still the five hundred pounds to pay each year to the Government! Robert, the fifth earl, son of Earl Henry, likewise petitioned Queen Elizabeth in 1603 to be helped in his financial embarrassments caused by the debts due to the Crown from his father and uncle.

Just as the ancient family house, Radcliffe Tower, had passed to the descendant of the second son of its builder, Sir James Radcliffe, so the earldom of Sussex, after the death of the fifth earl, for lack of an heir in the direct line, passed in precisely the same way to Edward, son of the first earl's second son, Sir Humphrey Radcliffe. This Edward, sixth Earl of Sussex, was childless, and with his death not only did the earldom become extinct, but the main branch of the Radcliffe family ended also.

Other branches of this once powerful family suffered the same fate. The fifth Earl of Sussex, whose contemporaries gave him a bad character with regard to his treatment of his wife, married his illegitimate daughter Jane to Sir Alexander Radcliffe, of Ordsall Hall, and with the

THE THIRD EARL OF SUSSEX

death of their son the line of Radcliffes of Ordsall came to an end. But no branch of the great family died out in such tragedy as that which marked the passing of the Radcliffes of Wymersley, founded by a younger brother of the builder of the Tower. In 1688 his direct descendant was Sir Francis Radcliffe, and he, when his son married an illegitimate daughter of Charles II., was created Baron and Viscount Radcliffe and Earl of Derwentwater. In due course his grandson succeeded him as third Earl of Derwentwater, and in 1716 was beheaded in London for his share in the Jacobite Rebellion of the previous year, having been made prisoner at Preston. The family estates were confiscated by the Government and set aside for the benefit of Greenwich Hospital.

Still were the Fates unsatisfied. The unfortunate Earl of Derwentwater's brother and heir, Charles Radcliffe, escaped to the Continent, where he assumed the title, despite its forfeiture by the English Government. When the young Pretender made the attempt to regain the throne of his fathers in 1745, Charles Radcliffe accompanied him. A year later he met the same fate as his brother; and when on December 8, 1746, the axe fell upon the scaffold on Tower Hill, and Charles Radcliffe's head was severed from his body, another branch of the great Lancashire family became extinct.

The Tower itself passed through many hands after it was sold by the first Earl of Sussex to Andrew Barton, of Smithells Hall, near Bolton. It remained in that family until about the middle of the eighteenth century, when it passed to Henry Bellasys, son of Lord Fauconberg, on his marriage with a Barton heiress. After that it knew several owners until it was purchased by the Earl of Wilton. So late as 1833 the old Hall was still standing, although used as a cowshed and hayloft, together with a range of buildings shown in the illustration of the Tower

as it appeared early in the eighteenth century. Eleven years later nothing was left save the Tower itself. "This interesting relic of old English architecture," says Samuel Bamford, writing in 1844, "was taken down many years ago to make room for a row of cottages for the workpeople of Messrs. Bealey & Sons, bleachers. It is understood that the Earl of Wilton, to whom the place belonged, sold the materials to the firm, and let them the land. . . . This venerable pile was highly interesting to all who loved to gaze on the relics of other days, and it was probably calculated to convey a more correct idea of the rude but strongly built habitations of our forefathers than any other object to which the curious in this neighbourhood had access . . . the materials were chiefly beams and planks of solid black oak, which together with the simplicity of the construction and the rudeness of the workmanship, testified to the great age of the edifice. . . . The square tower, or fortified part of the ancient residence, still remains, but is tottering with decay. The vaulted roof of the lower room almost hangs by a single stone, and, unless it be protected from further wanton outrage, it must soon share the fate of the hall, and leave only its name in remembrance of things that have been."

Such protection has been given to the birthplace of the great family that time alone can destroy it. Only one other relic of the family remains at Radcliffe; this is an alabaster tombstone, upon which is carved the recumbent figure of a medieval knight and his lady, in the church. The knight is in full armour, and both he and his lady have their hands raised in the attitude of prayer. Close beside the pillar on which their heads are resting are two shields—the one near the lady's pillow showing the coat-of-arms of the

Langleys, that near the knight's pillow the coat-of-arms of the Radcliffes. At the foot the remains of figures of children can be traced; and round the edge is a broken inscription in Latin, in which all that can be deciphered is that the beholder is bidden to pray for the soul of James de Radcliffe. The date of his death is missing. Dr. Whitaker, the father's eating by order of her wicked stepmother. So deeply rooted was the belief in the tradition, and so intense was the veneration for the entirely fictitious memory of Fair Ellen, that the villagers and others used to break small pieces of alabaster from the tombstone, convinced that they would serve as amulets to ward off disease or trouble. This form of

RADCLIFFE TOWER AS IT APPEARED IN THE EIGHTEENTH CENTURY

most learned of Lancashire historians, believed this was the tombstone of James Radcliffe, the grandson of the builder of the Tower, but the herald's art has proved him to be wrong. The Langley shield proves that the chipped and broken alabaster once covered the body of James Radcliffe of the next generation—the builder's great-grandson.

Superstition takes no heed of historical facts or heraldry, and the country folk around Radcliffe were firmly convinced that this alabaster slab was none other than the tombstone of the Fair Ellen of Radcliffe, who was made into a pie for her veneration accounts for the broken and dilapidated condition of the stone, which ultimately had to be hidden beneath the floor of the church to prevent its total disappearance. When the church was being restored, about forty years ago, the tombstone was rediscovered, and may now be seen in the chancel near the communion rails.

Radcliffe Tower, perhaps more than any other ruin in Lancashire, stands as the symbol of vanished glories. For four centuries the Radcliffes were men of might and power in Lancashire; for two centuries afterwards they were lords of renown, high in the service of their sovereign; now all that is left of their strength and wisdom, their ambition, their success, their baronies and earldoms, is a mutilated tombstone and this crumbling mass of stones, surrounded by belching chimneys, and the hum of industries undreamed of when they hunted the deer over the very ground upon which those chimneys stand.

THE OLD ALABASTER TOMB IN RADCLIFFE CHURCH

THE MISTRESS OF ROSSALL GRANGE

ONE of the saddest stories in the religious differences that distracted Lancashire in the reign of Queen Elizabeth is that of Mrs. Allen, of Rossall Grange in the Fylde. The history of the persecution to which she was subjected shows with unmistakable clearness how Queen Elizabeth and her advisers used religion as a cloak for purely political ends.

The Allens were an ancient family which, like so many others in Lancashire, had remained faithful to the Roman Catholic religion, despite the persecutions, the pains, and the penalties inflicted during the reigns of Henry VIII. and Edward VI. One member of the family, William Allen, had suffered persecution and imprisonment whilst he was a young man of nineteen at Oxford, for in the council book there is an entry under the sixth of October, 1551, which records a " complaint made in council that one Allen—a fellow of Oxford, being committed to close prison, was suffered to have conference with others, and to translate a supplication into Latin for Peter Paulo, an Italian." During the reign of Mary, and the re-establishment of the Roman Catholic religion, this William Allen rose to considerable eminence in the Church, but when Queen Elizabeth succeeded her sister, and the national religion was changed once more from Roman Catholicism to Protestantism, William Allen gave up the canonry he held at York and left the country. It was William Allen who was the cause of the persecution of his brother's wife and family.

The recusant priests, as they were called, who fled the country, were closely watched by Elizabeth's agents abroad, and when it was discovered that William Allen was engaged at Louvain in educating the sons of English Roman Catholics, he became a marked man. So closely were his movements followed that when he paid a secret visit to England, the fact immediately became known to the authorities, and they issued a writ to the Sheriff of Lancashire ordering him to apprehend Allen and others, " late Ministers in the Church, who were justly deprived of their office for their contempt and obstinacy, and who are yet, or lately have been, secretly maintained, in private places in that our county of Lancaster." Notwithstanding a most vigorous search, Allen remained securely hidden in the neighbourhood of Poulton ; tradition says that the secret chamber in Mains Hall was for a long time his hiding-place. He succeeded in returning to Belgium and in 1568 achieved his crowning offence in the eyes of Elizabeth's Government. In conjunction with Dr. Venteville, he established the college at Douai, thus providing for the English Roman Catholics education for their sons which it was impossible for them to obtain in England. Douai speedily became the centre of plots and intrigues which went on ceaselessly against the English Queen, and in these plots and intrigues Allen was believed to be the prime instigator.

That Queen Elizabeth and her advisers had reason to regard Allen as something more dangerous than an ordinary recusant priest is shown by the fact that when Philip II. was preparing the great Armada, the Pope commanded Allen to write " The Admonition to the Nobility and People of England," in which he called upon them to rise in favour of the King of Spain. Allen was also in constant correspondence with Mary Queen of Scots, who, in answering one of his letters, said,

" The many good reports and multitude of rare virtues flowing from you, which long ago had made your name beknown, not only unto me, but to the greatest and every one of good in Christendom, have no less made me esteem your comfortable letter in this my affliction as a singular sign of some good to ensue therefore." It is a singular instance of the divisions of the times that whilst William Allen was in active correspondence with three of Queen Elizabeth's most deadly enemies —the Pope, King Philip II. of Spain, and Mary Queen of Scots—his uncle, Thomas Allen, was described as " her Majesty's merchant," and his uncle's wife was one of the gentlewomen of the Queen's privy chamber and afterwards mother of the maids of honour.

William Allen's services to the Roman Catholic cause in England were rewarded by the Pope making him a cardinal on the urgent recommendation of the King of Spain, who said, " In the person of Father Allen everything which can be desired concurs, for he belongs to no party ; he has learning, morals, judgment, great acquaintance with everything in the kingdom (England) and with the negotiations for its conversion, and the instruments of all these have been and are his disciples, of whom so many have suffered martyrdom. The purple of his hat may be said to be dyed in the blood of martyrs whom he has educated."

It has been written of Cardinal Allen, and by one who had no sympathy with the faith for which he was exiled, " It would not be easy to name a single Englishman of the Elizabethan age whose life and writing could furnish a better insight into the character of the political and religious conflict between England and the Pope than those of Cardinal Allen. His intellectual and literary gifts, the virtues of his private life, his un-doubted orthodoxy, his energy and tact, marked him out as the foremost amongst his co-religionists at a time when they could boast of numbering two-thirds of the population of England."

Mrs. Allen of Rossall, the Cardinal's sister-in-law, had been left a widow in 1579. Four years later, the incessant plotting against Elizabeth, both at Rome and Madrid, led to stringent measures being taken against English Roman Catholics, and amongst those in Lancashire Mrs. Allen was especially singled out. It has been argued by more than one historian of the period that the English Roman Catholics suffered persecution, and even martyrdom, at the hands of Elizabeth, not because of their faith but for their participation in treasonable plots. Elizabeth, in her bitter and unceasing struggle with Spain and Rome, was fighting for her life ; emissaries from Spain, from France and Italy, the majority of whom were priests, and some of them her own countrymen, were constantly coming to England for the sole object of encompassing her death, and some of them actually bore with them the papal absolution for her murder. The Government, therefore, saw a potential conspirator in every Roman Catholic, and Mrs. Allen's close relationship to the Cardinal marked her out for the full rigour of the law. As a preliminary step she was outlawed.

Towards the close of the year 1583, because of the plotting abroad mentioned above, the Privy Council came to the decision that harsher measures were necessary against the Roman Catholics, and sent a list of over three hundred names to Sir Edmund Trafford, the Sheriff of Lancashire, amongst which Mrs. Allen headed the list in her district. News having reached Mrs. Allen that the sheriff and his officers were coming to

Rossall, she hid herself with an old priest, called George Bramley, and Mrs. Coniers, a relation of her late husband's. Her place of hiding is not mentioned, but it must have been in close proximity to Rossall as she only used it as a refuge lest she should be suddenly surprised in the night, returning to the house each day. The most careful watch was kept during the day, and in order to secure the furniture and other property to her three daughters, of whom the eldest was only sixteen, she made a deed of gift, which, together with their father's will, should have secured to them their lawful inheritance.

One night a messenger, purporting to come from the sheriff, appeared at Rossall; in reality he was a spy. He asked for Mrs. Allen, and on being told that she was not at home he said he must await her return. The man remained in the house all night, prying into every corner. On the following morning, the under-sheriff, together with a magistrate and a rabble of men, appeared at Rossall, and " with the greatest roughness of speech and bearing, they commanded the servants in the Queen's name to open all the doors, and to deliver up into their hands all the keys and all the arms that were in the house." This the servants declined to do unless they saw the Queen's order or commission, to which the magistrate replied, " Let it be commission enough for you that the High Sheriff's deputy orders it to be done."

" That is indeed something which your worship tells us," answered one of the servants, " still for us it is not enough, as we want to look at the Queen's mandate."

Roughly pushing the protesting servants aside, the under-sheriff and his followers forced their way into the house, demanding to know the whereabouts of Mrs. Allen and her priest Bramley. When the servants answered that neither of these two people were in the house, " they were straightway ordered in the Queen's name to take an oath, that, unless they wished to be clapt in prison they should instantly disclose, not only where the afore-named persons were in hiding, but also everything that should be asked of them." This oath the servants, whose loyalty and devotion to their mistress never wavered, refused to take, saying that it was both audacious and unlawful.

The under-sheriff went first to the dining-room, and seeing there a large portrait of Cardinal Allen, began to abuse and revile the original, a proceeding in which he was joined by the magistrate. From words they fell to action, and they and their followers, after stabbing and hacking at the canvas with their knives and daggers, finally tore it from its frame and trampled it underfoot.

By means of threats they secured the keys from the eldest daughter, and made a thorough search of the house and of every chest and cupboard in it. They made no secret of their anger at finding no money, and took the few articles of jewellery which belonged to one of the daughters; they even carried away the clothing of the three girls.

Meanwhile Mrs. Allen, who was hiding near by, and was kept fully informed of all that was passing at Rossall, hit upon an ingenious idea by which to rid herself of the under-sheriff and his rabble. Rossall was in a remote situation; there was no town or village near in which provisions could be obtained, and the officers and men of the law were therefore entirely dependent for their food upon Rossall itself. With the hope of so seriously diminishing the supplies in the house that the men would be starved out, she sent word secretly to some seven-and-twenty people, some of whom were her servants, and others her neighbours and friends, to go to the house that night. The under-sheriff, alarmed by the appearance of so large a number of people, many of whom, according to the custom of the time, carried arms, feared that he and his party were about to be attacked. But Mrs. Allen's servants, who knew their mistress's intentions, reassured him, saying that he had no need to be afraid of the country-people, who had not come there to do him any harm, " but to visit their lady after the custom of the country at this holy season (for it was the New Year), and to recreate her by their presence, and to take dinner with her if she were at home ; that therefore the deputy and his companions might freely sit down to table, and fearlessly finish the dinner they had begun." "Very well;" said the deputy, after he had plucked up his spirits somewhat at the servants' words ; " let food then be given them."

After they had finished dinner the deputy ordered the country-folk to depart in the Queen's name. Twenty of them obeyed the order, but seven remained. They paid for their temerity by being cited to appear at the next assizes at Lancaster, when they were fined seventeen English shillings for disobeying the magistrate's order.

Convinced that Mrs. Allen was hiding in the neighbourhood, the deputy decided to remain some days at Rossall and sent some of his men to Manchester. This party had not proceeded far on their road when they met a spy who told them that he had seen Mrs. Allen only a few days previously in the house of a man called Annion, and he was sure that if they went there at once, they would either catch the lady herself or find something she had hidden. The men forthwith proceeded to Annion's house where, after ransacking the place from top to bottom, they found £500 in gold pieces enclosed in a little box, hidden in a flour-chest, and also a large quantity of linen. In addition to this they found £3 which belonged to Annion, but this they took, declaring it to be Mrs. Allen's, and, notwithstanding the fact that Annion was a poor man, they emptied the flour, the winter's supply for himself and his family, upon the floor and trampled it underfoot. Two of the servants at Rossall, as well as Annion, were carried before the sheriff, who threatened them with all kinds of torments if they did not immediately confess Mrs. Allen had hidden the money with the intention of sending it to Cardinal Allen at Rheims. The servants replied that they " could not confess to a matter whereof they had no knowledge, even if he were to inflict on them a thousand kinds of torments." Annion's answer was that he had received the money from Mrs. Allen " to the intent that if any misfortune should befall the mother in these ups and downs he should deliver the money over to the daughters."

Meanwhile the deputy remained at Rossall, and soon a greater anxiety than the loss of her money, her house and her furniture assailed Mrs. Allen. Her three daughters were left alone with no protection save that of the servants, and their position consequently gave her cause for a double anxiety—for their honour and their religion. From threats let fall by the deputy the unhappy girls learnt that they were " to be removed elsewhere, where they would be taught a different mode of loving, believing and worshipping God from what they had hitherto been accustomed to under their mother." Word of these threats was instantly conveyed to Mrs. Allen in her hiding-place and she decided that they must escape.

After remaining four days at Rossall

the deputy decided to take the three girls to the sheriff's house, but finding this would delay his own journey, he left them in charge of some of his men with orders between the distracted mother and her daughters through a faithful intermediary, and it was finally decided that the best way of escape was through the outer

"AND DRAWING BACK THE BOLT, STEPPED OUT INTO THE DARKNESS"

to follow immediately. The men, however, were in no hurry to depart from such pleasant quarters and they lingered for several days.

Many anxious discussions took place door, the keys of which could be abstracted in the daytime. During the next three days the outer doors were most carefully watched by one of the girls in turn. On the third day chance favoured them, and, unobserved by any of the sheriff's men, the girl who was watching removed the keys and hid them away, thus at night-time the door could only be shut by a bolt pushed to on the inner side, which would hinder access from without, but could be moved back with ease by anybody within. That same night when the sheriff's men, whom the faithful servants plied with ale, were all soundly asleep, the three girls crept quietly down the stairs to the outer door, and drawing back the bolt, stepped out into the darkness.

With all speed they made their way to the nearest ferry, where fortune again favoured them, for they found a boat and immediately crossed over to the other side of the river. During a whole fortnight they wandered about the country, hiding by day and walking by night, for the whole district was being carefully searched by the sheriff's men. The unhappy girls dared scarcely trust themselves to any one's hospitality, and when finally they were united to their mother they were half-starved.

The High Sheriff had confiscated the whole of Mrs. Allen's property on the ground that she was an outlaw, and that by the law anything she possessed became the property of the Crown; Mrs. Allen and her daughters consequently were reduced to beggary. So cruel an application of the law against a woman whose only crime was that she was a Roman Catholic, and the sister-in-law of a Cardinal, aroused the indignation even of the Protestant gentry of the district, and some of them, despite the risks they ran in so openly espousing the cause of the unhappy widow, went to the sheriff and pointed out that he had acted illegally in confiscating the property, as it belonged to the daughters by inheritance and deed of gift. In reply to these representations the sheriff agreed that the question should be settled by law.

The case was tried at Manchester, and although it was urged upon Mrs. Allen that it would aid her daughters' cause if they appeared in court, and claimed their property in person, she refused, because they would not have been allowed to plead until they had promised to become Protestants, and as they were under age, she chose six gentlemen to appear in their name : four other gentlemen also went to Manchester to testify to the deed of gift. The sheriff's action during the trial made it speedily clear that the verdict had already been decided upon. He declined to accept the evidence of witnesses on Mrs. Allen's behalf lest " he should appear to show favour to papists, traitors, and enemies of the commonwealth," and the jury, faithful to his bidding, gave this finding : " Whereas the children, in whose name this suit is instituted, are not here present, we declare that they are either deceased, or else have fled the realm, and therefore are accounted as civilly dead. Whence it followeth that whatsoever property hath been found, the same doth all belong to the mother and not to the children ; and since the mother hath been proclaimed an outlaw, we adjudge that all the property doth appertain to the Crown and ought thither to resort."

This verdict having been given the sheriff immediately took possession of Rossall Grange and Mrs. Allen's other house, Taddenstaffe Hall, driving away all the cattle, and taking all the furniture, including the remainder of the girls' clothes, claiming the whole of the widow's property for himself and his partner, Worsley, as a reward for the obedience they had shown to the Queen's Majesty.

But they were not allowed to remain

long in possession. Two ladies declared that Mrs. Allen's property now belonged to them " by a general grant made by the Queen's Majesty for all property which should accrue to the royal treasury in the county of Lancaster through the outlawry of persons convicted." The dishonest sheriff was in treaty with these two ladies, when lo! a third claimant came upon the scene, a man called Baptist, who stated that Queen Elizabeth had bestowed on him all the property of the widow and children, under the title of wages and rewards, "on the condition that he should carefully look after the tender maidens, and cause them to be honourably brought up."

To these claimants a fourth was added in the person of the all-powerful William Cecil, the High Treasurer of England, who most ingeniously silenced all the others. Beginning with the unhappy Mrs. Allen and her daughters, he answered their petition by saying they had been lawfully deprived of their property by the finding of the jurors against which no appeal could be allowed. The sheriff, Trafford, and his partner Worsley, were informed that they had executed the confiscation in virtue of their office, " for which they have the ordinary fees from the Sovereign, and therefore they ought not to look for aught else, unless the Queen's Majesty should chance to bestow on them something else of inferior value, and that spontaneously." The claim of the two ladies presented a more serious difficulty, but Cecil evaded it by declaring that the Queen had made the promise with regard to property which might be confiscated at the time the promise was made, and that Mrs. Allen's property had been confiscated under laws which did not exist when the Queen made the grant to the two ladies. As for

Baptist he sternly told him that the Queen's promise was for £500 only and not for the widow's property, which was worth over £3000.

Meanwhile Trafford and Worsley held all Mrs. Allen's property, and, as they showed no signs of delivering it over, Cecil summoned them to London. Trafford was ill with the gout, so sent his son as his deputy. No sooner had the young man and Worsley arrived in the capital than they were summoned before Cecil and thrown into prison, until they entered into recognizances that they would give a full account of all their confiscations in Lancashire to my Lord Treasurer Cecil. The latter was accused at the time of disposing of the various claimants to Mrs. Allen's property for his own benefit, but he was really acting on behalf of the Crown, the rents from a portion of Mrs. Allen's estate, and from the whole of her son's property, which had also been confiscated, being paid to Queen Elizabeth and James I., until 1612, when the son's property was restored to his sister Mary, who had married Thomas Worthington of Blaniscowe.

But Mrs. Allen speedily discovered that the confiscation of her property, because of her faith, was not the ending of her troubles. Being an outlaw she no longer had any civil rights, and by the law of the land her daughters could be taken forcibly from her custody, and brought up as Protestants. She therefore determined to leave her native country. But the design was easier than the accomplishment. She was a marked woman, and it was two months before she and her two elder daughters succeeded in reaching the coast of France. During those two months they had been obliged to walk by night, hiding in " woods and thickets or other secret places," by day. When they landed on French soil they were utterly destitute and half-starved.

The youngest daughter, Mary, who was only nine years of age, remained in England, and, as we have seen, ultimately became her brother's heir. This brother, John Allen, was a "recusant," and having left the kingdom without Queen Elizabeth's permission, was, in consequence, deprived of his property.

Mrs. Allen joined her brother-in-law, Cardinal Allen, at Rheims, and there she passed the remainder of her life. The two daughters both became nuns at Louvain in Flanders.

THE FROG AND THE CROW

THERE was a jolly fat frog liv'd in the river Swim, oh,
And there was a comely black
crow liv'd on the river brim, oh;
"Come on shore, come on shore," said the crow to the frog, "and then, oh."
"No, you'll bite me; no, you'll bite me," said the frog to the crow again, oh.

"But there is sweet music on yonder green hill, oh,
And you shall be a dancer, a dancer in yellow,
All in yellow, all in yellow,"—said the crow to the frog,—"and then, oh."
"Sir, I thank you; sir, I thank you," said the frog to the crow again, oh.

"Farewell, ye little fishes, that are in the river Swim, oh,
For I'm going to be a dancer, a dancer in yellow."

"Oh, beware! Oh, beware!" said the fish to the frog again, oh.
"All in yellow, all in yellow,"—said the frog to the fish,—"and then, oh."

The frog he came a-swimming, a-swimming to land, oh;
And the crow he came a-hopping, to lend him his hand, oh;
"Sir, I thank you; sir, I thank you,"—said the frog to the crow,—and then, oh.
"Sir, you're welcome; sir, you're welcome," said the crow to the frog again, oh.

"But where is the music on yonder green hill, oh?
And where are the dancers, the dancers, the dancers in yellow?
All in yellow, all in yellow?"—said the frog to the crow,—and then, oh.
"Sir, they're here; sir, they're here," said the crow to the frog, and ate him all up—*Oh!* (Screamed.)

IN former days the "sermon taster" was a prominent figure in most Lancashire congregations; a self-appointed critic of the parson's discourses, and a veritable thorn in his side. It is related of one of these "sermon tasters" that he never missed a sermon for years at the church he attended, and that regularly, every Sunday, he lay in wait for the parson at the church door after the conclusion of the service, in order to "speak his mind" upon what he had heard. His opinions were given with uncompromising frank ness. One Sunday the parson, seeing his critic waiting for him, and a little weary of the weekly complaints and comments, thought he would carry the attack into the enemy's country. "How is it, John," he asked, before the "sermon taster" had time to speak, "how is it, that although I displease you week after week you still continue to attend my church? Why don't you stay away?"

John's mouth fell open with astonishment. "Me stay away?" he gasped. "Me stay away? Why, if I stopped away there's no telling what sort of stuff you'd be preaching!"

DID SHAKESPEARE ACT IN LANCASHIRE?

THIS very interesting point is raised in a letter written by Mr. E. J. L. Scott to the *Athenæum* in January 1882. He quotes a letter from Henry le Scrope, ninth Baron Scrope in the service of his cousin, Queen Elizabeth, were called. It is known that Shakespeare was a member of this company. Thus runs Lord Scrope's letter, with its old-world spelling—

SHAKESPEARE. AFTER THE DROESHOUT ENGRAVING

of Bolton, Governor of Carlisle, and Warden of the West Marches, to the English Ambassador, William Asheby, at the Court of King James VI. of Scotland, from which it appears that King James had desired to witness the performance of the Queen's Players, as the actors

"After my verie hertie comendacions: vpon a letter receyved from Mr. Roger Asheton, signifying vnto me that yt was the kinges earnest desire for to have her Majesties players for to repayer into Scotland to his grace: I dyd furthwith dispatche a servant of my owen vnto them wheir they were in the furthest parte of Langkeshire, wherevpon they made their returne heather to Carliell, wher they are, and have stayed for the space of ten dayes, whereof I thought good to gyve yow notice in respect of the great desyre that the kynge had to have the same come vnto his grace; And withall to pray yow to gyve knowledg thereof to his Majestie. So for the present I bydd yow right hartelie farewell. Carlisle the XXth of September, 1589.

"Your verie assured loving frend,
"H. Scrope."

Mr. Scott says—

"There is no further letter relating to the subject among Asheby's correspondence, but it is very interesting to think that Shakespeare visited Edinburgh at the very time when the witches were tried and burned for raising the storms that drowned Jane Kennedy, mistress of the robes to the new Queen, and imperilled the life of Anne of Denmark herself. In that case the witches in *Macbeth* must have had their origin from the actual scenes witnessed by the player so many years previously to the writing of that drama in 1606."

The Manchester City News in reprinting this letter in February 1882, says—

"The letter is, however, specially worthy of note in these columns, because it shews not only that Shakespeare was in Edinburgh at the period named (1589), but that he and his company of players were summoned to go from Lancashire—here spelt 'Langkeshire.'"

The Queen's Players were not kept for the exclusive pleasure of Queen Elizabeth, but during the absences of the Court made tours throughout the country. Thus they were at Stratford-on-Avon in 1587, the date upon which Shakespeare is supposed to have joined them. The Queen's Players were at Lathom House, giving performances before the Lord Derby of that time on October 10, 1588, and again at Knowsley in June 1590. This evidence would point to a two years' tour by the Players in the north, and to two visits to Lancashire, one before, and one after the command visit to Edinburgh, which would give Shakespeare a considerable knowledge of the country.

The warm interest taken both by King James and his Queen, Anne of Denmark, in Shakespeare and his plays after they became King and Queen of England, might reasonably be taken to have been founded on their former acquaintance with him at Edinburgh, and if Shakespeare was amongst the Queen's Players commanded to Edinburgh, then he must have acted in Lancashire, for it is proved beyond all doubt that the company of players summoned by King James, through the English Ambassador, went to Scotland directly from Lancashire.

THE UNSWORTH DRAGON

ACCORDING to tradition the family of Unsworth occupied the same residence, some mile and a half from Bury, ever since the time of the Conquest. The house itself gradually changed from a manor-house to a farm with the declining fortunes of the family. But there still remained many relics of the past, and amongst them a carved oak table which was directly connected with an old legend.

Tradition has it that in the olden times a fierce and terrible dragon ravaged the country round Bury, its lair being near Unsworth, and which " resolutely defied the prowess of sundry brave heroes who would fain have immortalised their names by freeing the country from such a scourge."

One Thomas Unsworth, however, a member of this family, succeeded, where others had failed, by the exercise of ingenuity as well as by courage. Finding that the scaly hide of the dragon made it invulnerable against bullets, he put his dagger into a petronel, and rousing the anger of the monster by a pretended attack, shot it under the throat when it raised its head, his dagger piercing the soft skin.

The table was made after this great event, being carved, as the story goes, with the very dagger which caused the dragon's death. Round the table were carved St. George and his dragon, the lion and unicorn ; the Derby crest,—the Unsworths being the oldest tenants of that family,—and a representation of the actual dragon which Thomas Unsworth had killed. Over this table hung a painting of the coat-of-arms of the Unsworths, above which was another carving of the family dragon. The crest showed a man in black armour holding a hatchet in his right hand ; this was said to be a portrait of the redoubtable slayer of the dragon. The monster, however, does not appear in the coat-of-arms. The armour which Thomas Unsworth wore when he killed the dragon was said to have been in possession of the family a few years previous to 1845, when, " not being considered of much value, it was partly spoilt and lost."

This legend would seem to rest on surer foundations than most of its kind, for a portion of land was granted to one of the ancestors of the Unsworths in return for his service in freeing the country from some " dire monster," which in all probability was either a wolf or a wild boar of exceptional size and ferocity. But the Unsworth family firmly believed in the dragon, and it was freely carved in various shapes and forms about the house. The illustrations show three of the different carvings. The first one hung above the coat-of-arms, and was carved on a panel of wood about two feet long and one inch thick. The tongue and eyes were painted red, the body brown with spots upon it to indicate scales, the shaded part was painted green. The other two were carved on separate panels of an old chest.

A NUMBER of canal boatmen drinking at an inn, had spent all their money and were at their wits' end to obtain another gallon. Suddenly an idea occurred to one of them, and calling the landlord he said, " I'll bet thi a shillin' tha connot think on to say ' three matches ' to three questions I'll ax thi."

" I'll bet I con," said the landlord.

" Well, how owd are ti ? "

" Three matches ! "

" And how mich are ti wo'th ? "

" Three matches ! "

" And what will ti tak' for a gallon o' ale ? "

The landlord, seeing the trap into which he had fallen, made no answer but ordered the shillingsworth of beer.

MR. FRANK ORMEROD once heard a group of people in a Lancashire town talking of Polar explorations and " sprawnging " about the extreme cold which was sometimes experienced by the men engaged in the work. " Whaw," said one, " I've yheard 'at it's so cowd sometimes 'at it freezes t'words as Captain speighks 'um, an' 'at sailors han to put 'um in a saucepan an' warm 'um afore they can tell what he says ! "

MANY good political stories of Lancashire are told by Sir William Bailey of Salford. A parliamentary candidate throughout his speech had been perpetually repeating the proverb, " Speech is silvern, but silence is golden."

" Thee keep thy mouth shut, an' tha'll grow rich," cried a man in the audience, to the utter discomfiture of the candidate.

Another candidate, a Bolton factory owner, had a passion for wearing diamonds, and one night when addressing a meeting he had " about seventy-five pounds worth of ironmongery on his hands." At the close of the meeting his supporters called for three cheers for the prospective member. Some of his opponents were present, and as the cheers died away, called out lustily, " And three cheers more for his jewellery ! "

A LANCASHIRE man, at the outbreak of the Boer War, wished to enlist in one of the county regiments in order to " feight again th' Boers." But he failed to pass the medical examination because of the bad state of his teeth. He was bitterly disappointed and disgusted, and said—

" Aw thowt as aw'd ha' to shoot th' Boers ! Aw didn't know as aw'd ha' to worry 'em ! "

AN EIGHTEENTH=CENTURY ADVENTURER

ALTHOUGH the story of John Hatfield and his imposture may perhaps be considered as belonging more particularly to Cumberland than to Lancashire, his robbery of the Liverpool merchant, Mr. Crump, and the widespread interest taken in the case throughout the county, justifies its inclu-

ability and began life as what would now be called a commercial traveller, but in those days was called a rider, for a linen-draper in Lancashire. During his many journeys in the North of England, selling the goods of his employer, Hatfield made the acquaintance of a young woman who was the illegitimate daughter of Lord

JOHN HATFIELD

sion here. Binns, who made the famous collection of prints and drawings of Lancashire men and Lancashire places, which is now kept in the Brown Library at Liverpool, included Hatfield in his Lancashire worthies and unworthies: the illustration here given is reproduced from that collection.

John Hatfield was the son of very poor parents, and was born at Mottram, in Cheshire, in 1759. He had great natural

Robert Manners, a close relation of the then Duke of Rutland. Lord Robert had announced his intention of giving his daughter a thousand pounds upon her marriage, provided that she married with his approbation. This news having come to Hatfield's knowledge he set himself assiduously to court the daughter, and having won her affections presented himself to Lord Robert and demanded her hand. Hatfield had an attractive appearance and good manners; his prospects for a young man of twenty were extremely promising, and relieved by such a fortunate settlement of his natural daughter's future, Lord Robert willingly gave his consent. So pleased was he indeed with Hatfield, that the day after the marriage he gave him a draft upon his bankers for fifteen hundred pounds in place of the promised one thousand. The money was Hatfield's undoing.

Shortly after the marriage Hatfield set out for London, where he hired a phaeton in which he drove in Hyde Park, frequented one of the fashionable coffee-houses in Covent Garden, and cut the figure of a man of means and fashion, giving himself out to be a close relation of the Rutland family. There would seem to have been no intention to defraud, or to gain money by this falsehood, only a desire to appear as a man of birth and quality. Fifteen hundred pounds would not support a fashionable life for long, and having come to the end of his money Hatfield retired from London, and for three years nothing was heard of him. In 1782 he re-appeared in his fashionable haunts, having deserted his wife, and the three daughters she had borne him, leaving her penniless. Mrs. Hatfield did not long survive this desertion.

When the Duke of Rutland was appointed Viceroy of Ireland, Hatfield with an amazing audacity descended upon Dublin. Immediately on landing he engaged the best suite of apartments in the leading hotel. He told the landlord that he was nearly related to the Viceroy, but that he could not appear at the Castle until his horses, servants and carriages arrived, and that he had given orders before he left England for them to be shipped from Liverpool. " The easy and familiar manner in which he addressed the master of the hotel, perfectly satisfied

him that he had a man of consequence in his house, and matters were arranged accordingly." These " matters " turned out more satisfactorily for Mr. Hatfield than for the landlord, since he was never paid a penny.

In those times the coffee-houses occupied the same place in the social life of the upper classes as clubs do to-day; and in Dublin, Lucas's coffee-house was the one most frequented by men of rank. Hither Hatfield went, and by clever references to a mythical estate in Yorkshire, and his equally mythical relationship to the Viceroy, succeeded in impressing himself most favourably upon its frequenters.

These pretensions availed him for about a month, and then his servants and horses and carriages still being detained by ever-differing reasons at Liverpool, the landlord of the hotel began to grow suspicious. At the coffee-house too it began to be remarked that it was strange a connection of the Viceroy should delay so long in paying his respects to his exalted relative. The fascinating Mr. Hatfield, scenting the growing suspicion, disappeared from Dublin as mysteriously as he had arrived, leaving behind him a train of debts to tradesmen, for gambling, and for borrowed money, and, above all, a thoroughly duped landlord.

His next appearance was in Scarborough, where again posing as a relative of the Duke of Rutland he introduced himself to several people of distinction in the neighbourhood, and insinuated that by the Duke's interest he would shortly be one of the Members of Parliament for Scarborough. Needless to say Hatfield stayed at the principal inn of the place and stinted himself in nothing. But when after many delays and subterfuges the bill was presented with an intimation that it must be paid immediately, he sneaked out of the town, and reaching

York by unfrequented roads took the coach to London. But the landlord of the Scarborough inn did not submit tamely to this robbery. He followed Hatfield to London and, by the then existing law, had him arrested for the debt and thrown into prison. In those days debtors remained in prison until they could pay their debts, and Hatfield having no means was kept in durance for eight and a half years, and would in every probability have remained there for the rest of his life, if a Devonshire lady, Miss Nation, who had made his acquaintance whilst visiting a poor family in the debtors' prison, had not been completely fascinated by the attractive adventurer. She paid his debts, took him out of prison and married him. They went to live in Devonshire, and Hatfield might have become a respectable member of society but for his love of display and pretence. Shortly after his liberation he " had the good fortune to prevail with some highly respectable merchants in Devonshire to take him into partnership with them, and with a clergyman to accept his drafts for a large amount." Upon the money thus obtained Hatfield once more appeared in London as a man of large means and position, and even went so far as to canvass the town of Queenborough before a general election. In the meantime the Devonshire merchants had grown suspicious, and receiving no reply to their demands for the return of their money, they made him bankrupt in order to bring his fraud to light. Hatfield was therefore once more obliged hurriedly to leave London, and, as on the former occasion, he deserted his second wife, by whom he had had two children.

He was heard of in several places, but nothing was definitely known of him until July, 1802, when he arrived at the " King's Head," Keswick, in a carriage without any servant—and gave himself out as the Honourable Alexander Augustus Hope, brother of the Earl of Hopetoun, and member of Parliament for Linlithgow. At Buttermere there lived an old couple called Robinson, who kept a small public-house by the side of the lake, and who had amassed a little property by their industry. They had an only daughter, Mary, whose beauty had been made famous by the author of " A Fortnight's Ramble to the Lakes of Westmoreland, Lancashire and Cumberland," and who was in consequence known as the " Beauty of Buttermere." To her Hatfield began to pay assiduous attention.

But shortly after his arrival at Keswick he had made the acquaintance of an Irish gentleman, a member of the then Irish Parliament, by a very clever trick. Hearing that this gentleman had been in the Army he introduced himself, and, taking an Army List from his pocket, pointed to his assumed name, " the Honourable Alexander Augustus Hope, Lieutenant-Colonel of the 14th Regiment of Foot." The Irish gentleman had no reason to doubt the evidence of the Army List or Hatfield's assertion, and the acquaintance thus begun, ripened rapidly into friendship. Living with the Irish gentleman and his wife was a young lady of good family and considerable fortune, and Hatfield wooed her so ardently that having consented to marry him she bought all her wedding clothes. But although she was carried away by the ardour of the supposed Colonel Hope, and fell a ready victim to his fascination, the young lady was possessed of some prudence. Before she would consent to fix the wedding day she insisted that both his relatives and her own should be informed. To this Hatfield at once agreed. The Irish gentleman and his wife were told, and " Colonel Hope " pretended to write a number of letters to his brother, Lord Hopetoun, and other members of his family.

From this time he played a double game. His attentions to his betrothed at Keswick were "assiduous and fervent," but all the while he was laying a siege no less assiduous to the heart of the Beauty of Buttermere. His betrothed having definitely stated that she would not marry him without the knowledge and countenance of his supposed relatives, and therefore realizing that his scheme for obtaining possession both of herself and of her fortune had failed, Hatfield decided to secure the local beauty and her small fortune. But it was essential to the success of this further devilry that the Irish gentleman and his betrothed should be kept in expectancy of his receiving letters from his Hopetoun relations, and this expectancy he fostered most cleverly. Even for an astute and accomplished swindler [like Hatfield the game was difficult, and fearing lest word of what he had been doing should reach either one or other of the ladies, he would go off on a fishing expedition whenever any company was expected at the inn at Buttermere, and he only attended the church at Keswick once.

His wooing of the Beauty of Buttermere was so successful that on October 2, 1802, they were married at Lorton, Hatfield thus committing bigamy. On the day before the marriage Hatfield wrote to the Irish gentleman at Keswick, saying he was obliged to go away for ten days into Scotland, and begged him to cash a draft for thirty pounds drawn on Mr. Crump, of Liverpool, and out of this pay some small debts of his in Keswick, and send him the balance, as he feared he might be short on the road. The draft was signed with the name of Colonel Hope.

The Irish gentleman cashed the draft, paid the debts and sent Hatfield the remainder, adding ten guineas to the amount. The next day came the news that "Colonel Hope" had married the Beauty of Buttermere. The Irish gentleman's suspicions were instantly aroused by what appeared to him the most dishonourable conduct, and he instantly sent the draft for thirty pounds to Mr. Crump at Liverpool, who at once accepted it. The gentleman was naturally satisfied by this, but seeing the unworthy trick played upon the young lady in his charge, deemed it his duty to write to the Earl of Hopetoun. Before an answer could be received the bride and bridegroom returned to Buttermere. About the same time a Welsh judge called Harding, who had some acquaintance with the real Colonel Hope, was passing through Keswick, and from what he heard was convinced that an imposture was being carried on. He therefore sent his servant over to Buttermere with a note for the pretended Colonel Hope, who, when it was handed to him, said that it was a mistake, and that "the note was for a brother of his." Calling for a carriage with four horses, Hatfield immediately went over to Keswick, where he drew another draft on Mr. Crump in the name of Hope, for twenty guineas: this was cashed by the landlord of the "Queen's Head." Of this sum Hatfield sent ten guineas to the Irish gentleman to repay his loan. The latter, hearing he was in Keswick, came to him with the Welsh judge to whom he introduced him as Colonel Hope. But Hatfield flatly denied that he had ever used the name; his name was Hope, he said, but he had never stated that he was the member for Linlithgow. A man who had been his constant associate and boon companion at Keswick, supported this statement, but the evidence against Hatfield was overwhelming, and he was arrested on a warrant for having forged and given several franks as the member for Linlithgow.

In those days the signature of a member of Parliament, and various other people who were accorded the privilege, upon an envelope, passed it through the post without a stamp.

Hatfield was given over to the care of the Keswick constable, but managed to escape and got on board a sloop off Ravinglass. Here he remained for a few days, and then taking the coach to Ulverstone, was afterwards seen at a hotel in Chester. There was a general hue and cry, and he was finally arrested near Swansea, whence he was taken to London, where he was brought before the magistrates as an absconding bankrupt. But a warrant from a Cumberland magistrate against Hatfield charging him with felony "by pretending to be a member of Parliament of the United Kingdom, and franking several letters by the name of A. Hope, to several persons, which were put into the Post-office at Keswick, in Cumberland, in order to evade the duties of postage," having been produced, he was sent to Carlisle to stand his trial at the next assizes.

Hatfield came up for trial in August, 1803, and upon most damning evidence was found guilty, and condemned to death, hanging being then the punishment for forgery. "Notwithstanding his various and complicated enormities," says an account of the time, "his untimely end excited considerable commiseration. His manners were extremely polished and insinuating, and he was possessed of qualities which might have rendered him an ornament to society." It was therefore thought that a reprieve would be granted, but no pardon arriving, Saturday, September 3, 1803, was fixed for his execution, a gallows being specially erected, on an island formed by the river Eden on the north side of the town between the two bridges. From the moment Hatfield was condemned he had behaved with great serenity and cheerfulness. He was driven from the gaol to the gallows in a carriage. "As soon as the carriage door was opened by the Under-sheriff, the culprit alighted with his two companions (the governor of the gaol and the Under-sheriff). A small dung-cart boarded over was placed under the gibbet. A ladder was placed to this stage, which he instantly ascended. He immediately untied his neckerchief, and placed a bandage over his eyes. Then he desired the hangman, who was extremely awkward, to be as expert as possible about it, and that he would wave his handkerchief when he was ready. Having taken his leave of the gaoler and the sheriff, he prepared himself for his fate. He was at this heard to exclaim, "My spirit is strong, though my body is weak."

Hatfield gave the signal, the cart was drawn away, and he was left dangling. Thus ended a man whose frauds had enabled him to live upon other people for the greater part of his life. The poor Beauty of Buttermere was obliged to leave home because of the countless visitors who flocked from all parts of Cumberland and Lancashire, to see the scene of Hatfield's last exploit. When her mother and father heard that the man was hanged, they both exclaimed, "God be thanked."

A CASE OF EXTRAORDINARY MEMORY

ONE of the most remarkable cases of memory which has been placed on record is that of the Rev. Thomas Threlkeld, who was a Presbyterian minister at Rochdale for twenty-eight years, and died there in April 1806 at the age of sixty-seven. Thomas Threlkeld had been born at Halifax in Yorkshire, his father also being a Presbyterian minister, but was sent to the famous Academy at Warrington to finish his education, having first attended the Grammar School at Daventry, where his remarkable memory, especially with regard to the Bible, first made itself manifest. When a passage was recited he could immediately give it chapter and verse ; and on the other hand if a chapter and verse were given he could at once repeat the passage. Both at Daventry and Warrington his fellow-students took unceasing delight in putting his memory to the test, and never once was it known to be at fault. Many instances of Threlkeld's powers of memory are given in a tract, entitled "A Sermon preached at Rochdale April 13, 1806, on the occasion of the death of the Rev. Thomas Threlkeld, a minister of a Dissenting congregation in that place. To which is added an appendix containing some account of the life and character of Mr. Threlkeld and particularly of the powers of memory and of the treasures of knowledge possessed by him ; by Thomas Barnes, D.D., fellow of the American Philosophical Society."

Dr. Barnes was a pupil at the Warrington Academy at the same time as Threlkeld and therefore wrote with personal knowledge. He relates that on one occasion, with no intention of testing Threlkeld, he told the story of "a parish clerk, who, having occasion to read the words 'Gebal and Ammon, and Amalek,' sang them out in a manner so ridiculous that no person could have heard him without a smile. Mr. T. immediately replied : 'Those verses are in the 83rd Psalm and 7th verse.' And then joined most heartily in the laugh which he had himself unconsciously heightened by the oddness and gravity of the quotation." Upon another occasion a minister challenged Threlkeld to give the place of a text from which he had been preaching. "Mr. T. asked for a Bible and found the passage, saying, 'Quote fair, sir, and you shall have a fair answer. But I knew that you had confounded two verses together, which stand at a considerable distance asunder. You have joined the fifth and tenth verses as though they were one. I knew your trick, and I asked for the Bible that the company might with their own eyes detect you.'" Threlkeld was proved to be right, much to the discomfiture of the preacher.

But Threlkeld's powers of memory were not applied to the Bible alone. He was also a linguist : "Nine or ten languages it is certainly known that he read, not merely without difficulty, but with profound and critical skill." In his library at Rochdale he had books in Latin, Greek, Hebrew (and its dialects), French, Italian, Spanish, German, Dutch, Swedish, Gaelic, Manx, Arctic, Portuguese, Danish, Flemish and Welsh. For the last language he had a particular fondness, of which Dr. Barnes tells the following anecdote. When the famous Dr. Priestley, of Warrington Academy, went to Wrexham to marry Miss Wilkinson, the daughter of a Wrexham iron-master, there seems to have been some difficulty as to the giving-away of the bride. Priestley therefore took Threlkeld, whose tutor he had been at the Warrington Academy and who was his life-long friend, with him, in order that he might perform that office.

The service commenced and all went well until the moment when the clergyman asked, " Who giveth this woman to be married to this man?" To the amazement and consternation of bride, bridegroom and wedding party, no Threlkeld was there. Shortly before the opening of the marriage service he had been seen in his place, so the church was thoroughly searched, and there, hidden in a tall pew, the missing "giver-away" was found greedily reading a Welsh Bible, and so deeply enjoying the beloved language that he had completely forgotten the wedding and his duties.

Dates were absolutely a passion with him, no matter how unimportant. His knowledge of historical dates, of chronology, heraldry and genealogy was encyclopædic, and one of his favourite amusements was to go through the succession in the Episcopal Sees, and trace the pedigrees of families. The collection of such material was his constant occupation, but he would appear to have had no sense of proportion or of importance in this daily addition to the stores of his memory. To learn the date when an every-day person was born or married gave him as much pleasure as to learn the dates of events in the life of the most distinguished man or woman ; and it was not unnatural therefore that his minute enquiries were sometimes mistaken for prying, and an unhealthy curiosity as to other people's affairs. All was grist that came to Threlkeld's mental mill, and this, perhaps, was the cause why his prodigious memory served no purpose beyond interesting and amusing himself, and exciting the admiration of his friends.

Personally he was very shy, awkward and ungainly, extremely modest as to his wonderful power of recollection, and had the simplicity of a child. Dr. Barnes frequently endeavoured to find out the method Threlkeld pursued in order to arrange the endless array of facts in his mind. Threlkeld told him that he "classed them together by the year, and referred every new entry to that which lay nearest to it."

He endeavoured to explain himself by saying, "The year you have just mentioned was 1631. In that year Mr. Philip Henry was born. I have therefore laid up that name along with his ; and they are now so associated that whilst I retain the one I shall not forget the other." From this it is clear that Threlkeld depended entirely upon the association of ideas, which is borne out by Dr. Barnes' opinion : "From his description, so far as I could understand it, his mind appeared to be divided and fitted up like a shop, furnished with shelves and drawers for every different kind of articles, so that every new article was immediately referred to its own place, and so joined with those which stood there before, that the whole now presented itself at once, like soldiers drawn up in a line."

In his later years Threlkeld was looked upon as a living concordance to the Bible in Rochdale and the neighbourhood, and was constantly asked the most puzzling questions by his brother-ministers, sometimes actually for information, but generally for mere amusement. He was never known to be wrong.

In only one direction would this wonderful memory seem to have been of direct service. Threlkeld was one of the managers of a fund for the benefit of the widows of Presbyterian ministers, and consequently was frequently appealed to on circumstances connected with the lives of dead ministers, "and such was the opinion of his memory, that if the books had been consulted, and had reported differently, the error would have been imputed to the secretary, and not to Mr. T.'s memory. This was deemed infallible."

THE MURDER AT "THE JOLLY CARTER"

TOWARDS the end of the month of May 1826 a murder of unusual brutality sent a thrill of horror throughout the whole of South Lancashire.

At Winton, near Worsley, was an inn called "The Jolly Carter," kept by Joseph Blears and much frequented by the drivers of the carts which the Stratford people sent to the Worsley mines for coal. The inn was also resorted to by "packmen," as pedlars were then called, and two of these packmen, brothers, Alexander and Michael M'Keand, were constant customers whenever they were in the neighbourhood.

On the night of the 22nd May the two brothers sat drinking late at "The Jolly Carter." Blears, the landlord, was asleep. He had had a tiring day, a meeting of a women's club having been held in the house. His wife was in the bar parlour tidying it up preparatory to closing for the night. Besides Mr. and Mrs. Blears, there was only a maid-servant, Elizabeth Bates, and a small boy called Higgins, both of whom had already gone to bed.

There was nothing in the previous conduct of the two brothers that roused any suspicion as to their honesty, but there is little doubt that they had arranged between themselves to rob the Blears. This day the takings had been considerable.

At a given signal Michael went to the bar, where he set upon Mrs. Blears with a knife, stabbing her about the head, whilst Alexander went upstairs to the room where Elizabeth Bates and the boy Higgins were sleeping. The latter was awakened by the sound of a struggle, and saw Alexander cut the unfortunate woman's throat. Rushing from the room with the murderer in hot pursuit, the boy leapt over the staircase and ran out of the house. Alarmed by his escape Alexander gave the warning to Michael, who, leaving the knife sticking in Mrs. Blears' head, joined his brother in the search for this witness of their crime. Meanwhile, the boy had hidden in a dry ditch, the murderers actually passing close by in their search for him. Failing to find the boy the M'Keands were convinced that he had gone to give the alarm, and made off.

Mrs. Blears, although severely wounded, was found to be alive; ultimately she recovered; but Elizabeth Bates was dead. The brutality of this attack upon two women roused the greatest horror, and there was at once a hue and cry after the murderers, who had disappeared leaving no trace behind them.

A week later a villager of Kitling, near the moors of Kirby Stephen in Westmoreland, saw two men bathing their feet in a stream. Whilst waiting his turn to be shaved in the barber's shop, he had read a description of the M'Keands issued by the police, and from this description he instantly recognised them. They were promptly arrested, but only after a most desperate resistance, fighting to the last with an energy and strength surprising in starving men. When taken it was found that the soles of their boots were completely worn out, their feet were covered with blisters and they had not a penny in their pockets. During their week of wandering they had scarcely touched any food. In the following August they were tried at Lancaster, and both hanged there.

Following the then prevailing custom the body of Alexander M'Keand after it was cut down was sent to the Manchester Infirmary for dissection; and at the Infirmary it was exposed for public inspection. Mr. Procter records being taken to see this grisly sight by his guardian on Friday, August 25, 1826, the execution having taken place on the previous Monday. He says, "The weather was exceedingly wet, and the sight far from being agreeable to us; yet the novel exhibition proved irresistible to many."

A song that was popular long after the murder had these lines :—

" Oh, Betsy Bates we murdered thee,
For which we're on the fatal tree

.   .   .   .   .

We stabbed the mistress in the bar,
And gave her many a cruel scar ;
And in her head we left the knife,
But William Higgins saved her life."

SHIP=BUILDING AT CARKE

IN the middle of the eighteenth century there was a brisk trade in shipbuilding at Carke, vessels from fifty to two hundred tons being launched there. These vessels traded exclusively with the Baltic, with the then British possessions in North America and the West Indies, where many Lancashire families had considerable property. Some of the posts of the ropewalk belonging to the old shipyard could still be seen as late as 1872, and when the railway was made across the Marsh below Carke, many caulking-irons and other shipwrights' tools were found. The last vessel built at Carke was called *The Mayflower*.

The vessels trading with the Baltic rarely ever made more than one voyage in the year. They were laid up for the winter when the Baltic was ice-bound, the place of mooring being opposite to an orchard, their cables being fastened to the boles of some large apple-trees.

AN OLD ALUM MINE

NEAR the western border of Pleasington, bounding a deep wooded glen below Woodfield Park, there formerly used to be an alum mine, but, like so many mines, its history, after the first few years, was not one of prosperity. The mine was originally opened by Sir Richard Hoghton of Hoghton

Tower, on whose property it lay, the land on that side of the Darwen being a portion of the Hoghton Park estate, and King James I. paid it a visit during his memorable visit to Hoghton in 1617. The fact that the Crown drew a royalty from the mine doubtless added to James's interest.

Sir Richard appears to have made it pay, for we read, "Sir Richard Hoghton set up a very profitable mine of Alum nigh unto Hoghton Tower, in the hundred of Blackburn, within these few years, where store of very good alum was made and sold." But the output was not large, as we learn from Fuller's *Worthies of England*. Describing the natural commodities of Lancashire in 1662, the old writer makes this mention of the Pleasington Alum Mine :—" Allume—I am informed that Allume is found at Houghton in this County, within the Inheritance of Sir Richard Hoghton, and that enough for the use of this and the neighbouring Shires, though not for transportation. But because far greater plenty is afforded in Yorkshire, the larger mention of this mineral is referred to that place." Fuller adds that a considerable quantity of alum was then " daily employed by clothiers, glovers and dyers."

Later on the Pleasington Alum Mine was taken on a joint lease from the Duchy of Lancaster by a Mr. Ramsay and Lady Sarah Hoghton, daughter of the Earl of Chesterfield, and the wife of Sir Richard Hoghton, grandson of the entertainer of King James. But much trouble was the result. Lady Sarah entered into articles of agreement with a Captain James Benson to work her portion of the mine, but the speculation proved a ruinous one. The works at the mine and Lady Sarah's portion of it were seized by Benson's creditors and he himself was thrown into prison. This was in 1659, only a year after the agreement had been made.

People with grievances in those times were very fond of stating their case to the public in small pamphlets or tracts, and Benson, believing himself to be injured, published " A Relation of James Benson's undertaking the making of Alum at the Alum Works in Lancashire, truely opened, and the instrumental causes of his present condition set forth." He referred to the kindness of his cousin, Mr. Justice Sharples of Blackburn, but reproaches a Dr. Fyfe, Major Ashurst, and Mr. Thomas Wilson, as having " been great contrivers and assistants to my lady," and who, from " professed friends had become secret and sure enemies." Benson appealed to Lady Sarah for some allowance in consideration of his losses, and offered to refer the matter between them to the arbitration of two or four godly divines, mentioning Mr. Tyldesley and Mr. Eaton ; but Lady Sarah refused any compensation, or arbitration, whereupon Benson declared that he had " received the hardest measure that ever poor man received from any person professing truly to fear God ' and vowed' he would never have any more to do with any business that concerned her ladyship's honour."

After Benson's failure the working of the alum mine ceased altogether, but some little time afterwards it was reopened by Sir E. Colebrooke, who, however, had no better success than his predecessor. Nevertheless alum-making was still carried on at Pleasington towards the end of the eighteenth century, though doubtless upon a very small scale, for the Blackburn Parish Burial Register shows that " Alexander Macknallin, of Pleasington, alum-worker," was buried in May 1769 ; and " John Kitchin, alum-striker," was buried in April 1771.

THE STORY OF THE MARTYR'S ALTAR

ON St. John's Day 1559, the saying of the Mass in England was declared to be illegal. As we have already seen death was the punishment of the priests who disregarded the law ; imprisonment and confiscation of their estates were the punishments of those who followed their ministrations. But no law could touch the devotion and fidelity to their faith of the old Roman Catholic families of Lancashire, amongst whom the Townleys of Townley were pre-eminent. A precious relic of their devotion is still preserved. This is the old missionary altar which was used at the secret services of the proscribed faith.

When the Act of Uniformity which made the saying of the mass illegal was passed, a Mr. Burgess was agent and bailiff to the Townleys, and it was he who made the altar, in order that the Townley family might hear mass in his house, which was close to Townley Hall. By worshipping in the house of his agent, John Townley and his family avoided the danger of the estate being confiscated, which would inevitably have happened if priest or altar had been discovered in their own home. When closed, the old missionary altar had the appearance of a double oak cupboard, and as it was kept in a sitting-room, no suspicion as to its actual use was roused in the minds of those who were constantly searching the houses of suspected Roman Catholics. When in use, the piece of wood at the top, carved with the sacred symbol surrounded by rays, and with cherubs' heads at either side, shown in the drawing, was held in position by two wooden pegs, so that it could be quickly and easily removed. It was kept in the lower portion of the altar.

This relic of the times of bigotry has had many vicissitudes. The John Town-ley for whose use it was originally made suffered a life-long persecution for adherence to his faith. He suffered imprisonment nine different times, and each time in a different prison. When he was seventy-three years old he became blind, and "was bound to appear and keep within five miles of Townley his house. Who hath paid into the Exchequer twenty pounds a month and doth still (1601), so that there is paid already above five thousands pounds." Thus says the inscription beneath his portrait in the gallery at Townley Hall.

John Townley's first imprisonment took place in 1564, and consequently the neighbourhood of Burnley became dangerous for the Burgess family, who removed to a large farm at Brindle called Denham Hall, about three miles from Hoghton Tower. Here, the altar was placed in a large room and was used at the secret services attended by the numerous Roman Catholic families living in the neighbourhood under the protection of the Hoghtons, who then belonged to that religion. But in 1611, the Hoghtons became Protestants, and the Burgess family, for safety's sake, left Denham Hall for a more retired house called Woodend in the parish of Clayton-le-Woods. It was here in the lifetime of the successor of the maker of the altar, that it became associated with a tragedy. Father Arrowsmith, the martyred priest whose hand is still venerated at Ashton-in-Makerfield, said mass upon this altar. Twenty-two years later its existence was nearly discovered by the authorities. Near to Woodend was Woodcock Hall, a beautiful old house still in existence but sadly fallen from its former condition, belonging to a family of the same name. The owner of the house was a Roman Catholic, but in order to save his estate, which had been in his family for over four hundred years, he became a Protestant. His wife, an Anderton, remained in the old faith, and sent their son John to the English College at St. Omar's in France, to be educated. Ultimately John Woodcock became a priest and returned to Woodcock Hall. Immediately after his arrival he made arrangements to celebrate a midnight mass for the Burgess family and their Roman Catholic neighbours on the missionary altar at Woodend, in honour of one of the feasts of their Church. But whilst he was standing in his vestments in front of the altar, waiting to begin the mass when the clock struck twelve, a man rushed into the room begging the little band of worshippers to disperse immediately, as they had been betrayed to the authorities and the poursuivants were already approaching the house. Father Woodcock quickly removed his vestments, closed the altar, and when the poursuivants arrived was safely hidden in the priest's hiding-hole.

When the men burst into the room, Mrs. Burgess, who had thrown herself into a chair, feigning illness, protested against such an intrusion into a sick woman's room at that time of night. The poursuivants replied that they had a warrant to apprehend a popish priest who was known to be in the house.

Mrs. Burgess answered, "You will not find a man in my room at this time of night."

"What are all these people assembled for if it be not to meet the popish priest?" they asked her.

"They are some neighbours," she said, "who have come to sit up with me."

The men gave no credence to this explanation, and despite the protestations of Mrs. Burgess and her husband, searched the house minutely, from the cellar to the roof, but found no trace of the priest's secret hiding-place. The assembled people were roughly bidden to return to their own homes. After the baffled poursuivants had gone Father Woodcock emerged from his hiding-place, opened the altar, and assuming his vestments said the mass to a little band of the faithful who had stolen back to the house after their dismissal. Before daybreak he hurried away to his father's house. It was lucky that he did so, for the traitor who had told the authorities of his presence at Woodend, went to them very early the next morning, saying—

"I had quite forgotten. There is a hiding-hole in that house, for I once went there courting the servant-maid when the mistress was absent, but she came back earlier than was expected, and I was put into the hiding-place. I think I can find it again, behind a certain panel."

So the poursuivants hastened to Woodend, taking the traitor with them. He went directly to the panel that concealed the hiding-hole, pushed it back, and lo! the hole was empty! The bird had flown.

News of the return of the poursuivants to Woodend, and their discovery of the hiding-hole speedly reached Woodcock Hall, and Mr. Woodcock, fearing a similar visit to his house, and the loss of his estate, if his son were discovered there, gave him some breakfast and ordered him to leave immediately. No tragedy upon the stage shows a scene so supremely terrible as that which took place at Woodcock Hall on this August morning of 1644. The father, who had already shown that he set his worldly possessions before his religious belief, driving his son forth into the hands of his enemies and to the certainty of a horrible death lest those possessions should be taken away; the mother torn between her duty to her husband, her fidelity to her Church and her love for her son. The son, serene, exalted, obeying his father as a son;

exhorting his weeping and distracted mother like a priest; and then riding away into the unknown. What a moment of human littleness, of human greatness! The father condemned his son to death!

There is a theory that intense agony of the human mind leaves its impress upon the environment in which that agony was undergone. It is a wide subject, theories upon which can neither be proved nor disproved, but it is certain that the scenes of great tragedies frequently inspire feelings of gloom and distress in people who are entirely ignorant of what has happened in the past. The heartrending moment at Woodcock Hall, therefore, may easily have given the old house that "air of mystery and aloofness" to which Dom Bede Camm refers in his story of the Martyr's Altar.

Driven forth from his father's house, Father Woodcock had scarcely gone a mile when he was overtaken at Bamber Bridge by the traitor and the poursuivants, returning from their fruitless search at Woodend. He was arrested, taken before the magistrates, and by their order conveyed to Lancaster Castle, where he remained in close confinement for two years. In August, 1646, he suffered his martyrdom, being hanged, drawn and quartered.

The taking of Father Woodcock so near to Woodend, brought such serious trouble upon the Burgess family, that they deemed it expedient to leave that part of the country. Taking the altar with them, now made doubly precious by the ministrations upon it of the two martyrs, Father Arrowsmith and Father Woodcock, they removed to Ashton-in-Makerfield, where they placed themselves under the protection of the great Roman Catholic family of Gerard of Bryn. And here they remained in comparative peace and quiet, until the persecution abating they were able to secure the lease of a farm called Hawkslough in Cuerden, near Bamber Bridge, for three lives. This was then the usual custom of renting farms.

Returned to their old country, the martyr's altar was placed in a large parlour of the farm, and for three generations of Burgesses was used for the worship of all the Roman Catholics in the neighbourhood. When the lease of the farm expired with the third life, the penal laws against those of his faith not being so strictly enforced, the then head of the family, Thomas Burgess, was able in 1784 to buy a plot of waste ground at Clayton Brook, close to Hawkslough Farm, upon which he built the present house. The altar was placed in a large room at the back of the new house, where it remained for nearly sixty years. But upon the death of Thomas Burgess, in 1843, the altar went forth once more on its wanderings. The house being let to a Protestant, the altar was taken to the house of Mrs. Abbot, Thomas Burgess's daughter, at Brockholes, near Preston, where it was placed in a private oratory. Upon the death of Mrs. Abbot, the altar was taken to the house of her daughter, Mrs. Clarkson, at Bolton-le-Sands. When Mrs. Clarkson became a widow in 1891, she left Bolton-le-Sands for Lancaster, and there the ancient altar was placed in a little oratory in Dale Street, by her brother, the Rev. Thomas Abbot. "Here," says Dom Bede Camm, "Bishop O'Reilly often used to visit it and make his meditation in the little chapel, in veneration of the glorious martyrs who had offered the Holy Sacrifice upon it. Here, too, we visited it in June 1906, not long after the death of the venerable priest who took such a holy pride in it." The "venerable priest," was the Rev. Thomas Abbot, who used to say mass upon the

THE ALTAR OPENED

THE ALTAR CLOSED

taken back to Bolton-le-Sands, and placed in a private oratory in the house of Mr. Thomas Clarkson. Thus from the time it was made in 1560, down to our own day and generation, this altar has never left the possession of the Burgess family. In one of the drawers the vestment is preserved which Father Woodcock wore when he said

altar every day after his retirement to Lancaster.

In more recent years, the altar was mass for the last time at Woodend, so worn by age and faded that it could be taken for either red or white.

THE SKULL IN THE "BORTRY TREE"

TRADITION has it that when the only road from Lancaster to Ulverstone passed through the upper end of Flockburgh, and so on to Sandgate, there stood not far from the end of the town, a little wayside inn, for the accommodation of travellers along this road. This inn was pulled down some two hundred and fifty years ago. Behind it grew a pear-tree, which in some storm had been partially torn up and thrown on one side, so that it nearly touched the ground. The then owner of the site upon which the inn had stood, instead of cutting the pear-tree down, allowed it to remain in this inclined position, probably because he knew that old pear-trees when thrown over in this way, if properly lopped and pruned, will go on bearing fruit much more abundantly than they did whilst they were perpendicular. But about the commencement of the nineteenth century, the venerable pear-tree became rotten and decayed; it encumbered much of the garden ground; and it was therefore cut down. But when the ground over which it had reclined for so long was trenched, a strange discovery was made. At a very little depth from the surface they came upon a human skeleton, the body—that of a large man—to judge from the position of the bones, having been apparently bent double, after it had been put in the hole. Some of the bones were in wonderful preservation, as was also the skull.

There is little doubt that this skeleton was that of some traveller who had been murdered at the old inn, and whose body had been hastily thrust into the ground beneath the pear-tree, as it would be less liable to be discovered there than in any other part of the garden. Such murders were not uncommon at wayside inns. Travellers were obliged to carry considerable sums of money on their journeys, as the expenses of the road were heavy. Some of these lonely wayside inns had the most sinister reputation, and the memory of one of them at Gilsland, near Carlisle, has been perpetuated by Sir Walter Scott as " Mumps Ha' " in *Guy Mannering*. At " Mumps Ha' " a deep yawning gulf lay beneath the bed, and into this the sleeping traveller was hurled headlong by Tib Mumps and her confederates. There is no tradition of such elaborate villainy as this at the old inn at Flockburgh, but the huddled position in which the skeleton was found, and the shallowness of the hole in which it was buried, give reasonable suspicion that it was buried hastily, and that time was an object with those who had to dispose of the body.

The skull for many years afterwards remained in the hollow part of an elder-tree—a " bortry " or " burtree " in the dialect—that grew near by, in which it was placed by the finder.

THE late Edwin Waugh was very fond of telling this story. A man had run some distance to catch a train, and arrived at the station just in time to see it leaving the platform. He stood looking at it for a second or two and then gave vent to his injured feelings, by shaking his fist at the departing train, and shouting, " Go on, thou greyt puffin' foo'! Go on! Aw con wait! "

A BOY went to a tobacconist's shop and asked for half-an-ounce of thick twist. When he had been served he threw a penny upon the counter, and turned to leave the shop.

" Here, lad! " cried the tobacconist, " tha'rt a ha'penny short."

" Nay," said the boy, as he bolted out of the doorway, " it's yo! "

LANCASHIRE WOMEN PREACHERS

THE spiritual exaltation which led men and women to suffer martyrdom for their faith was not dead in Lancashire in the eighteenth century, and found expression in the lives of many who joined the newly formed sect of the Methodists. Of these Ann Cutler is the most striking example. She was born near Preston in 1759, and although always quiet and serious she evinced no particular interest in religion, beyond that shown by most young girls, until she was twenty-six, when, hearing some Methodists preach at Preston, she "was convinced of her sin, and found a sinking in humility, love and dependence upon God."

To compare this humble Preston girl with St. Catherine of Siena and Joan of Arc may sound extravagant, but the same spirit which animated and inspired the Italian gentlewoman and the French peasant-maid animated and inspired Nanny Cutler. St. Catherine, her every thought fixed upon the Divinity, saw visions which enabled her to give counsel to the Pope and to Emperors ; Joan of Arc, tending her sheep, her mind filled with the thoughts of her country's woe and misery, heard mystical voices which bade her save France from ruin. By her belief in her visions St. Catherine became a power for good ; and by her faith in the mystical voices Joan of Arc defeated the English, and crowned her king at Rheims. Absolute faith in the divine nature of their "call," absolute conviction that a mission was imposed upon them by the divine will, was the inspiration which made the Italian lady a saint, and the French peasant-girl a soldier.

The same faith and conviction inspired Nanny Cutler. Speedily after her conversion she felt that her vocation and her duty were " to cry for sinners." " I cannot be happy," she said, " unless I cry for sinners." I do not want any praise : I want nothing but souls to be brought to God. I am reproached by most. I cannot do it to be seen or heard of men. I see the world going to destruction and I am burdened till I pour out my soul to God for them."

Preaching and praying by women were not favourably regarded by the early Methodists, and any attempt at religious teaching on the part of a woman met with active opposition. But Nanny Cutler, supported and upheld by her belief in the divine message, went steadily on. Like St. Catherine and Joan of Arc and other religious mystics she had visions, and believed herself in continual union with the Deity. Unlike her early forerunners she did not describe these visions to all who would come and listen ; but she wrote of them to the leader of the Methodists, the great John Wesley, whose answer shows that he knew what was accepted in fourteenth and fifteenth century Italy and France as miraculous, would be openly scoffed and jeered at in eighteenth-century England.

"*Walton, April* 15, 1790.

" MY DEAR SISTER,

"There is something in the dealings of God with your soul which is out of the common way. But I have known several whom He has been pleased to lead exactly the same way, and particularly in manifesting to them distinctly the Three Persons of the ever blessed Deity. You may tell all your experiences to me at any time ; but you will need to be cautious in speaking to others, for they would not understand what you say. Go on in the name of God and the power of His might. Pray for the whole spirit of humility; and I wish that you would write and speak without reserve to, dear Nanny,

"Yours affectionately,
"JOHN WESLEY."

From this letter it would appear that Nanny Cutler's visions were of the Trinity, and having compared her spiritual exaltation with those of St. Catherine of Siena and Joan of Arc, it is interesting to note that in her visions St. Catherine believed that she saw and communed with the Almighty, and that she was the Spouse of Christ; whilst Joan of Arc affirmed that the voices whose command she obeyed were those of St. Catherine of Fierbois, St. Margaret and St. Michael.

Whether an ill-nourished body and want of proper sleep caused mental hallucination so vivid as to impress the subject with reality, is for the doctor, not the story-teller, to determine. Nanny Cutler's daily food consisted of milk and herb-tea; at midnight she rose for an hour of prayer, and winter and summer she invariably got up at four o'clock. She vowed herself to a life of celibacy.

For nine years, with unswerving fervour and zeal, she continued her task, undergoing physical exertion upon this meagre diet which would have taxed the strength of a strong man. The Rev. William Bramwell, who has written a biography of Nanny Cutler, says: "She met with the greatest opposition that I ever knew one person to receive, and I never saw or heard of her being in the least angry. She never complained of ill-usage. She was sent for by many, both rich and poor; and though she was exceedingly sensible of opposition, yet she would say, "I am not received at such a place; but the will of the Lord be done." In many essentials Nanny Cutler might

have sat to George Eliot for the character of Dinah in *Adam Bede*, but Dinah was drawn from George Eliot's aunt Elizabeth Evans, who curiously enough was a member of Mr. Bramwell's congregation; it was whilst listening to a prayer by him that Elizabeth Evans "found peace."

Despite the opposition of the Methodist leaders and the dissuasion of her friends, Mr. Bramwell amongst them, Nanny held a series of "revivalist" meetings throughout Yorkshire. This was followed by others through Lancashire, the last being at Oldham, Manchester, Derby and Macclesfield. From Manchester Nanny wrote: "The last week but this at Oldham and Delph, and another place, and near a hundred souls were brought to God. Many cried for mercy and the Lord delivered them. In this town I cannot exactly tell the number. God has sanctified many; some preachers and leaders."

At Macclesfield she fell ill, but she continued to preach and pray, to visit the sick and to labour in the task to which she had devoted her strong soul. She felt that she would not recover and died a few days later at the age of thirty-five, worn out by her unceasing labours. She was buried at Macclesfield, and this inscription is on her tombstone:—

UNDERNEATH LIE THE REMAINS OF

ANN CUTLER,

WHOSE SIMPLE MANNER, SOLID PIETY, AND
EXTRAORDINARY POWER IN PRAYER,
DISTINGUISHED AND RENDERED HER EMINENTLY
USEFUL IN PROMOTING A RELIGIOUS REVIVAL
WHEREVER SHE CAME.
SHE WAS BORN NEAR PRESTON IN LANCASHIRE,
AND DIED HERE DECEMBER 29TH, 1794.
AET. 35.

"The charm of her praying," says one of her biographers, "seemed to be in the intense force of her sympathy for the sinful, and for those who were immersed in the cares and pleasures of daily life. It was for these that she cried aloud and spared not." In appearance Nanny Cutler was weak and insignificant, but she had " a smile of sweet composure which seemed in a sense a reflection of the Divine Nature."

Although by her fervour and exaltation Nanny Cutler is one of the leading figures of early Methodism in Lancashire, she was not the only woman preacher amongst the sect. Whilst she was still a girl of twelve, Sister Bosanquitt and others, such as Sister Crosby, Sister Ryan, and Sister Hurrell, were holding public religious meetings, in spite of the strong disapproval of the founder of their sect, John Wesley. His prejudice notwithstanding, Wesley was obliged to admit that in special cases it would be wrong to prohibit women from preaching, but he insisted that women who preached should have an " extraordinary call," as is shown by a letter he wrote in 1771 to Sister Bosanquitt: " I think the strength of the cause rests here, in having an extraordinary call; so I am persuaded has everyone of our lay-preachers; otherwise I would not continue his preaching at all."

Another Methodist woman-preacher, Mary Barritt, preached in Manchester, making many converts by her open-air sermons at Shude Hill.

The preaching of women has never been wholly approval of by the Methodist body, and when a very definite line was taken on the matter, Mrs. Child in her letters from New York wrote: " This seemed a strange idea for Methodists, some of whose brightest ornaments have been women preachers. As far back as Adam Clarke's time, his objections were met by the answer: 'If an ass reproved Balaam, and a *barn-door fowl* reproved Peter, why

shouldn't a woman reprove sin?' This classification with donkeys and fowls is certainly not very complimentary. The first comparison I heard wittily replied to by a coloured woman, who had once been a slave: ' Maybe a speaking woman *is* like an ass,' said she; ' but I can tell you one thing—the ass saw the angel when Balaam didn't.' "

During periods of religious excitement such as were frequently witnessed in Lancashire at these " revivals," zeal and fervour often approached dangerously near to hysteria, and the use to which such mental exaltation could be put by unprincipled persons is exemplified by the case of a child-preacher called Elizabeth Bradbury, of whom the following account is given by Charles Hulbert. He says that she was born of poor parents at Oldham, as far as he recollects, in 1798, " At the age of nine months she could almost articulate every word in common occurrence, with the sole instruction of her mother. At twelve months she could read, and shortly after learned to write, and acquired some knowledge of the Latin language. At the age of three years she stood upon a table placed in the pulpit of the Methodist Chapel at Middleton, seven miles from Manchester, and preached to a numerous and respectable congregation. The effect upon the minds of the hearers was most extraordinary, some absolutely fainted from excess of feeling and surprise. She was at this period considered as a prodigy, or rather as one endowed with miraculous gifts. The crowds who came daily to visit her, and the money which was presented to her parents from visitors, prevented their acceptance of numerous offers from respectable individuals to take this extraordinary child under their protection and to provide for her education and future happiness

About the year 1803 the editor (Charles Hulbert) saw her at the Bull's Head, Swinton, five miles from Manchester, where her imprudent father exhibited her as a prodigy of talent and literature, and induced her to act the preacher for the amusement of public-house company. She appeared equally playful as other children of her years, but seemed remarkably shrewd in her observations on the different characters in the company, especially on those who were not quite so liberal in their gratuities as she could wish. The editor requested her to write something in his pocket-book as a proof of her talent, when she immediately wrote her own and her father's name with each hand (right and left) in a most beautiful style. He has had no information respecting her since the above period."

BALLAD OF MARRIAGE

IN yonder wood there is a dene
 Where I myself was late reposing;
 Where blossoms in their prime have
  been,
And flowers fair their colours losing;
A love of mine I chanced to meet,
 Which causèd me too long to tarry,
And then of him I did intreat,
 To tell me when he thought to marry.

" If thou wilt not my secret tell,
 Ne bruit abroad in Whalley parish,
And swear to keep my counsel well,
 I will declare my day of marriage.
  * * * *
" When summer heat will dry no mire,
 And winter's rain no longer patter;
When lead will melt withouten fire,
 And bear-brades do need no water [1];
When Downham stones with diamond rings,[2]
 And cockles be with pearls comparèd;
When gold is made of gray goose wings,
 Then will my love and I be married.

" When buck and hart in Hodder lies,
 And graylings on the fells are breeding;

When mussels grow on every tree,
 And swans on every rock are feeding;
When mountains are by men removèd,
 And Ribble back to Horton carried,
Or Pendle Hill grows silk above,
 Then will my love and I be married.

" When moor or moss do saffron yield,
 And beck [3] and sike [4] run down with
  honey;
When sugar grows in every field,
 And clerks will take no bribe of money;
When men in Bowland dieth here,
 And at Jerusalem be buried;
Or when the sun doth rise at noon,
 Then will my love and I be married."

" Now farewell, friend; if it be so,
 And this thy once expected wedding;
For neither I, nor none of my kin
 Will ever need to look for bidding.[5]
I swear and vow, if this be true,
 And thou of such an evil carriage,
If I should live ten thousand year,
 I'd never more expect thy marriage."

[1] The young green shoots of bear, or bigg, a coarse kind of barley, to which rain is indispensable when they first appear above ground.
[2] At Downham crystals are found, usually called Downham diamonds, which in lustre equal Bristol stone. These are mostly found on Wossà Hill, near Downham.

[3] Beck is the Scandinavian name for a brook or burn.
[4] Sike is a small rivulet or stream; in Lancashire often called a rindle.
[5] Bidding to a wedding is inviting. So at a funeral, two or four persons called bidders are sent about to invite the friends, and distribute the mourning.

STONYHURST AND THE SHERBURNES

THE Sherburnes were an ancient family whose pedigree has been traced back to the time of Richard I.; but the earliest mention of their being settled at Stonyhurst is in the reign of Edward III., some two centuries later. Stonyhurst descended from Sherburne fathers to Sherburne sons, who intermarried with all the leading Lancashire families—the Stanleys, the Radcliffes, the Townleys, the Talbots of Bashall, the Bolds of Bold,—until 1717, when Sir Nicholas Sherburne, having survived his only son, died, leaving Stonyhurst to his daughter, the Duchess of Norfolk. The beautiful old house which had been begun by a Richard Sherburne in 1594, was finished by his son; and it was the last Sir Nicholas who added the two great cupolas which are seen from far, and the beautiful waterways of the garden; he also laid out the garden in the Dutch style.

Stonyhurst in the days of the Sherburnes, and especially in the time of Sir Nicholas, was famous for its hospitality. He kept a pack of staghounds, and of all the Roman Catholic families of Lancashire maintained the most princely state. From the earliest period of their occupation of Stonyhurst the Sherburnes had been buried in Mitton Church, and in the reign of Henry VIII. Hugh Sherburne built the Sherburne Chapel, which is now almost filled with their monuments. This chapel was an enlargement of a small chapel, originally dedicated to St. Nicholas, on the north side of the choir. And here, amongst many epitaphs giving the history and extolling the virtues of dead and gone Sherburnes, we find the epitaph of the last direct representative of the race, Sir Nicholas, written by his daughter, the Duchess of Norfolk. It begins, "This monument is to the sacred and esteemed memory of Sir Nicholas Shireburn and his Lady," and after detailing his marriage, the births of his three children, goes on as follows:—

"Sir Nicholas Shireburn was a man of great humanity, simpathy and concern for the good of mankind, and did many good charitable things whilst he lived; he particularly set his neighbourhood a-spinning of Jersey wool, and provided a man to comb the wool, and a woman who taught them to spin, whom he kept in his house and allotted several rooms he had in one of the courts of Stonyhurst, for them to work in, and the neighbours came to spin accordingly : the spinners came every day, and span as long a time as they could spare, morning and afternoon, from their families : this continued from April 1699 to August 1701. When they had all learn'd, he gave the nearest neighbour each a pound or half a pound of wool ready for spinning, and wheel to set up for themselves, which did a vast deal of good to the North side of the Ribble in Lancashire. Sir Nicholas Sherburne died Dec. 16, 1717. This monument was set up by the dowager dutches of Norfolk, in memory of the best of fathers and mothers, and in this vault designes to be interr'd herself, whenever it pleases God to take her out of the world.

" Lady Sherburne was a lady of an excellent temper and fine sentiments, singular piety, virtue, and charity and constantly employed in doing good, especially to the distressed, sick, poor and lame, for whom she kept an apothecaries shop in the house ; she continued as long as she lived doing great good and charity ; she died January 27th, 1727. Besides all other great charities which Sir Nicholas and Lady Sherburne did, they gave on All Souls' Day, a considerable sum of money to the poor ; Lady Sherburne serving them with her own hands that day."

The Duchess of Norfolk died childless, in 1754, and was buried beside her father and mother in the vault in the Sherburne Chapel in Mitton Church. Stonyhurst then reverted to the family of her aunt—Sir Nicholas's sister Elizabeth, who had married Humphrey Weld, of Lullworth Castle, a Dorsetshire gentleman of considerable estate—in the person of Edward Weld, her cousin. It was under his son, Thomas Weld, that the stately mansion of the Sherburnes with its superb views of Ribblesdale and Calderbottom was converted into a Roman Catholic seminary.

For over two centuries education had been forbidden to Roman Catholics in England except in Protestant schools. The consequence was that all those Roman Catholics who could afford to do so, sent their sons abroad to foreign seminaries, but more particularly to the Colleges of St. Omer and Douai in France, which were practically English. The College of St. Omer belonged to the English Jesuits, and here Thomas Weld himself had been educated, being an eye-witness of the violent seizure of the college and the ejection of his masters in 1762, under the decree of the expulsion of the Jesuits from the realm of France. The English Jesuit fathers took refuge in the Austrian Netherlands, but here again they "were dislodged, pillaged and ejected under an edict for the suppression of the Order, promulgated by Pope Clement XIV. in 1773." They went to Liège, where for some years they continued their work in educating the English boys and youths of their faith.

But in 1794 the armies of the French Republic overran the Netherlands, and once more the Jesuit fathers found themselves ruined and proscribed. Three years before, the spirit of religious tolerance, which had been slowly growing in England, had found expression in an Act of Parliament permitting Roman Catholics to open schools for pupils of their religion, provided the masters took the oath of civil allegiance. In "their uttermost distress," the English Jesuits of Liège, finding themselves driven from their last resting-place and the whole continent closed against them, gladly took advantage of this Act.

Stonyhurst had fallen into sad disrepair, having been neglected both by the Duchess of Norfolk, her cousin and his son, but it offered a safe asylum, and a long lease of the house and a neighbouring farm was gladly given by Thomas Weld to his old master, upon extremely moderate terms, so moderate indeed, that he was regarded as founder and benefactor.

There is a graphic story of the priests leading the small remnant of their pupils from Liège through the Lancashire woods, and arriving at a desolate and deserted Stonyhurst, where the wind and the rain found entrance through broken windows and crumbling roofs. The early days of masters and pupils at Stonyhurst were days of misery, but soon the old decaying buildings round about the house were pulled down, the roofs and windows were mended, the garden walks cleared of weeds and overgrowth, and twenty-four years later, Dr. Whitaker tells us, " It is filled at present by more than two hundred and fifty students of the Roman Catholic religion, sent thither from most parts of the world. . . . Stonyhurst College at the present day is a monument of the liberal spirit of His Majesty's Government ; and the benefits arising from it form a strong contrast with the mischiefs of that ancient jealousy, which reduced such numbers of British subjects to the alternative of living in ignorance at home, or of resorting for liberal education to foreign climes."

In the course of time a new wing and other additions were made to the old house, the Elizabethan style of Sir Richard Sherburne's house being faithfully followed ; the result is that to-day Stonyhurst is one of the most beautiful and most stately buildings in the country, surrounded by gardens of exquisite beauty. Its vast library contains countless treasures. Amongst them is one of touching interest—a Book of Hours which belonged to the unhappy and unfortunate Mary, Queen of Scots. This is the book she is said to have held in her hand when she mounted the scaffold in the hall of Fotheringay Castle, and which she gave to her confessor, before she laid her head on the block. The confessor gave this precious relic to the library of Douai College, and thence it was taken by the Jesuit fathers to Liège, and in 1794 was brought by them to Stonyhurst. Amongst other treasures is a Roman altar dedicated to the " mother goddess " by a Captain of the Asturian Legion, which was rescued in 1834 from the rubbish of a neighbouring farm-yard. This proved to be the identical altar which Camden the chronicler saw, and described, near Ribchester in 1603.

The view from the old home of the Sherburnes, now the centre of one of the most perfect systems of education in the country, is the finest in all Lancashire. To the south one sees the high grounds about Blackburn and the windings of the Ribble as it runs towards Ribblesdale ; to the east are the beautifully wooded valleys of the same river and the Hodder, with Clitheroe Castle standing upon its lonely hill, the rolling map of Pendle Forest serving for background.

In Mitton Church, amongst the many monuments to the Sherburnes there is an echo of the Jacobite Rebellion of 1715, in the shape of an epitaph to Peregrine Widdrington, the youngest son of that Lord Widdrington who played so important a part in deceiving the Jacobite Generals as to the support of Manchester.[1]

" In this vault lies the body of the Hon. Peregrin Widderington. The Hon. Peregrin Widderington was the youngest son of William, Lord Widderington, who died April the 17th, 1743. This Peregrin was a

[1] See " The Battle of Preston."

man of the strictest friendship and honour with all the good qualities that accomplished a fine gentleman; he was of so amiable a disposition, and so ingaging, that he was beloved and esteemed by all who had the honour and happiness of his acquaintance, being ever ready to oblige and to act the friendly part on all occasions, firm and steadfast in all his prin-

The Sherburne Duchess of Norfolk seems to have had a *penchant* for writing epitaphs. Those to her father and mother already quoted, and this one to Peregrine Widdrington were written by her own hand, her Grace's inconsistency in spelling even the name of her own family being faithfully followed by the marble - cutters. Another interesting

THE SHERBURNE CHAPEL IN MITTON CHURCH

ciples, which was delicately fine and good as could be wished in any man; he was both sincere and agreeable in life and conversation. He was born May 20, 1692, and died February 4th, 1748-9. He was with his brother in the Preston affair, 1716, where he lost his fortune, with his health, by a long confinement in prison. This monument was set up by the Dowager Duchess of Norfolk, in memory of the Hon. Peregrin Widderington."

point in the Sherburne Chapel is that the statues upon the tomb of Sir Nicholas Sherburne's father and grandfather, are the latest instances of recumbent, cross-legged figures being placed upon gravestones. They were made by a stonemason in London called Stanton, by Sir Nicholas's direction in 1699, and cost, for those times, the large sum of two hundred and twenty-three pounds.

136

SACRED MUSIC IN LANCASHIRE

FROM the earliest time a love of music has been inherent in the Lancashire character. It was helped and fostered by the feudal lords, who used to set apart pieces of land in order that the income arising therefrom might be devoted to the payment of the village musicians. Such endowments were made as late as the fourteenth century. Thus supported and encouraged, it is not surprising that music played an important part in the lives of the Lancashire people. Whatever the occasion—at the rush-bearings, the wakes, the guisings, the public festivals in summer and winter in the villages and manor-houses, at births, christenings, weddings, and funerals—there was always music and singing. Michael Drayton, whose *Polyolbion*, a description in verse of the whole of England, was published in 1612, gives this picture of Lancashire gaiety and response to music :—

> "So blyth and bonny now the lads and lassies are,
> That ever as anon the bag-pipe up doth blow,
> Cast in a gallant round about the hearth they go,
> And at each pause they kiss, was never seen such rule,
> In any place but here, at bonfire or at Yule;
> And every village smokes at wakes with lusty cheer,
> Then 'Hey' they cry for Lun; and 'Hey' for Lancashire."

But as early as 1590 some of the Puritanically inclined clergymen had complained bitterly of brides and bridegrooms being escorted to and from the churches with "piping," and when the Commonwealth held sway, music was silenced in Lancashire as well as in the rest of England. Although music accorded ill with the sour, narrow, and fanatical view of life held by the Puritans, the measures promulgated against it were in reality

ordained to prevent its use in places of worship. Organs were destroyed in churches and cathedrals, and every where choirs were disbanded. In one church, whilst the Puritans were breaking up the organ—which they considered a sign of Popery—they fell out amongst themselves and used the organ-pipes as weapons in a free fight.

For nearly half a century music was unheard in the Lancashire churches and the singing of the psalms had been forgotten. Even the restoration of Charles II., although it set the pipes and the fiddles playing once more, and brought back the May-pole and the merry-makings and dancing to village wakes and fairs, did not affect the churches, which were still organless and choirless. And it was not until a year before Charles's death that the then Warden of Manchester Collegiate Church, Warden Stratford, in spite of strenuous and bitter opposition, re-established the choir, and built an organ, at the same time restoring the old services of daily Matins and Evensong. This was the first sign in the country of revolt against the fanaticism and prejudice which had robbed the church services of all their beauty. But it was eleven years before other places were affected by the example of Manchester, chiefly because there was no one who knew how to sing sacred music, and also because of the opposition of the older generation of Puritans.

Oldham was the next town to establish a musical service in its old church, being aided thereto by a man called Abraham Hurst who started a school there, for the teaching of sacred music, in 1695. But apparently there was no organ at Oldham even then, for in the following year Hurst took his pupils, who numbered sixty, to Manchester to sing to the organ in the Collegiate Church. This large number of pupils shows how eagerly the younger generation welcomed the change in the dreary Puritan services. The elder generation, however, looked upon the introduction of singing into the churches as being directly inspired by the devil, and when one of these—an old Oldham Puritan—was told that a boy of his acquaintance was about to join Hurst's school of music, he "prayed that God would strike him dumb"; an expression of opinion which gives a clear idea of the lengths to which religious intolerance was carried.

Hidden away in the vestries of some of the churches, in long-disused chests, were quantities of old music books which had never been opened for nearly a century. But no one could read them, and for a long time there was only one hymn tune known, which had to serve both for morning and evening service. Abraham Hurst, however, had some smattering of knowledge of the old books, and after he gave up his music school at Oldham, his place was taken by one of his pupils, Elias Hall, to whom singers and musicians in the county owe the Old Lancashire Notation. Hall and several other of the pupils had learnt something of the method of the old books from Hurst, and research upon the basis of this slender knowledge soon cleared away the hitherto insuperable mysteries of the old tune-books.

In the same year that Abraham Hurst took the pupils of the Oldham music school to sing to the organ in the Collegiate Church at Manchester, Hall took them to Rochdale by the invitation of the Vicar of that place. There they sang without an organ, for one was only placed in the church seven years afterwards, but the worthy and enterprising Vicar was so pleased with the service that he gave Hall and the singers a banquet at the "Royal Oak."

A further impetus to the use of music in churches was given shortly afterwards by the appointment of Warden Stratford of the Manchester Collegiate Church to the Bishopric of Chester. In 1701 he gave public support to the movement by granting Elias Hall permission to establish schools of music wherever he chose in the diocese; and in consequence the teacher spent a considerable portion of his time in going from place to place giving the necessary instruction. As a further help he wrote the *Psalm-singer's Compleat Companion*, wherein may be found the Old Lancashire Notation.

A few years later the love of singing had so spread that a singers' gallery was built in Oldham Church, and the list of the names of those who occupied it is the first record of a regular choir.

MOTHER to her small son, standing at the door one night :-

"Come in and shut th' door, John. What ar't doin' theer?"

"Aw'm lookin' at th' moon."

"Lookin' at th' moon. Come in aw tell thee, an' let th' moon alone."

"Who's touching th' moon?"

THE FIRE AT HOLKER HALL

A DISASTROUS fire occurred at Holker Hall, the beautiful seat of the Duke of Devonshire (now the property of Lord Richard Cavendish, the brother of the present Duke), on 10th March, 1871, when, in three hours, the whole of the south wing, in which the principal rooms were situated, was completely gutted, and their valuable contents destroyed. Mr. James Stockdale, in his *Annals of Cartmel*, has left us a graphic account of an occurrence which is still remembered by the older folk in the neighbourhood. The then Duke of Devonshire, the grandfather of the present peer, had been in residence for some little time at Holker—it was his favourite home—when his brother, Lord Richard Cavendish, and his second son, Lord Frederick Cavendish,[1] arrived at the Hall on the 9th of March. "Lord Frederick Cavendish's bedroom," says Mr. Stockdale, "was in the south-west wing of the Hall. On retiring to rest about two o'clock in the morning, he passed through his dressing-room, where there was a fire, to his own bedroom, and then fancied he smelt a somewhat strong smell of burning wood; not, however, at the time supposing it to arise from anything more than the wood that might have been used in lighting the fire. In the course of about three hours afterwards, and whilst fast asleep, he was suddenly aroused by a very loud noise in the dressing-room, which at once caused him to arise from his bed to ascertain the cause, when to his utter astonishment, on opening the dressing-room door, he perceived that the legs of the table had been burnt off, causing it to fall heavily to the

floor, and that the rest of the furniture and the whole of his own wardrobe were enveloped in flames. Instantaneously his lordship made his way through another door into the great corridor, and seizing the alarm bell, soon had the whole of the household about him. As this was a little before five o'clock in the morning, all the labourers then being at their own homes in the neighbouring villages, considerable confusion, as is always the case, arose at first. However, this did not last long. The great bell was rung—servants were sent out in every direction for help and assistance—and in a most unprecedentedly short time the whole neighbourhood, it may be truly said, had arrived at the Hall, and with a willingness to give assistance, never on any occasion surpassed.

"The active fire-brigade of some forty men were the first to appear on the scene, and at once manned the excellent fire engine always on the premises, throwing volumes of water into the midst of the roaring flames; but, owing to the vast quantity of wood in the walls of every part of the building, and the corridors throughout having been studded with wood to prevent damp from injuring the valuable pictures and portraits hung up there, as well as the excessively inflammable nature of the furniture and everything else in the rooms, it became quite obvious that the whole of the south wing of the Hall, and everything therein not already removed, could not be saved from falling a prey to the flames. From that moment the efforts of all (and these were hundreds!) were directed to cutting off the lurid flames, already roaring, flaring and rushing towards the great body of the hall; as well as in removing the furniture and valuables from this part of the premises. The fire-engine, therefore, was forthwith

[1] Lord Frederick Cavendish was Chief Secretary for Ireland. He took the oath for his office on May 0, 1882. On the afternoon of that day whilst walking with Mr. Burke, the Under-Secretary, in Phœnix Park, they were both attacked by Fenians and foully stabbed to death.

made to play with all its power (efforts of men in extremity!) on the approaching flames, and particularly on the adjoining old part of the Hall; the roof and the partition and the flooring of which had been cut away. Water obtained from some large tanks on the roofs was conveyed to the place and poured down copiously on the flames, by numbers of persons who had come up to give assistance; still for a time (and it was an anxious time!) the prospect of these exertions being successful was most doubtful; and to add to the dilemma, the water supply seemed to be in the course of being exhausted. No way daunted, however, by these disheartening appearances, the noble fire brigade, now aided on all sides by hundreds of volunteers, worked the fire engine with redoubled effect, till at last there did appear something like a reliable hope that this neck-and-neck struggle with the devouring element would end successfully, particularly as the wind, till then rather strong, had abated a little, and had shifted somewhat so as not to blow directly on the old part of the building.

"In the meantime seasonable help arrived from another quarter, for the Lowood fire engine, which had been sent for, appeared on the scene of action, and began at once to play with great effect on the north side of the burning building, so that in a short time there could not remain any doubt that the progress of the flames would be arrested, and that the great body of the Hall would be saved. About nine o'clock, before which time all the roofs and floors of the burning south-west wing had fallen in, the Ulverstone fire brigade reached Holker accompanied by many gentlemen and tradesmen of the town, and at once began to direct their powerful engine on the burning embers, so as to prevent their again becoming dangerous; and at eleven o'clock even the strong fire brigade of the town of Barrow reached the place, and aided the Ulverstone fire brigade with their engine in keeping down the flames, still from time to time breaking out from amongst the smouldering rubbish.

"By this time all fear of any further destruction of Holker Hall had ceased, so that hundreds of persons who had assembled on the place from all parts of the country now, aided and assisted in returning to the Hall the furniture, pictures, and other valuables, which had, on the fire first breaking out, been carried out into the park and lawns from all parts of the Hall, and laid promiscuously in large heaps, amongst which were a few books saved from the Duke's most valuable library, and some of the costly articles of *vertu* and pictures of priceless value which stood in the south-west wing thus destroyed.

"So rapidly did the flames destroy the beautiful south-west wing of Holker Hall, that of the attics, sleeping-rooms, entrance, hall, corridors, dining-room, drawing-room noble staircase (with its stained glass window, containing the coats of arms of the Preston family from the first Preston of Holker down to the Lowthers, Cavendishes and the present Duke of Devonshire, and the families allied to them), most valuable furniture, marbles, statuary, family portraits, pictures and family relics —scarcely anything remained by eight of clock—three hours from the commencement of the fire—but bare stone walls, shattered columns, cracked and crumbling stone mullions, and smoking and smouldering wood and ashes."

There were one hundred and sixty-two portraits and pictures in the south-west wing at Holker, and of these one hundred and three were totally destroyed, whilst of the fifty-nine saved, some were only rescued at the risk of the lives of those who ventured into the smoke and flames.

Holker Hall originally belonged to the Prestons, a younger branch of one of the oldest Lancashire families. It passed with the last of their line, an heiress, to Sir William Lowther, of the Lowther family of Mask. At his death in 1756 he bequeathed it to Lord George Cavendish, second son of the third Duke of Devonshire, who left it to his brother Lord Frederick Cavendish, who was a Field-Marshal. Lord Frederick in his turn left Holker to his nephew, another Lord George Cavendish, who was ultimately made Earl of Burlington, and from him it descended to his grandson who became seventh Duke of Devonshire, when the sixth Duke died unmarried in 1858. It was during the reign of this Duke that the fire took place. Upon the death of the eighth Duke (known for so many years as the Marquis of Hartington) history repeated itself, the beautiful old house being left to its present owner, his nephew, Lord Richard Cavendish.

When the first Lord George Cavendish went to Holker in 1756, the roads were so narrow and full of ruts that his carriage could not be driven nearer the house than Grange, according to some accounts, or to Cart's Lane according to others. At one of these places—four miles from the Hall —the carriage used to be drawn over the beach and over the sands of the estuary into an old barn, where it remained until Lord George wished to go to London again. Whilst at Holker he used a "small fourwheel and partially-covered curricle, drawn by one horse, on which a postilion rode." It was a very narrow vehicle in order that it might pass through the roads and lanes. His brother, Lord Frederick (the Field-Marshal) years afterwards used a similar vehicle, painted green. It was kept at the stables at Holker, far into the nineteenth century, where Mr. Stockdale saw it when he was a child.

There was no public conveyance or any means of travelling except on horseback in the Cartmel district until 1757, when a stage-waggon was started. This was followed by a stage-coach in the year 1763, but progress by it was slow, for it rarely exceeded four or five miles an hour. The roads were intolerably bad, and Mr. Stockdale says, "Between Prescot and Liverpool, about the year 1808 and afterwards, there were deep ruts in almost every part of the pavement of the main London road, so that travelling at a trot in a chaise or carriage, there was, I well remember, scarcely any keeping with any certainty on the seat. The highway from Prescot to Ormskirk, I also remember, was even worse still."

At that time, too, "hipping" or stepping-stones were common in all the streams in the parish of Cartmel, in place of bridges. There is an amusing story told of the first Lord George Cavendish, and some stepping-stones across Carke Beck. There was a good deal of water in the Beck, and Lord George, who was then getting on in years, had got as far as the middle of the stream when he began to hesitate, wondering whether it would be wiser to go on or turn back. A woman, who lived in a cottage near by, seeing his difficulty, waded out into the water, with the idea of carrying him to the other side. Lord George did not hear her, and turning round suddenly, and at the same time perceiving her kind, if embarrassing intention, stepped at once into the water up to his knees, thus placing the stepping-stones between them.

"Good woman," he cried angrily, "I am bound to thank you for your good intentions, but see what you have done! Had you not come to my assistance I should have got over the river quite dry.

As it is, I am as wet as I well can be, and so are you." Then he took a crown piece out of his pocket and gave it to the woman, "looking, however, more vexed than pleased, and then marched in a stately manner right through the stream to the other side of the river."

LANCASTER SANDS

THREE STORIES

A YANKEE, says Mr. Frank Ormerod in "Lancashire Life and Character," boasting of the way American hens hatched chickens, was put to silence by a Lancashire man, who, after listening in silence to the stranger's story of "dozens in a sitting," quietly remarked, "Whaw, that's naught. I' Ribchester we allus fill a barrel wi' eggs, and set th' owd hen on t' bunghole!"

A NEW curate was asked to mention the name of Lucy Gay in the intercession. Thinking Lucy Gay was the name of a sick parishioner he prayed for her several Sundays in succession. Then he was told that he could stop as the mare had done what was wanted, having won the steeplechase by a length and a half.

A TERRIBLE fire in Manchester in 1789, in which a mother and her four children were all burnt to death, gave rise to this useful advice, which was sold upon a fly-sheet—

"Opeing this will be a caution to all how they rake their fires; likewise how they lie their things to dry! and how they take their candles to bed."

TYRONE'S BED

IT is a far cry from the savagery of Ireland during the sixteenth century to the beautiful dell near Rochdale known as "Tyrone's Bed," but there was a close and romantic association between them.

In the wild doings in Ireland during the reign of Queen Elizabeth, Hugh O'Neale stands out as a leading and prominent figure by reason of his generalship and his undaunted courage. His support of the English gained him the Earldom of Tyrone from the Queen. But the new Earl wearied of what he considered servitude, and wishing to liberate his country from the English dominance, he entered into a correspondence with Spain, and having obtained a supply of arms and ammunition from that country, placed himself at the head of a number of Irish chieftains, and instead of a friend, became a most dangerous enemy to England. He and his followers were pursued into bogs and woods, where they kept up a guerrilla warfare which was spun out for

some years by Tyrone's clever strategy and diplomacy. Sir John Norris, who commanded the English army in Ireland, is said to have died from the vexation of being continually outwitted by Tyrone.

At the time of his death Tyrone's half-savage forces were besieging Blackwater, and his successor, Sir Henry Bagnall, immediately advanced to the relief of that place. But he was surrounded by Tyrone's wild "kerns," and his soldiers, already much alarmed by the explosion of part of their store of gunpowder, were put to flight. Fifteen hundred men, including the general himself, were killed.

This victory, while it gave the Irish arms and ammunition, caused Tyrone to be regarded by his countrymen as their saviour and deliverer, and when, shortly afterwards, the Earl of Essex, Queen Elizabeth's favourite, took command, such was the Irish leader's reputation, that many of the English troops deserted or pretended illness rather than face him or his wild soldiers. If the Earl of Tyrone was regarded as a national hero by the Irish, he was considered a fiend incarnate by the English. Essex, finding his forces crippled by constant desertions, gladly "hearkened to a message from Tyrone who desired a conference." A plain near the two camps was chosen for the meeting, it being stipulated that neither of the generals should have any attendants. A river ran between the two men, and into this Tyrone rode until the water reached his saddle-girths, whilst Essex stood upon the opposite bank. Tyrone having " behaved with great submission to the lord-lieutenant, a cessation of arms was agreed on. Essex also received a proposal of peace, into which Tyrone had inserted unreasonable and exorbitant conditions, and there appeared afterwards some reason to suspect that the former had commenced a very unjustifiable correspondence with the enemy." From this strange interview dated the beginning of the Earl of Essex's downfall, and its tragic ending on Tower Hill.

Having arranged a truce with Essex, the Earl of Tyrone kept it until he had had time to collect the Irish chieftains and their forces together, then he promptly broke it, and " joining with O'Donnel and others, overran almost the whole kingdom." He stood forth as the champion of the Roman Catholic faith, and openly exulted in the present of a phœnix plume which Pope Clement VIII., "in order to encourage him in the prosecution of so good a cause, had consecrated and conferred upon him." Essex was recalled in disgrace, being superseded by Mountjoy, who instantly advanced against Tyrone in Ulster, which was the chief seat of the rebels. " He found the island in a desperate condition," says Camden, but being a man of capacity and vigour, " he chased the rebels from the field and obliged them again to shelter in woods and morasses; and by

these promising enterprises he gave new life to the Queen's authority throughout the island."

Although driven into the fastnesses of Ulster, Tyrone still looked for the promised help from Spain; the English, too, made every preparation to resist a Spanish invasion. The Spaniards were expected to land in the south of Ireland, and thither Mountjoy hastened, leaving Tyrone at the last extremity in Ulster. " At last the Spaniards, under Don Juan d'Aquila, arrived at Kinsale," old Camden tells us, " and Sir Richard Piercey, who commanded in the town with a small garrison of one hundred and fifty men, found himself obliged to abandon it on their appearance. These invaders amounted to four thousand, and the Irish discovered a strong propensity to join them, in order to free themselves from the English government with which they were extremely discontented. One chief ground of their complaint was the introduction of trials by jury, an institution abhorred by that people, though nothing contributes more to the support of that equity and liberty for which the English laws are so justly celebrated. The Irish also bore a great favour to the Spaniards, having entertained the opinion that they themselves were descended from that nation; and their attachment to the Catholic religion proved a new cause of affection for the invaders. D'Aquila assumed the title of general in this ' holy war ' for the preservation of the faith in Ireland; and he endeavoured to persuade the people that Elizabeth was, by several bulls of the Pope, deprived of her crown; that her subjects were absolved from their oaths of religion, and that the Spaniards were come to deliver the Irish from the dominion of the devil."

In order to prevent a general insurrection of the Irish, Mountjoy hastened with all speed to Kinsale. He acted with such promptitude that before the Spaniards could strike a blow they found themselves besieged by land and blockaded by sea. But the siege had only lasted a little while when another force of Spaniards to the number of two thousand, under Alphonso Ocampo, landed at Berehaven, and being joined by the Earl of Tyrone marched to the relief of Kinsale. Tyrone's plans, however, became known to Mountjoy through intercepted letters, and when the former, at the head of an advanced guard of the Irish and Spanish forces, approached Kinsale, to his intense surprise he found the English posted and ranged for battle. Attack was impossible with the number of men under his command. Tyrone therefore gave the orders for a retreat. He was hotly pursued by Mountjoy, who, having thrown the advanced guard into confusion, followed it up to the main body, which he attacked and also put to flight, killing twelve hundred men. Ocampo was taken prisoner, and D'Aquila was forced to surrender Kinsale. Tyrone, hotly pursued, managed to escape into Ulster, whence, with a price upon his head, he crossed over into Lancashire, finding a safe refuge in the great woods near Rochdale. Tradition, according to Roby, tells a romantic story of the Earl of Tyrone and Constance Holt, the daughter of Thomas Holt of Grizelhurst, an ancient mansion about a mile from Tyrone's Bed.

The story goes that one evening whilst walking with her old nurse along the dell, Constance had ascended to the edge of a steep cliff overhanging the river to watch the sunset. Suddenly the ground gave way beneath the young woman's feet. She was precipitated into the stream and borne rapidly away by the current. Before the horror-stricken nurse could call out, a stranger, wearing a rough grey cloak, had burst from a thicket on the opposite bank, and throwing off the cloak plunged into the river and brought the unconscious Constance to the shore. Then laying her gently down, he beckoned to the nurse and disappeared. In a few moments he returned with a cordial. When Constance regained her senses once more the stranger disappeared.

Great was the consternation at Grizelhurst when the old nurse described the rescuer of her young mistress. "It is the wild man of the woods!" cried one of the servants.

"It is about a three month agone since this wild man was first seen," said the old house-steward. "I saw him myself once, but I shook until the very flesh seemed to crawl over my bones. They say he neither eats nor drinks, but is kept alive in the body by glamour and witchcraft. He'll stay here until his time is done, and then his tormentor will fetch him to his prison-house again. He dares not abroad, if so much as the value or size of my thumb-nail of the sun's rim were left above the hill!"

Thus had superstition woven a story of magic and evil about Tyrone, who did not dare to leave his hiding-place in the dell during the daytime.

Thomas Holt, if we can believe the tradition, seems to have had knowledge of the great outlaw's presence in the neighbourhood, and the startling manner in which, according to the legend, Tyrone, on two occasions, made sudden and dramatic appearances at Grizelhurst shows him to have been acquainted with the house.

Late one evening the door of the room in which Constance had been listening to a minstrel was opened abruptly, and her rescuer stood before her.

"Madam," he said, "I am pursued. The foe are on my track. My retreat is discovered, and unless thou wilt vouchsafe to me a hiding-place I am in their power. The Earl of Tyrone—nay, I scorn the title—'tis the King of Ulster that stands before thee. I would not crouch thus for my own life, were it not for my country. Her stay, her sustenance, is in thy keeping."

The danger of the man who had saved her life removed Constance's fears, roused by Tyrone's unexpected and alarming appearance. The minstrel she knew could be relied upon, indeed it was he who suggested an old lead-mine near by as a safe hiding-place.

" Nay," replied Constance, " it must be in the house. The pursuers will not search this loyal house for treason."

Forthwith the young girl led Tyrone through passages and galleries to a secret chamber contrived in a great chimney-stack, where for some days he lay securely hidden, Constance visiting him each day and taking supplies of food.

Believing that his pursuers were completely thrown off the scent, Tyrone made preparations to return to Ireland. But even whilst he was taking farewell of his fair saviour a posse of the sheriff's men was heard approaching the house. Constance besought him to return to his hiding-place, but Tyrone pointed out that if, as in all probability, the men had a search warrant, her father's life would be in jeopardy were the great rebel found in the chimney-stack.

But where to hide him was the agonising question, since both her father and Tyrone's lives were at stake. Tyrone himself gave the answer.

" In thy chamber, lady." Then seeing her dismay and shrinking, he added, "They will not care to scrutinise for me there with much exactness ; and by the faith of my fathers, I will not wrong thee ! "

Time was pressing, and anxious only to save the man who had rescued her from drowning, Constance led the way to her bedchamber, where she hid him in a secret cupboard concealed by a curtain at the head of her bed, the door of which could only be opened by pressing a spring on one of the bed-posts. Scarcely was Tyrone hidden when a thundering knock upon the hall-door told of the arrival of the sheriff's men. They were led by a sheriff's officer, who showed Holt a warrant for the apprehension of Hugh O'Neale, Earl of Tyrone, a traitor then suspected of being harboured in the mansion of Grizlehurst. Holt, upon pain of being considered an accomplice, was commanded to deliver Tyrone to justice.

Holt, whose loyalty had never been called in question, was outraged by the charge of harbouring a rebel and a traitor, and in all good faith denied that Tyrone was in the house. The sheriff's officer then produced a search warrant, which added still further to Holt's indignation.

" I tell thee I have no plotters lurking here," he cried. " Search and welcome— but if thou findest aught in this house that smells of treason, the Queen may blot out my escutcheon ! "

The officer pointed out that he must obey his orders, which should be carried out with all courtesy and dispatch, and that the authorities had received information they could not ignore. Led by the enraged and fuming Holt the officers went all over the house, making the most careful examination into closets and cupboards, even lifting the pictures to see whether they concealed any secret panel. Holt showed the officer the concealed hiding-place in the chimney-stack with no little malicious satisfaction, but when the man insisted upon searching

Constance's bedroom his anger burst forth again.

"I have but one daughter," he cried hotly. "Dost think that treason may be stitched to her petticoat? Thinkest thou she would hide the invisible gallant in her bed-chamber. S'death that it should have come to this!"

They found Constance outside her bedroom door. "Thy chamber smacks of treason," her father said; "it must be purged from this suspicion. Hast aught plotting in the hem of thy purple, or in thy holiday muff and fardingale? Come with us, wench—the gallant Earl of Tyrone would sport himself bravely in thy bed-chamber, pretty innocent!"

To a running accompaniment of similar mockery, the officer made an examination of the room, tapping the wainscoting, and looking into the presses and closets. Satisfied that no one was concealed there, he was about to retire, when Holt in a scornful, taunting voice cried out—

"I wonder thou hast not tumbled the bed topsy-turvy; I am glad to see thou hast some grace and manners in thy vocation. Now, Sir Messenger, to requite thee for this thy courtesy and forbearance, I will show thee a secret tabernacle, which all thy prying has not been able to discover."

As he said this Holt approached the bed-post in which was the spring that opened the door of Tyrone's hiding-place. But before he could reach it, Constance, who had lost all control of herself in the danger her father was bringing upon them, interposed.

"Do not, my father—he must not look there!" she murmured, her voice quivering with fear. "For my sake, oh spare this——"

She could say no more, and half fainting she leant against the bed-post. It is not surprising that the officer's suspicions were aroused.

"Now, fair dame," he said; "it is but an ungracious office to thwart a lady of her will, but I must see what lurks in that same secret recess. Master Holt, I prithee help me to a peep behind the curtain."

Holt, who was utterly astonished at his daughter's attitude, hesitated. The officer spoke peremptorily, and Holt in obedience struck the spring upon the bed-post. Instantly the head of the bed flew aside, showing an opening behind, and as quickly the officer darted into it. There was the sound of a door being shut with great violence, and then of a struggle. Constance hid her face in her hands, unable to meet the awful suspicion in her father's eyes. Both stood listening. Then groans were heard followed by an intense stillness. Holt shuddered. Was murder being done behind the secret door?

Constance had the same thought. "Save them! oh, save them!" she implored, falling on her knees and seizing her father's hands. "Their strife is mortal!"

But with a gesture of disgust Holt shook himself free, and so violently that Constance fell to the floor. He was about to enter the hiding-place when the door flew open and the officer rushed out. He darted across the room, and the next moment they heard him running quickly down the staircase.

Holt, and with every reason, drew the worst conclusions. A terrible scene ensued between the father and daughter, in which the latter pleaded her innocence in vain. She was obliged to confess that she had secreted Tyrone in the secret cupboard; her father could only think that she had added treason to her own dishonour. Determined to wreak his vengeance upon the man he believed to be his daughter's lover, Holt forced the secret door, but instead of Tyrone, he found the sheriff's officer, gagged and pinioned, and without his uniform. The grey cap and cloak always worn by Tyrone lay upon the ground.

It then became clear that after mastering the officer in the struggle, the sounds of which had so greatly alarmed Constance and her father, Tyrone with ready resource had stripped him of his clothes, and donning them himself had passed out of the house unquestioned, and so escaped.

Tradition says that a tender interest had sprung up between Tyrone and Constance Holt, and the former, fearing that she and her father would be ruined by his concealment at Grizelhurst and his escape, made his way to London, and after making his submission obtained a free pardon from Queen Elizabeth, chiefly on account of the influence he was known to possess among his countrymen. Tradition, too, gives a tragic ending to the story—the death of Constance from a mysterious and wasting illness brought on by her father's suspicions and her love for Tyrone. But as the great Irish rebel was married at that period to his fourth wife, we may question the tender interest brought by legend into the story of his hiding in Tyrone's Bed.

QUEEN ELIZABETH
(From the painting attributed to Marcus Gheeraedts in the National Portrait Gallery)

THE POOR COTTON WEAVER

THIS ballad is still a favourite in many parts of Lancashire. It was written shortly after the Battle of Waterloo in 1815, at a time of great depression in the cotton trade. The "great mon," whom Marget declares she would go to London to see, if she had any clothes to put on, was the Duke of Wellington.

Aw'm a poor cotton-wayver, as mony a one
  knaws,
Aw've nowt t'ate i' th' heawse, un aw've
  worn eawt my cloas,
Yo'd hardly gie sixpence for o' aw've got on,
Meh clogs wi' booath baws'n, un stockin's
  aw've none;
    Yo'd think it wur hard, to be sent into
    th' ward [1]
    To clem [2] un do best 'ot yo' con.

Eawr parish church pa'son's kept tellin' us
  lung,
We'st see better toimes, if aw'd but howd
  my tung;
Aw've howden my tung, till aw con hardly
  draw breoth,
An' think i' my heart he means t' clem
  me to deoth;
    Aw knaw he lives weel wi' backbiten' the
    deil,
    But he never pick'd o'er [3] in his loife.

Neaw, owd Bill o' Dan's sent bailies one day,
Fur t'shop scoar aw'd ow'd him, 'ot aw
  couldn't pay,
But he're just too lat, fur owd Bill o' Bent
Had sent tit un' cart, un ta'en goods fur
  t' rent;
    They laft nowt but a stoo' 'ot've seaots
    fur two;
    Un' on it keawrt Marget un' me.

The bailies sceawlt reawnd os sly os a mea-
  wsè,
When they seedn o' th' things wur ta'en
  eawt o' th' heawse;
Un th' one says to th' other, "O's gone,
  theaw may see;"
Aw said, "Never fret, lads, you're welcome
  ta'e me:"
    They made no more ado, but nipt up th'
    owd stoo;
    Un' wey booath leeten swack upo' th'
    flags.

Aw geet howd o' eawr Marget, for hoo're
  strucken sick;
Hoo said, hoo'd ne'er had sick a bang sin'
  hoo're wick,
The bailies sceawrt off, wi' th' owd stoo' on
  their back,
Un they wouldn't ha'e caret if they'd brok-
  ken her neck.
    They'm so mad at owd Bent, 'cos he'd
    ta'en goods for rent,
    Till they'm ready to flee us alive.

Aw said to eawr Marget, as wey lien upo'
  th' floor,
"Wey ne'er shall be lower i' this wo'ald,
  aw'm sure,
Fur if wey mun alter, aw'm sure wey mun
  mend,
Fur aw think i' my heart wey're booath at
  fur end,
    Fur mayt weey han none, nur no looms to
    wayve on,
    Ecod; th' looms are as well lost as fun."

My piece wur cheeant off, un' aw took it him
  back;
Aw hardly durst spake, mester look'd so
  black;
He said, "Yo're o'erpaid last time 'ot yo
  coom."
Aw said, "If aw wur,' 'twur wi' wayving
  beawt loom;
    Un i't' moind 'ot aw'm in, aw'st ne'er pick
    o'er again
    Fur aw've wooven mysel' to th' fur end."

So aw coom eawt o' th' wareheawse, un' laft
  him chew that,
When aw thowt 'ot o' things, aw're so vext
  that I swat;
Fur to think I mun warck, to keep him un'
  o' th' set,
O' th' days o' my life, un then dee i' the'r
  debt;
    But aw'll give o'er this trade, un work wi'
    a spade,
    Or goo un' break stone upo' th' road.

Eawr Marget declares, if hoo'd cloas to put on,
Hoo'd go up to Lunnon to see the great mon;
Un' if things did no' awter, when theare hoo
  had been,
Hoo says hoo'd begin, un feight blood up to
  th' e'en,
    Hoo's nowt agen th' king, but hoo loikes a
    fair thing,
    Un' hoo says hoo con tell when hoo's hurt.

---

[1] World.   [2] To starve.
[3] Threw the shuttle.

THE GLEN OF THE DEADLY NIGHTSHADE

FURNESS ABBEY was the stateliest and most magnificent of all the Lancashire abbeys, as its monastery was the richest and most powerful, rivalling the great Yorkshire abbeys of Fountains and Jervaulx in splendour. But its story throughout the four hundred years of its existence was one of aggrandisement, disputes with neighbouring lords, and with other orders.

The Abbey was founded on July 7, 1127, by a body of thirteen monks who had come from the great Benedictine monastery at Savigné in Normandy and settled in the Vale of Bekansgill, or the "Glen of the Deadly Nightshade," which their abbot, with the far-seeing eye of a monk, had observed possessed all building materials near at hand. The lonely and remote situation was one, too, in which monastic authority would be supreme. Stone, timber, lead and iron were there in abundance, and under the patronage of the Earl of Boulogne, afterwards King Stephen, the work of building was begun. Stephen's grant to the first Abbot of Furness invested him with almost regal powers. It gave him possession of Furness, including Dalton, Ulverstone and Walney; the fishery rights as far afield as Lancaster; freedom from all county payments or service, and to have a market, a fair, and gallows at Dalton. The Abbots of Furness had thus the power of life and death.

Some twenty-one years after the founding of Furness Abbey a serious peril threatened its flourishing community of monks. The abbot of the parent house at Savigné in Normandy, surrendered his monastery and all his possessions to the Abbot of Clairvaulx in order that he and his monks might become Cistercians. Such a change boded ill for the monks of Furness, and their Abbot, Peter of York, hurried to Rome to appeal in person to the Pope, Eugenius III., against this surrender. After hearing his argument the Pope gave him authority that the abbey of Furness should remain Benedictine; and with the papal edict in safe keeping he set out upon the long return journey to England. His appeal to Rome and its result was not only displeasing to the mother-house, but it was regarded as a flagrant act of disobedience. As he was passing through Normandy he was seized by the monks of Savigné and forced to resign the abbacy of Furness and become a monk at Savigné itself, taking the vows of the Cistercian order. This was equivalent to imprisonment for life, and Peter of York's successor, doubtless taking warning by his fate, reconciled Furness with Savigné, and thenceforward, the great abbey in Lancashire was Cistercian.

Pope after Pope issued bulls to the abbots of Furness confirming them in their ever-increasing possessions, and taking the Abbey under their special protection. During the interdict laid by the Pope on England in the reign of John, during which no religious service might be celebrated, the monks of Furness Abbey had the right to say mass upon the private altars and use wax candles. King John Lackland had many dealings with the abbots of Furness. He deposited his gold and silver plate there, doubtless in return for a loan from the monks, and nine days after he signed Magna Charta at Runnymede, he wrote directing that it should be sent to him by "two of your monks and others of your people whom you well trust."

Within less than a century after its foundation, in addition to the land given by King Stephen over a dozen estates had been given or bequeathed to the Abbey.

The only other proprietor in Furness, besides the monks, was Michael le Fleming. With the accession of Henry III., the then Abbot saw an opportunity of realising the secret ambition of the house— that was the mastery of the whole peninsula. Henry III. was badly pressed for money at the beginning of his reign, and the wily Abbot of Furness therefore sent him four hundred marks for a confirmation of the charters given by King Stephen and his successors, adding " and to have the homage and service of Michael le Fleming for all the land which he held of the king for ten pounds yearly." The proffered ten pounds a year apparently moved the King to sign the charter, and orders were sent to Michael le Fleming ordering him to yield homage and service to the Abbot of Furness.

Michael le Fleming's position must have been particularly galling. Both he and his father had been lavish in their gifts to the Abbey in money as well as in land. They had materially helped in the creation of the fortunes of the establishment whose head was now endeavouring to crush them ; they were now to be the vassal of those whom they had raised by their bounty. Michael le Fleming must have entered a protest against the tenure of his land from the crown being changed for tenure from the Abbots of Furness, for, in the following year Henry III. issued a writ of inquiry to the Sheriff, which said, " We have been given to understand by our faithful, that we have been deceived in the concession which we made to the Abbot of Furness of the homage and service of Michael Flandrensis." A jury was forthwith summoned and their finding, sent to Henry III. by the Sheriff was, that if the transaction were confirmed it would be to the King's detriment. Nevertheless Henry signed a confirmation, and as the Abbey accounts state that the acquisition

of the homage and service of Michael le Fleming cost the Abbot fifteen hundred pounds, an enormous sum in those days, it is evident that Henry sold his vassal's rights.

The Fleming family were thus at the mercy of the Abbots of Furness. By the rights of manorial lordship they had the disposal of the hands and fortunes of the widows, and in 1277 they had exercised this power with regard to Alicia, the widow of another Michael le Fleming. If their ambition soared to the ultimate ownership of the le Fleming property they were disappointed, for this Michael dying without issue, his estate went to his sister, and ultimately to the Harringtons of Hornby Castle.

The position of the Abbots of Furness in the fourteenth and fifteenth centuries was that of sovereign princes. Henry V. exempted the Abbot from personal appearance in any Court of Justice within the realm, " with licence to prosecute and defend all causes in the courts within or without the county, by his attorneys appointed under the seal of the abbot and convent of Furness." They were Lords Paramount in Furness. But they were not always above reproach. Haughty and dictatorial, they were constantly involved in quarrels with their vassals and their tenants, and one of them, Abbot Robert, in 1423 was accused by the merchants of Calais, in a petition presented to Parliament, of smuggling wool out of the kingdom without paying the export duty upon it, in a ship of two hundred tons which sailed from the Peel of Fouldrey in June of that year to Ernemuthe in Holland.

But this splendour, this power was to have an end. All through the reign of Henry VII. there had been mutterings against the vast landed possessions of the monasteries. This king's mother, the

Countess of Richmond and Derby, dispossessed monasteries in order to found colleges. Very early in the sixteenth century there were indications at Furness of the coming change. "As we approach the great crisis in the history of the monastic institutions, we find the tenants growing bolder in their resistance of the various manorial rights, though the monks and his monks and twelve of the saide tenants, hath sett their seales." But the day for such documents was quickly passing.

Strange and alarming rumours found their way to the remote Abbey. The great monastic establishments were in constant communication, and wandering friars from all parts of the country brought

THE CHAPTER HOUSE, FURNESS ABBEY

still fitfully insist upon them. Thus in 1509 we have the Abbot and convent complaining that their tenants on Furness Fells have been making enclosures without their leave, 'more largelie than they aughte to doe.' The result was a compromise which nominally saved the lord's rights, but really left matters where they were, except that a small money-payment was agreed upon, and a formal document —'The Custome of Low Fournes' (Furness)—was drawn up, to which the Abbot gossip of the Court that filled the Chapter with foreboding. "The abbey must make friends; on 6th September, 1520, the abbot and convent grant an annuity of £10 to Thomas Howard, Duke of Norfolk." Never was the seeking of a friend at Court more obvious. The Duke of Norfolk was a powerful noble, and had the ear of the King. Ten years later a pension of five pounds a year was granted to Sir William Fitz-William, the Chancellor of the Duchy of Lancaster, for no apparent reason, save that the Duchy belonged to the King. Even Cardinal Wolsey, who, whatever his faults as a man and a statesman, was ever loyal to his Church, cast questioning eyes upon the vast powers vested in the Abbot of Furness. He suggested that the Earl of Derby should be made steward of the Abbey, a suggestion which was obsequiously accepted. But the Abbot endeavoured to strike a bargain; the monastery, he said, would appoint the Earl of Derby steward, provided he returned to them a grant, " made and sealyd wyth oure Convent seale and delyv'd unto the late Erle of Derby." And so matters went on, the Abbots trying vainly to break the impending fall, the authorities leaving no stone unturned to bring it about. In 1531 the Abbot was charged with deceiving " the King's grace of the last subsidy—the sum of £250," as well as with other withholdings, and with illegal exactions from his tenants. A horrible murder, committed by one Roland Taylor, was believed to have been instigated by Abbot Bank, and a clamour was made in London for the indictment of the Abbot. Bank strenuously denied the charges made against him, but Henry pardoned the murderer, which was taken as evidence against the Abbot; it was fortunate for him that he died in 1532.

His successor, Roger Peel, was the last Abbot of Furness. He had to send reports of his proceedings to Thomas Cromwell, and from these it appears that so relaxed had the abbatial authority become that even the monks openly rebelled against it. Abbot Peel complained to Cromwell of one of his monks, " I was constrained of very equity to put him in prison, howbeit there are divers of his friends that saith they will have him out of prison." Later, he tried to bribe Cromwell with ten gold nobles to dissuade Henry VIII. from insisting upon a demand he had made that the Abbot should give him the presentation to the living of Hawkshead. Thus matters went on for three years; increasing demands from the King and Cromwell and ineffectual shufflings and bribery on the part of the Abbot. Then came the visitation of the Royal Commissioners in 1535.

The next year the Pilgrimage of Grace brought down the storm on all the monastic establishments of Lancashire, Furness amongst them. The part taken by the monks in this rebellion and the encouragement they had given to their tenants and dependants to join in the insurrection was made an excuse for dissolving all the larger monasteries. Although the surrenders of monasteries were so numerous in the reign of Henry VIII., only one original deed has been found, and this is of Furness Abbey. Neither Abbot Peel nor any of his monks appear to have been implicated in the rising which cost Abbot Paslew of Whalley his life.

" All the members of the community, with the tenants and servants, were successively examined in private; and the result of a protracted inquiry was, that though two monks were committed to Lancaster Castle, nothing could be discovered to criminate either the Abbot or the brotherhood. The commissioners proceeded to Whalley, and a new summons compelled the Abbot of Furness to reappear before them. A second investigation was instituted, and the result was the same. In these circumstances, says the Earl (of Sussex) in a letter to Henry, which is still extant, ' devising with myself if one way would not serve, how and by what means the said monks might be rid from the said abbey, and consequently how the same might be at your gracious pleasure, I determined to assay him (the Abbot) as of myself, whether he could be contented to surrender, give a grant unto (you) your heirs and assigns the said monastery; which thing so opened to the Abbot fairly, we found him of a very facile and ready mind to follow my advice in that behalf.'"

The hangings of the abbots of other monasteries besides Paslew of Whalley, no doubt had some effect in bringing Abbot Peel to a "very facile and ready mind," and led him to sign the following deed :—

"I, Roger, Abbot of the monastery of Furness, knowing the misorder and evil life, both unto God and our Prince, of the brethren of the said monastery, in discharging of my conscience, do freely and wholly surrender, give and grant unto the King's Highness," etc.

Officers were immediately dispatched to take possession of Furness Abbey in the King's name. A few days later the Commissioners followed, taking Abbot Peel with them, and the whole community, in solemn chapter, ratified the deed of surrender signed by their head, and the glories of Furness Abbey were at an end. The monks were dispersed, a few with small pensions, and the Abbot was given the rectory of Dalton, which was then worth thirty-three pounds six shillings and eightpence a year; a mighty fall from the splendours of the Abbot's House at Furness Abbey!

Whatever the faults of the Abbots of Furness, their ambition and love of aggrandisement, they exercised a princely hospitality, and were most generous to their tenants. Their generosity was shown by some depositions taken in 1582, in the course of a dispute between the tenants of Low Furness, who had formerly been tenants of the Abbey, and the attorney-general of the Duchy of Lancaster, in which the Abbey lands had been merged.

"One deponent, aged seventy-eight, said that he had many times seen tenants resort to the monastery, on tunning days, sometimes with twenty, sometimes with thirty horses, and had delivered unto every of them firkins or barrels of beer or ale each containing ten or twelve gallons; and the same was worth tenpence or twelvepence a barrel at that time. A dozen loaves of bread were delivered to every one that had a barrel of beer or ale, which bread and beer, or ale, was delivered weekly; and every dozen loaves was worth sixpence. Another deponent had known divers children of the tenants and their servants to have come from the plough, or other work, into the said abbey, where they had dinner or supper; and the children of the said tenants came divers times to the said abbey, and were suffered to come to school and learning within the said monastery. This was confirmed by John Richardson, who said that there were both a grammar school and a song school in the monastery, to which the children of the tenants that paid provisions were free to come and resort; and that he was at the said school: and Richard Banks deposed, that the tenants, their families and children did weekly have and receive at and out of the said monastery, of charity and devotion, over and besides the relief and commodities afore rehearsed, to the value of 40s. sterling."

Furness Abbey flourished for four centuries, each century seeing an extension of its property and its revenues. All the great families of the neighbourhood gave it money or land, the Barons of Kendal, the Flemings, Broughtons, Huddlestons, Kirkbys and Penningtons; the Abbots kept a large force of armed retainers, and in addition could claim military services from many of the neighbouring landowners and squires who were their vassals. And throughout these four centuries they used the same seal. Within a circle were the Virgin, with a halo round her head and a globe in her left hand, and the Child. She stood between two shields of the House of Lancaster, showing the three lions of England, which were suspended from bundles of nightshade. At the bottom, each shield was supported by a monk in

the eighteenth century, they sent thrills of horror and wonder through their readers. Yet Mrs. Radcliffe, the author of *Udolpho*, in the midst of much we can only consider absurdity, gave a vivid picture, not only of the situation of the stately Abbey, but of the power of its abbots.

" In a close glen," she says, " shrouded by winding banks, clumped with old groves of oak and chestnut, are the

FURNESS ABBEY

his full habit, and over the head of each was a sprig of nightshade, whilst two plants of the same weed were shown in the foreground. An heraldic bird, called a wivern, which was the crest of Thomas, Earl of Lancaster, filled the lower compartment of the shield. Round it in Latin were these words : " The Common Seal of the House of the Blessed Mary of Furness."

No one reads *The Mysteries of Udolpho* in these days. They only raise a smile where, in the late years of

magnificent remains of Furness Abbey. The deep retirement of its situation, the venerable grandeur of its Gothic arches, and the luxuriant yet ancient trees that shadow this forsaken spot are circumstances of picturesque, and, if the expression may be allowed, of sentimental beauty, which fill the mind with solemn yet delightful emotions. The glen is called the Vale of Nightshade, or, more literally, from its ancient title Bekangill, the Glen of the Deadly Nightshade ; that plant being abundantly found in the neighbourhood. Its romantic gloom and sequestered privacy particularly adapted it to the austerities of monastic life; and in the most retired part of it King Stephen, earl of Mortmain and Boulogne, founded (in 1127) the noble monastery of Furness, and endowed it with princely wealth and almost princely authority, in which it was second only to Fountains Abbey in Yorkshire.

"The privileges and immunities granted to the Cistercian order in general were very abundant, and those to the Abbey of Furness were proportioned to its vast endowments. The abbot held his secular court in the neighbouring castle of Dalton, where he presided, with the power of administering not only justice but injustice; since the lives and the properties of the villein-tenants of the lordship of Furness were consigned, by a grant of King Stephen, to the disposal of the Lord Abbot. The monks also could be arraigned, for whatever crime, only by him. The military establishment likewise depended on the abbot. Every manse lord and free homager, as well as the customary tenants, took an oath of fealty to the abbot, to be true to him against all men, excepting the King. Every manse lord obeyed the summons of the abbot or his steward in raising his quota of armed men, and every tenant of a whole tenement furnished a man and horse of war for guarding the coast, for the border service, or any expedition against the common enemy of the king and kingdom. The habiliments of war were a steel coat or coat of mail, a falchion, a jack, the bow, the bill, the cross-bow and spear.

"The ruins of the Abbey and its dependencies extend over a considerable space, and cannot fail to excite admiration, not only at the riches and splendour that once prevailed here, but the exquisite taste of the founder both for the beauties of nature and the refinements of art. One of the most florid specimens of the manner after which this gorgeous pile was raised and finished, is preserved in the remains of the Chapter House. It was a Gothic saloon, divided by two rows of clustered columns, sustaining a groined ceiling; the interior was lighted by a series of small pointed windows with stone mullions, and, from the pedestals of the columns and enclosing walls that remain, appears to have been well-proportioned and sufficiently cheerful. The ceiling was once ornamented with Gothic fretwork, the only part of the Abbey thus decorated, its architecture having been characterised by an air of grand simplicity, rather than by the elegance and richness of embellishment which, at a subsequent period, distinguished the Gothic style in England."

DICK O' STANLEY GREEN

THE following song, which used to be a great favourite in the north of the county, is the Lancashire version of a song which existed in various parts of England and Ireland. In each version the subject is the same—the rustic lover offering himself to a lady, and retiring in anger because he considers her expectations extravagant. Some of the English songs had the titles of "Galloping Dreary Dun," "Richard of Taunton Dean," "Harry's Courtship," "The Clown's Courtship"; the Irish version was called "Dick of Ballyvan."

Last New-'Er's day, as I've heard say,
I mounted on my dappled grey,
My buckskin breeches I put on,
My country clogs to save me shoon,
Beside an owd hat to cover yed,
'Twas all hung round wi' a ribbon red.

Straightway I went unto the hall,
Aloud for Mistress Jane did call,
Some trusty servant let me in,
That I my courtship might begin:

"Why don't yaw ken me, Mistress Jane?
I am poor Dick, fro' Stanley Green.

"My fayther's sent me here to woo,
And I con fancy noan but yaw;
And yaw loove me, as I loove yaw,
What need ye mak so muckle to do?

"It's I con plough, and I con sow,
An' I con reap, an' I con mow,
An' I con to the market go,
An' sell my daddy's corn an' hay,
An' addle a sixpence ivvery day."

"Sixpence a day will never do;
I must wear silk and satin too;
Sixpence a day wain't find us meat."
"Ods-ducks!" says Dick, "I've a stack o' wheat,
Besides an owd house, stands close by;
It'll all be mine when my feyther die."

"Your compliments, Dick, are so polite;
They mek' the company laugh outright."

.   .   .   .   .

"If yaw have got noah more to say
I'll bid yaw good neet, an' I'll away."

THE PIMPERNEL

THE pimpernel was believed to be a charm against the power of witches and wizards, and in an old manuscript, preserved in the Chetham Library, it is said: "The herb pimpernel is good to prevent witchcraft, as Mother Bumby doth affirm," but a special verse was to be said whilst it was being gathered, as follows—

"Herb Pimpernel, I have thee found,
Growing upon Christ Jesu's ground;
The same gift the Lord Jesus gave unto thee,
When He shed His Blood upon the tree.
Arise up, Pimpernel, and go with me,
And God bless me,
And all that shall wear thee.—AMEN."

These words were to be said for fifteen days together, twice a day, "morning early fasting, and in the evening full."

TOCKHOLES CHAPEL AND NON= CONFORMITY IN LANCASHIRE

O NE of the first questions which had to be settled when Charles II. was restored to the throne in 1660 was the form of Church government. The country was practically divided into two parties, the Churchmen, who desired the return of the bishops to their sees, and the old forms of ecclesiastical authority; and the Puritans, who were bitterly opposed to any form of a State church. A large number of the clergy were what were called Independents, because of their refusal to accept any form of Episcopacy, and these petitioned Charles praying for religious liberty. They, however, were outnumbered by the moderate men, who were quite ready to accept a plan proposed by Archbishop Usher in which the bishop was only the president of a diocesan band of presbyters; they were likewise willing to accept the Book of Common Prayer, with certain amendments and the omission of the "superstitious practices." Charles, who was far ahead of the age in which he lived in broad-mindedness, not only proposed to grant the petition of the Independents, but to extend the same toleration to all Christians in the kingdom.

But here Churchmen, Puritans, Presbyterians and Independents all joined issue. They would admit no toleration of the Roman Catholics, and a Blll which embodied the King's declaration was thrown out by the House of Commons. This brought matters to a deadlock. A further conference was promised, but Parliament taking no action in the matter the Episcopal party asserted its legal rights. Bishops and clergy, who had been ejected from their sees and parishes during the Commonwealth, returned to their palaces and parsonages,

and the dissolution of the Parliament shortly afterwards put an end to any possibility of ecclesiastical compromise. It is strange to reflect that the re-establishment of the Church of England upon its old lines, was directly due to the intolerance of opposed and warring sects of the Roman Catholic form of religion.

The new Parliament approached the religious question in a very different spirit. Charles himself was all for compromise, but in the year succeeding his restoration, the tide of loyalty rose higher and higher, with the result that his second Parliament had only fifty Puritan members. "The new House of Commons," says Green, "was made up for the most part of young men, of men, that is, who had but a faint memory of the Stuart tyranny of their childhood, but who had a keen memory of living from manhood beneath the tyranny of the Commonwealth. Their very bearing was that of wild revolt against the Puritan past." Imbued with this spirit, the new Parliament went far beyond the wishes of Charles and his ministers. "A common suffering," Green continues, "had thrown the squires and the Episcopalian clergy together, and for the first time since the Reformation the English gentry were ardent not for the King only, but for the Church and King." And this spirit was shown at the very opening of the first Session of the 1661 Parliament. Every member was ordered to receive the Communion, and the League and Covenant which had been entered into by the English Parliament and Scotland in 1643 for the abolition of episcopacy, and the articles of which were the foundation of the Puritan principles, was ordered to be burnt by the common hangman in Westminster

Hall. This was turning the tables with a vengeance. But even greater changes followed in quick succession. The Bill passed by the Commonwealth excluding Bishops from the House of Lords, was repealed, and, led by the Earl of Clarendon, the Lord Chancellor, Parliament placed the Church practically on the same level as the State. Clarendon maintained that the Parliament and the Church were essential parts of the system of English government in the exercise of the powers of the Crown, " and under his guidance Parliament turned to the carrying-out of the principle of uniformity in Church as well as in State on which the minister was resolved."

The greatest difficulty was the Presbyterians, who formed the majority on most of the corporations of boroughs which practically returned the borough members. In order therefore to force them into line, or to drive them from their office in the corporations, an Act was passed by Parliament called the Corporation Act, which insisted upon the reception of the Communion according to the rites of the Anglican Church, a renunciation of the League and Covenant, and a declaration that it was unlawful on any grounds to take up arms against the King, before any man could undertake municipal office. Each of these points was a matter of conscience with the Presbyterians, and consequently they were driven from the corporations. A measure even more drastic and comprehensive was directed against the Puritans by the Act of Uniformity. This Act enforced the use of the Prayer-Book and the Prayer-Book only, in all public worship, and further, the unfeigned consent and assent to all that it contained was demanded from every clergyman; like the corporations, they too had to give a pledge they would seek to make no changes in Church or State.

The Bill was opposed hotly in the House of Lords; even Clarendon sought to soften some of its more sweeping measures, but the House of Commons would listen to no compromise and Charles was compelled to give his reluctant assent.

St. Bartholemew's Day, 1662, was the last day allowed for compliance with the Act of Uniformity, and on that day nearly two thousand vicars and rectors, comprising nearly a fifth of the English clergy, were driven from their parishes, and on that day too a new word came into our language, the word " Nonconformist," which to us means no more than one who is not a member of the Church of England. In 1662 the word had a tragic significance—it meant poverty, obloquy, and persecution for conscience' sake.

The rectors and vicars were not alone in their refusal to accept the Act of Uniformity, in many places they were followed by their parishioners. This was the case at Tockholes and several other places in the Blackburn Hundred, and at Tockholes itself there was one of the earliest congregations of Nonconformists. It probably had no regular ministry, but it was one of the first places to have a meeting-house.

Finding that the Act of Uniformity had not brought about its desired effect, the Parliament, with the hope of rendering the position of all those who dissented from the State Church an intolerable one, passed an Act for suppressing Conventicles, which came into force 1st July, 1664. The Act was ruthless. Any person present at a meeting for religious exercises, " in other manner than is allowed by the Liturgy of the Church of England, where shall be five or more persons than the household, shall suffer three months' imprisonment, or be fined five pounds, for the first offence, six months, or ten pounds fine, for a second offence, and seven years' banishment to the American plantations, or one hundred pounds fine, for a third offence." Those who lent their houses or barns for use as conventicles suffered the same penalties. This was followed the next year by the Five Mile Act, which provided that "Nonconformist ministers shall not, after

constitutional monarch he was obliged to acquiesce in the will of the Parliament. Whatever his faults, and they were many, Charles was tolerant. In 1670 the Act for Suppressing Conventicles was amended, but only in the direction of greater severity. Two years later Charles expressed his personal feelings upon the persecution of so many of his subjects, by exercising his prerogative as supreme head

TOCKHOLES CHAPEL

the 5th of March 1665, unless in passing the road, come or be within five miles of any city, town-corporate, or borough ; or within five miles of any parish, town or place wherein they have been parson, vicar, or lecturer—upon forfeiture for every such offence, of the sum of forty pounds, one-third to the King, one-third to the poor, and one-third to him that shall sue for it."

This relentless persecution had been entirely against Charles II.'s wishes. As a

of the Church. He published a Declaration of Indulgence, in which he "declared his will and pleasure to be, that the execution of all and all manner of penal laws in matters ecclesiastical, against whatsoever sort of Nonconformist, or recusants, be immediately suspended." Following upon the Declaration of Indulgence licences were issued by the Government to applicants for Nonconformist meeting-houses and places for preaching.

A register of these licences has been kept at the Public Record Office in London. The strength of Nonconformity in the parish of Blackburn is shown by the list of licences given below, and from the list Tockholes appears to have been the first place to have a special meeting-house, probably some adapted building.

Licenses to Preach and for meeting-houses.[1]

License to John Harvie to be a Pr. Teacher in a meeting-house in Tockley (Tockholes) erected for that purpose, in the Parish of Blackburn, Lancaster, 1 May '72.

The meeting-house in Tockley (Tockholes) in the parish of Blackburn. Pr. Meeting. 8 May, '72.

The house of John Horwood (or Harwood) in the Hundred of Blackburn, Lancaster, licensed for a Congr. meeting-place, 2 May, '72.

Thomas Jollie to be a Congr. Teacher in his house at Wymondhouses in the Hundred of Blackburn, Lancaster, 2 May.

The house of Thomas Jollie at the Wymondhouses in the Hundred of Blackburn, in Lancashire. Congr. Meeting-place. 2 May, '72.

The house of Robert Whitaker in the Hundred of Blackburn, Lancaster. Congr. place. 2 May, '72.

The house of Richard Cottham in the Hundred of Blackburn, Lancaster. Congr. place. 2 May, '72.

The house of Richard Sagar in the Hund. of Blackburn, Lanc. Congr. place, 2 May, '72.

(Sept. 20). A new built house on Langoe Green in Blackburn, Lancaster.

(Dec. 9). An erected meeting-house in Blackburn, in Lancaster. Pr.

Dec. 25, '72. A meeting-place erected

by the people adjoining to Langoe Greene in ye P'ish of Blackborne in Lancash. Congr.

License to Charles Sagar. Pr. Teacher of Blackborne, Lancashire, Feb. 3.

The house of Thomas Anderton, at Samsbury. Pr. meeting-place.

The house of William and Henry Berry in Upper Darwin to be a Pr. meeting-place.

The barn of John Pickop in Dedwinclough (in Newchurch-in-Rossendale) to be an Indep. meeting-place.

The house of John Durden in Yatebanke to be a Pr. meeting-place.

The house of John Harris in Withnell to be a Pr. meeting-place.

But the Nonconformists and Roman Catholics enjoyed the free exercise of their religion for only a year. The Parliament considered Charles's Declaration of Indulgence as a subversion of its own authority, and resisted to the utmost the theory it implied that a statute law passed by Parliament could be relaxed or in any way interfered with by the mere fiat of the King. So fierce was the opposition to his tolerance, that Charles was absolutely compelled to revoke his Declaration of Indulgence, and to suspend the licences which had been granted for places of worship. Measures of even greater severity were taken, and between 1675 and 1679 many of the Nonconformist ministers and members of their congregation in the Blackburn region were persecuted. The chief sufferers were two of the preachers who appear on the list of licences, Thomas Jollie of Wymondhouses, near Clitheroe, and Charles Sagar, who had been schoolmaster of Blackburn Grammar School. Justice Nowell of Read Hall, and Ratcliffe of Mearley were the principal accusers of these men.

The crisis between the civil authority

---

[1] Pr. stands for Presbyterian; Congr. for Congregational; and Indep. for Independent in the licences.

and the passive resisters amongst the Nonconformists came after twelve years of unceasing struggle on both sides. In 1684, the year before Charles's death, the notorious Judge Jeffreys took the Northern Circuit, and several Nonconformist preachers being brought before him at Preston he inflicted the heaviest sentences upon them permitted by the law, giving his judgment with indescribable ferocity and violence. This, and the two following years were the darkest times of Nonconformity. Charles II. died in 1685, and was succeeded by his brother James II., a Roman Catholic, yet the persecution of the Dissenters still continued. James was naturally anxious to relieve his co-religionists from the ban under which they suffered no less severely than the Nonconformists, but he could not relieve one religion, whose followers would not accept the Act of Uniformity, without relieving others in a similar situation. In freeing Roman Catholics he was therefore compelled, sorely against his will, to free the Nonconformists, and his Declaration of Liberty of Conscience to Nonconformists and Recusants was the result.

CHARLES II
[*After the engraving by Vanderbanc*]

Thus, after fourteen years, the persecution of the Nonconformists came to an end, a persecution bred wholly of intolerance, and carried out in spite of the publicly declared wishes and opinions of King Charles II.

The congregation at Tockholes, whose first licensed minister, as we have seen was John Harvey appears to have been founded on a Presbyterian-Congregational basis. Despite the persecution all round them they pursued their way, unflinching and undismayed, for in 1674 we hear of a Mrs. Yates of Blackburn being dismissed from Mr. Thomas Jollie's church at Wymondhouses to "Mr. Harvey and his society." After several years John Harvey left Tockholes for Chester, and was succeeded by John Waddington of Whalley, who had been an elder in Mr. Jollie's church. Waddington's desire to become a preacher, and to give a sermon on trial is recorded in 1677, during the height of the persecution, but he was only ordained a minister in 1682. Jollie made this entry in the Church Book of Wymondhouses in 1681, " Mr. Waddington not ordained when expected, from ministers and people failing, but done afterwards honourably."

"The meeting-house in Tockley," mentioned in the licence of 1672, was in all probability some barn, or already existing building, adapted for the purposes of Nonconformist worship. Whether it fell into disrepair, or was too small to accommodate an increasing congregation, can only be conjectured, but after the Revo-

of those who attended St. Michael's Chapel attended the Presbyterian Meeting on the following Sunday when no service was given at the Chapel-of-Ease. Thus, in 1714, we read in the records of St. Michael's Chapel, "Most of the inhabitants frequent a Presbyterian Meeting-house there is within the chapelry those Sundays there is no service in their own chapel."

OLD LICENSED PREACHING PLACE AT GREENACRE

lution of 1688, when James II. fled from the kingdom, the Nonconformists of Tockholes used the Chapel-of-Ease belonging to Blackburn parish church on alternate Sundays, the Church of England service being held there only once a fortnight. It was only when this unusual proceeding was ended by the Bishop that the Presbyterians erected the chapel shown in our illustration. This was in 1710. Four years later there was very little distinction at Tockholes between conformity and nonconformity, for many

The Hoghtons of Hoghton Tower at that time were Nonconformists, an unusual circumstance amongst the landed gentry, but Sir Richard Hoghton, son of Sir Gilbert Hoghton, who unsuccessfully besieged Blackburn during the Great Rebellion, adhered to the Presbyterian party after the Restoration of Charles II. He was a great protector and supporter of Nonconformist ministers ejected from their livings under the Act of Uniformity. His fifth son, Charles, who succeeded him, died in the year Tockholes Presbyterian

Church was built, and it was his widow Mary, Lady Hoghton, who gave it support. The panels to the doors to the two Hoghton pews were decorated with shields bearing her monogram of M.H., the letters being interlaced. The chapel was surrounded by a graveyard which was extended several times, and many of the families worshipping there had vaults beneath their pews.

The old pew-rents read curiously. They were collected at Martinmas and in March. At Martinmas 1716, Mary, Lady Hoghton, paid seven shillings for one pew and seven-and-sixpence for the other, for the half year. In the following year the rent was increased to eight shillings for the first, and twelve-and-sixpence for the second. Five yeoman each paid one pound a year for their pews; the half-year's pew rents of the chapel in 1717 brought nine pounds fourteen shillings to the minister, Mr. Peter Valentine; by no means a large salary, but he had a house, and from time to time sums of money were given to an endowment for the minister's stipend.

"KNIGHTS OF THE ROYAL OAK"

WHEN Charles II. was restored to the throne in 1660, he decided to found a new order of knighthood, as a reward to those who had been specially distinguished by their loyalty to his cause during his exile, and whose incomes were not less than one thousand pounds a year. The new order was to be called "The Knights of the Royal Oak," in commemoration of Charles's escape from Cromwell's troops by hiding in an oak-tree at Boscobel after the Battle of Worcester. The new knights were to have a special badge—a silver medal with a device of the King in the oak-tree stamped upon it, hanging to a ribbon placed round their necks. Six hundred and eighty-seven gentlemen had been chosen for the new honour when the idea was abandoned—" from the apprehension that such an order of knighthood might create heats and animosities, and open those wounds afresh which it was thought prudent should be healed." So marked a distinction would doubtless have had this effect.

The following gentlemen in Lancashire whose incomes are given after their names, were amongst those who missed the knighthood :—

Thomas Holt, Esqre.	£1000
Thomas Greenhalgh, Esqre	£1000
Colonel — Kirby	£1000
Robert Holte, Esqre.	£1000
Edmund Assheton, Esqre	£1000
Christopher Banester, Esqre	£1000
Francis Anderton, Esqre	£1000
Colonel James Anderton	£1500
Roger Nowell, Esqre.	£1000
Henry Norris, Esqre.	£1200
Thomas Preston, Esqre.	£2000
— Faringdon of Worden, Esqre .	£1000
— Fleetwood of Penwortham, Esq.	£1000
John Girlington, Esqre.	£1000
Willian Stanley, Esqre.	£1000
Edward Stanley, Esqre.	£1000
Thomas Stanely, Esqre.	£1000
Richard Boteler, Esqre.	£1000
John Ingleton, Esqre., sen.	£1000
—Walmesley of Dunkenhalgh, Esqre .	£2000

A FAMOUS LANCASHIRE ACTOR

IN the seventeenth century it was an unheard-of thing for a man of family to go upon the stage, actors and actresses still being considered as vagabonds. The public support of the theatre, by both Charles II. and his brother the Duke of York (afterwards James II.) had done much to remove the prejudice against the stage created by the Puritans, but as a profession it was not considered a fitting one for a gentleman to follow. Barton Booth broke through this prejudice, and achieved not only fame in his own time, but a lasting memorial to his powers in the monument erected to him in the Poets' Corner of Westminster Abbey.

Barton Booth was descended from an ancient family, the Booths of Barton, near Eccles, which was closely related to the old Earls of Warrington, and in the reign of Henry VI. had given two Archbishops to the See of York. He was the third and youngest son of "John Booth, Esq., of Barton," and was born in Lancashire in 1681. He was only three years old when his father was forced to remove to London, being in embarrassed circumstances, and at the age of nine he was sent to Westminster School, whose headmaster was the famous Dr. Busby, whose name has come down in history as an incarnation both of severity and of the "flogging master."

BARTON BOOTH

Barton himself used to say when speaking of the place of his education, that he had been "under the correction of Dr. Busby."

But he would appear to have been a favourite with the terrifying pedagogue, probably because he was a good scholar. At school his histrionic abilities were speedily noticed, and the little Lancashire boy, in the routine of lesson-saying, "repeated passages from the classics with such action and feeling that he was taken notice of by the whole school." This was said by Knipe, who succeeded Dr. Busby as headmaster. At the annual performance of a Latin play—a custom still kept up at Westminster—Booth made such an impression by his performance that Busby openly praised him, speaking in the highest terms of his talent as an actor. This praise from his master is supposed to have turned the boy's mind in the direction of the stage, for Busby dying shortly afterwards, Booth's father, angry at his son's growing inclination, used to say that "the old man had poisoned him with his last breath."

Barton Booth was intended by his father for the Church, and at seventeen he was told to be ready to go to the University. According to one story, rather than give up his ambition he ran away with a company of strolling players; and to another, that he went to Trinity

College, Cambridge, but shortly afterwards decamped from there with some players, to the great rage and mortification of his family. Booth had a graceful presence, a fine musical voice, and a natural aptitude for recitation, and very soon after his flight he was playing the most important parts in tragedy in Dublin, a remarkable circumstance for a boy of seventeen, and which points to the possession of unusual gifts. During three seasons he remained in Dublin, each year adding to his reputation, and then was advised to try his fortune in London. This was in 1701. First of all he effected a reconciliation with his family, fear of whose anger, it was said, had prevented Betterton giving Booth an engagement in his London theatre before he ran away. But in Dublin the young man had made several influential friends, and upon the introduction of one of them, Lord Fitzhardinge, a Lord of the Bedchamber to Prince George of Denmark, the husband of Queen Anne, Betterton at once gave him an engagement.

Booth made his first appearance in London in the first year of the reign of Queen Anne. His success was immediate, and very shortly afterwards a former school-fellow of his at Westminster, Nicholas Rowe, having written a play called *The Ambitious Stepmother*, the leading part was given to him. Again he made a marked success. Betterton, who for many years had been the leading actor upon the English stage, was growing old, and " it was not long before public opinion decided that his successor would be this handsome and stately young Lancashire gentleman."

Betterton, who had been taught by Davenant how Hamlet was played in Shakespeare's own time, died in 1710, and Booth was at once given his place in public estimation. Booth, indeed, had only one rival, Wilks, who whilst he was more versatile and a better performer in comedy, could not approach him in tragedy.

In the year following Betterton's death, Wilks, Colley Cibber, and Doggett, the comedian (whose coat and badge are still rowed for by the London watermen on the first of every August), became patentees and managers of Drury Lane Theatre. Booth was engaged as a member of their company, and before very long he, too, had a desire to be a patentee. The licence of Drury Lane was held direct from the Crown, and the Crown nominated the patentees. Booth, therefore, did not so much need capital as Court influence. But Cibber, Doggett, and Wilks had no wish that Booth should be a patentee, chiefly because they wished to keep all the profits for themselves, and also because all three had a personal animus against the handsome and brilliant actor. A curious contest ensued. Booth, because of his family traditions, was a Tory, and at that time the Tories were in office, the famous Lord Bolingbroke being Secretary of State. And on more than one occasion Lord Bolingbroke had befriended the actor. The Court was then at Windsor, where Lord Bolingbroke and other highly placed friends of Booth's were in constant attendance upon Queen Anne. The patentees did not dare to dismiss Booth ; he was too great an attraction to the theatre, and dismissal might mean his entering into rival management. They, therefore, determined to keep him away from Windsor and his influential friends by giving him part after part. Booth quietly accepted the situation, which enabled him to gain even a firmer hold upon the public, but at the same time he was outwitting the three patentees. Chetwood, a prompter who had the story of this curious interweaving of politics and the stage from Booth himself, tells us, "To prevent his soliciting his patrons at Court, then at Windsor, they (the patentees) gave out plays every night, where Mr. Booth had a principal part. Notwithstanding this step, he had a chariot and six of a nobleman's horses waiting for him at the end of a play, that whipt him the twenty miles in three hours, and brought him back to the business of the theatre the next night. He told me not one nobleman in the kingdom had so many sets of horses at command as he had at that time, having no less than eight, the first set carrying him to Hounslow from London, ten miles; and the next set ready waiting with another chariot to carry him to Windsor."

Politics, too, played no inconsiderable part in completing Booth's reputation and placing him in the forefront of the actors of his time. The feeling in 1712, between the Tories, who were in office, and the Whigs was bitter in the extreme. Addison, of *Spectator* fame, was a Whig, and having written a "Liberal" tragedy called *Cato* he thought it might be desirable "to animate the public with the sentiments of Cato," in other words, the production of the tragedy was to be a hit at the Tories. Addison was then a great man of letters; his play was, therefore, at once accepted by the three patentees of Drury Lane, and the chief part—Cato—assigned to Barton Booth, a fact which emphasizes the position he had achieved. The patentees considered they had a grudge against him, and he was their servant, but they did not even consider the possibility of another actor playing the part.

The first night roused a fever of excitement. The Whigs and their supporters spoke openly of tyranny being exposed, and looked forward to the performance as an opportunity of demonstrating against the Government. On the eventful evening—14th April, 1712—both sides mustered in strong force in the theatre, Lord Bolingbroke occupying the stage-box. But to the rage and discomfiture of the Whigs, the Tories applauded the "Liberal" sentiments of the play as vigorously as they themselves. "The numerous and violent claps of the Whig party," wrote Pope, who had written the prologue, to Sir William Turnbull, "on the one side of the theatre was echoed back by the Tories on the other, while the author sweated behind the scenes to find their applause proceeding more from the heart than the head."

The play was a success, and Addison, the Whig dramatist, had a triumph; but, with consummate skill and readiness, Lord Bolingbroke converted it into a triumph for the Tories. Whilst the Whigs had been in office they had attempted to secure the nomination of their military favourite, the great Duke of Marlborough, as Captain-General. In the play, Cato denounces military dictatorship. After one of the acts, Lord Bolingbroke sent for Booth and presented him with fifty guineas, "for defending the cause of liberty so well against a perpetual dictator," thus completely turning the tables on the Whigs, who had sought to place the Duke of Marlborough in that position.

Booth touched the high-water mark of his talents in *Cato* and the part ever after remained the best in his repertory; it likewise gained for him the position of one of the patentees of Drury Lane, which he occupied with Cibber and Wilks nearly to the end of his life.

The remainder of Booth's life was passed in ease and tranquillity. He was twice married; first to the daughter of a Norfolk baronet, and secondly to Hester

Santlow, a beautiful dancer who became an actress. She made him a most tender and affectionate wife. Seeing the effect of drunkenness upon other actors, Booth, early in his career, had forsworn the bottle, but he was inclined to be a *gourmand*, and Chetwood, the prompter, says, "I have known Mrs. Booth, out of extreme tenderness to him, order the table to be removed, for fear of overcharging his stomach."

He died in 1733, a man of wealth, leaving much property both in London and the country, and was buried at Cowley, in Middlesex, where he had a house. Behind Westminster Abbey there are two quaint little streets—Barton Street and Cowley Street. These were built by Booth, who gave them their names—the first after his native place of Barton, in Lancashire; the second after his country home.

Booth was essentially a "scholar and a gentleman." When the audience was small he was apt to act carelessly, and on one occasion, having suddenly dropped his languor and become fiery and energetic, when asked the reason, he said, "I saw an Oxford man in the pit, for whose judgment I had more respect than for that of the rest of the audience." Booth was "no great speaker in company, but when he did, it was in a grave, lofty way, not at all unlike his pronunciation on the stage," and Cibber's son said of him:

"He had the deportment of a nobleman, and so well became a star and garter he seemed born to it."

OWD PINDER

By Edwin Waugh

OWD Pinder were a rackless foo',
　An' spent his days i' spreein';
　At th' end ov every drinkin'-do,
He'm sure to crack o' deein';
"Go sell my rags, an' sell my shoon,
　Aw's never live to trail 'em;
My ballis-pipes are eawt o' tune,
　An' th' wynt begins to fail 'em.

"Eawr Matty's very fresh an' young;—
　'Twould any mon bewilder;—
Hoo'll wed again afore it's lung,
　For th' lass is fond o' childer;
My bit o' brass 'll fly—yo'm see—
　When th' coffin-lid has screen'd me—
It gwos again my pluck to dee,
　An' lev her wick beheend me.

"Come, Matty, come, an' cool my yed;
　Aw'm finish'd, to my thinkin'."
Hoo happed him nicely up, an' said,
　"Thea'st brought it on wi' drinkin'."
"Nay, nay," said he, "my fuddle's done,
　We're partin' t'one fro t'other;
So promise me that when aw'm gwon,
　Thea'll never wed another!"

"Th' owd tale," said hoo, an' laft her stoo';
　"It's raly past believin',
Thee think o' th' world thea'st goin' to,
　An' lev this world to th' livin';
Whet use to me can deeod folk be?
　Thea'st kilt thisel' wi' spreein';
An' iv that 's o' thae wants wi' me
　Get forrud wi' th' deein'!"

THE DESTRUCTION OF AN ESTATE

THE tract of salt marshy land stretching from Humphrey Head to Cowpren Point originally formed part of the commons and waste grounds belonging to the parish of Cartmel, and in 1798 it was bought by Mr. James Stockdale of Carke Hall and Mr. Robinson of Ulverstone. For nine years afterwards the marsh remained as a pasture, and then the owners agreed to build an embankment to prevent the sea from overflowing the land. A large number of men were employed and in 1808 an embankment three miles in length, and ten to fifteen feet in height, was completed. It was made of sea-sand dug out of two large trenches on either side, and its surface was entirely covered with marsh sods, each three and a half inches in thickness. The embankment enclosed six hundred acres of land and its makers were rewarded with the Ceres gold medal of the Society of Arts for their achievement.

In order to test the efficacy of the embankment some little time was allowed to pass; then when it was shown that it kept back the sea, the two proprietors divided the reclaimed land between them, Mr. Stockdale taking all the part to the west of the Cockle Road which he called the "West Plain," and Mr. Towers of Duddon Hall (who had succeeded Mr. Robinson) taking the part to the east of the Cockle Road. This he called the "East Plain."

"In about two years," says Mr. Stockdale's son, "the entire tract of land was divided into convenient enclosures, cop and quickthorn fences constructed, plantations made, and large farm buildings erected, and then my father let his part (West Plain) to farm, at the rent of seven hundred and fifty pounds per annum; Mr. Towers preferring to keep his part in his own hands. The land continued very

fertile for many years; the straw of the oat and other grain crops sometimes attaining the height of six feet and more; the quality of the grain (oats, wheat and barley), being far superior to any that ever appeared in the market; and in this prosperous condition the estate was when it was almost entirely destroyed in the autumn of the year 1828."

The first warning came in 1827. It has been generally supposed that the embankment was destroyed by the inrush of the sea, but the actual cause of destruction was the River Leven. In 1819 the embankment certainly did suffer severely from repeatedly high and stormy tides, but on the suggestion of the younger Mr. Stockdale it was covered with a species of concrete which rendered it impervious to water. The River Leven undermined the sandbanks upon which the embankment rested. Mr. Stockdale mentions this curious fact—"It will have been observed," he says, "by those who have lived long in the neighbourhood of estuaries, that the freshwater rivers passing through them are continually changing their courses; sometimes, however, the rivers leave the high sand-banks on one side of the estuary *undisturbed* for a great length of time, and then these banks, from the continual deposit of sand and mud during the time they are covered by the sea (twice each day), rise so high as ultimately to be out of the reach of any but high tides; a sward then begins to form, and after a while the whole sand-bank becomes a marsh. Sooner or later, however, the freshwater rivers are sure to resume their old courses and return to the places they have occupied before." This is precisely what happened to the Riven Leven.

Beyond the memory of man its course had been on the Bardsea side of the Ulverstone estuary, but in 1827 it was observed to be gradually flowing through the sand-banks in the direction of the embankment at the Winder Low Marsh, back to the course it was known to have occupied a hundred years before. By the vast segment of a circle nearly three miles in length, and cutting a bank for itself in the soft sand some twenty feet in height. Thus took place, Mr. Stockdale tells us, the final act of this tragedy of Nature :—

ULVERSTONE SANDS

twenty-ninth of July 1828, it had advanced so far that it was only four hundred and ten yards away from the most westerly point of the embankment. Steadily the river drew nearer, approaching the embankment in the shape of a

"The water-edge or margin of the river, particularly at the flow of the tide, sawed away and undermined the soft sand-banks, and caused them to fall with a tremendous plunge here and there all along the edge of this segment of a circle of two and a half to three miles, in immense masses, each of not less than twenty yards in length, eight or ten yards in width, and twenty feet in height, into the river beneath, with a continuous roar like the firing of heavy guns from a fort, or the noise of loud thunder. On the 26th October, the first or lowest row of sods of the embankment fell into the river, so that between the 29th of July and the 26th of October the river had passed through a sand-bank four hundred and ten yards in width, two and a half to three miles in length, and twenty feet in height, and taken the whole mass in a suspended state in the water, in other parts of the estuary. Soon after this the foundation of the embankment was precipitated into the river, and when it (the river) reached the plantation on the inside, the trees (thirty feet or more in height) fell topsy-turvy into the stream, the tops sticking in the sand or clay under the water, showing in miniature what takes place in the Mississippi and other large rivers, the trees there forming the ' snags ' so dangerous to navigation. From this time the sea flowed again over the West Plain estate, and has continued to do so ever since. The river having met with gravel, stones and clay retired on the 8th of December, 1828; but the plantation is destroyed, the fences are all washed away, the lower large farm buildings are knocked down, and, as the break of the precipice proceeded forward long after the river had retired, no less than about two hundred acres of the arable land which were within the embankment, have " been undermined and washed away by the waves and the action of the sea. As no one," Mr. Stockdale continues, " looking at the present broken-down fences and buildings, and the wide sandy waste called the 'Low Marsh' could possibly imagine that so valuable an

estate had once existed there, I may be excused for saying that it certainly was, without any exception, much the finest farm in this country. My late father had spared neither pains nor expense in laying it out into large and convenient fields (thirty-eight in number) divided by well formed quickthorn hedges, erecting two sets of excellent farm buildings, with all the conveniences known at that day, as well as belting; the estate inside the embankment with a plantation a mile and a half in length, to keep off the prevailing west winds; indeed at the time of its destruction in 1828, it might have been, and was, considered a model farm—a model farm in those days, at any rate."

Happily for the owner of the East Plain that portion of the reclaimed land was at a considerable distance from the river, and Mr. Towers further protected it by building a cross embankment near the Cockle Road.

The destruction of the West Plain estate is probably not the first time that valuable land had been so engulfed in the Ulverstone estuary, and some of it not far from the Cartmel shore. West, in his *Antiquities of Furness*, says : " These encroachments have been progressive, for great part of the parish of Aldingham has been swept away within these few centuries. There is a tradition in Furness that the church of Aldingham stood in the centre of the parish ; at present it is within reach of the tide. It is within the memory of man that some part of the ruins of a village called Low Scales was visible on the sea-sands, and the villages of Cringleton and Rope, which the first Sir Michael le Fleming exchanged with the monks (of Furness Abbey) for Bardsey, are only known in record." During Mr. Stockdale's lifetime the land all round Limbrick Point was washed away to a width of from ten to fifteen yards, and the same erosion was going on at Quarryflat Point until the building of the railway embankment kept back the sea.

A proof that large portions of land have been washed away in previous times by the combined action of the rivers and the sea, is shown by the large "scars" which lie in the estuary hundreds of yards from what is now the river bank. At the time the River Leven destroyed the West Plain estate in 1828 it laid bare a very large scar, called the "Cowp Scar" close by, which was the remains doubtless of some high land washed away in former days and where a village—either Hert, Forde Bodle or Lower Lies—once stood. There are other "scars" in the estuary nearer the Furness shore, in all probability the sites of villages of which now only the names are known to antiquarians.

THE FOUNDER OF THE "GRINDLETONIANS

A CURIOUS sect called the "Breirlists" or "Grindletonians" was founded by Roger Brereley or Breirley, a clergyman, who was one of the Brereleys of Marland, near Castleton. For some years he was at Grindelton in Yorkshire, whence the sect took his name. But later he was perpetual curate of Burnley Church; he died at that place in 1637. During his time in Yorkshire, Brereley suffered much persecution, and at one time was a prisoner at York pending the hearing of fifty charges against him for false teaching. Not a single charge could be proved, and he was set at liberty. Brereley was a poet as well as a preacher, and his sermons and poems were published in 1677, under the following lengthy title:—"A Bundle of Soul-convincing, Directing and Comforting Truths; clearly deduced from diverse Texts of Holy Scripture, and practically improven both for Conviction and Consolation: being a brief summary of several sermons preached at large by that faithful and pious Servant of Jesus Christ, Mr. Rodger Breirly, Minister of the Gospel at Grindleton in Craven." In the preface of the book we are told that Brereley's "life and conversation were comely in the eyes of the sons and daughters of Sion, and beautiful in the streets of that city, so that none could lay shame thereon." This gentleman of the "comely" life and conversation had some merit as a poet, as is shown by the ingenuity of the lines which conclude a poem called "Self Civil War":—

"I can not with my self, as I conceive
  Wretch that I am, my self, my self deceive.
Unto my self, I do my self betray,
And from my self, banish my self away,
My self agrees not with my self a jot,
Knows not my self, I have my self forgot,
Against my self I have mov'd wars
    unjust,
I hurt my self and I my self distrust,
My self I follow, and my self I fly,
Besides my self and in my self am I.
My self am not my self—another some
Unlike my self and like my self I am,
Self's son self furious and then wayward
    else
I cannot live with—nor without my self."

A SEVENTEENTH CENTURY BISHOP ON DRUNKENNESS

THE district round about Rochdale was famous for its good ale, and James Holt of Castleton seems to have been so appreciative of the local product that he drew down upon himself the censure of no less a personage than Nicholas Stratford, Bishop of Chester. The Holts had originally settled at Stubley Hall in the reign of Henry VIII., and this curious entry concerning one of them was made by Norroy King at Arms during a visitation he made in Lancashire in the thirtieth year of that reign, for the purpose of recording coats-of-arms—

" Robarde Holte of Stubley, hase mar. an ould woman, by whom he has none issewe, and therefore he wolde not have her name entryed." This ungallant entry notwithstanding, the " ould woman " had a daughter whose grandson in due time succeeded to Stubley. But finding the old house too bleak and exposed, in the reign of Charles I. he removed to another house at Castleton which was in a warmer and more fertile situation. It was his son, James Holt, who received the episcopalian warning in the reign of William III. He had apparently written to the Bishop of Chester about a curate, and this is the answer he received, dated November 1699—

" Sir,—Your request on behalf of Mr. Halliwell was easily granted ; for I am myself inclined to give the best encouragement I can to the poor curates, as long as they continue diligent in the discharge of their duties. But I have now, Sir, a request to make to you, which I heartily pray you may as readily grant me ; and that is, you will for the future abandon the sottish vice of drunkenness, which (if common fame be not a great liar) you are much addicted to. I beseech you, Sir, frequently and seriously to consider the many dismal fruits and consequences of this sin, even in this world—how destructive it is to all your most valuable concerns and interests ; how it blasts your reputation, destroys your health, and will (if continued) bring you to a speedy and untimely death : and, which is infinitely more dreadful, will exclude you from the kingdom of heaven, and expose you to that everlasting fire where you will not be able to obtain so much as one drop of water to cool your tongue. . . I have not leisure to proceed in this argument nor is it needful that I should, because you yourself can enlarge upon it. I assure you, Sir, this advice now given you proceeds from sincere love and my earnest desire to promote your happiness both in this world and the next ; and I hope you will be pleased so to accept from,

" S^r
" Your affectionate friend
"and humble servant
" N. CESTRIENS."

WARRIKIN FAIR

THIS is one of the oldest ballads in the Lancashire dialect which has been preserved, its date being fixed by the name Randle Shay in the fifth verse. Randle Shay, or Shaw, was bailiff to Sir Thomas Butler at Warrington in the second year of the reign of Edward VI. (1548). It was evidently preserved by oral tradition for a time, and then incorrectly dictated by, or taken down from, its singer. The second line of the second verse should read thus: "Hoo tuck up th' kippo, an' swat him o'er th' face." That is, She took up the big stick and struck him over the face. The next line reads, She pushed or pitched him upon the hillock, and he fell with a whack. "Welly," is well-nigh, nearly. The second line of the third verse, in English, is : I will give thee all the light, wench, in me that lies. "Udgit" may mean a soft fool, or a clumsy fellow ; or it may be a form of hedgehog. "By lakin" is a corruption of "By our Lady," a Roman Catholic expletive often to be met with in old plays. The third line of the fourth verse reads : And he gave me a luncheon of dainty snig (*i.e.* eel) pie. The first line of the fifth verse means : Then Grace she prankèd her (*i.e.* dressed, adorned herself) featly and fine. The third and fourth lines of this verse mean that she stayed at Warrington five market-days, till the man with the mare came and put up at Randle Shay's. "Gloppen" means startled, surprised ; "loppen," to have leaped. In the seventh verse are two similar colloquialisms, "her heart in her hand and her wind (breath) well-nigh gone." "Snood" is a hair-fillet or band. "Woode" is mad, wild. The two first lines of the eighth verse read : To Randle's she went, and she

heaved up the latch before the man had tied the mare properly or completely to the hay-rack. "Poo'd" is pulled ; thrumper'd," thumped, beat. "Sompan" is probably what is still meant by sumph —a foolish, stupid fellow. "I'll hold thee a groat" means : "I'll bet thee a wager of a groat." In the last verse Randle Shay accosts Grace Scott familiarly as "Naunty," or aunt, a common mode of salutation to elderly women.

Now, au yo' good gentlefoak, an yo' won tarry,
I'll tell yo' how Gilbert Scott soud his mare Barry ;
He soud his mare Barry at Warrikin fair,
But when he'll be paid, he knaws no', I'll swear.

So when he coom whom, and toud his wife Grace,
Hoo stud up o' th' kippo, and swat him o'er th' face,
Hoo pick'd him o' th' hillock, and he fawd wi' a whack,
That he thowt would welly a broken his back.

"O woife," quo' he, " if thou'll le'mme but rise,
I'll gi' thee aw' th' leet, wence, imme that lies."
"Tho udgit," quo' hoo, "but wheer does he dwell ? "
"By lakin," quo' he, "that I conno tell."

"I tuck him for t' be some gentlemon's son,
For he spent tuppence on me, when he had dun ;
An' he gen me a lunchin o' denty snig poy,
An' by th' hond did he shak' me most lovingly."

Then Grace hoo prompted her neatly and fine,
An' to Warrikin went o' We'nsday betime;
An' theer, too, hoo staid for foive markit days,
Till th' mon wi' th' mare cum to Randle Shay's.

An' as hoo wer' resting one day in hur rowm,
Hoo spoy'd th' mon a-riding th' mare into the town;
Then bounce goes hur heart, and hoo were so gloppen,
That out o' th' winder hoo'd like for to loppen.

Hoo stampt an' hoo stared, an' down stairs hoo run
Wi' hur heart in her hont, an' hur wint welly gone;
Her head-gear flew off, an' so did her snood;
Hoo stampt an' hoo stared, as if hoo'd bin woode.

To Randle's hoo hied, an' hoo hov' up the latch,
Afore th' mon had tied th' mare gradely to th' cratch.

"My gud mon," quo' hoo, "Gilbert greets you right merry
And begs that yo'll send him th' money for Barry."

"Oh, money," quo' he, "that connot I spare."
"Be lakin," quo' hoo, "then I'll ha' the mare."
Hoo poo'd an' hoo thrumper'd him sham' to be seen,
"Thou hangman," quo' hoo, "I'll poo' out thy e'en.

"I'll mak' thee a sompan, I'll houd thee a groat;
I'll auther· ha' th' money, or poo' out thy throat;
So between 'em they made sich a wearisom' din,
That to mak' 'em at peace, Randle Shay did come in.

"Cum, fye, nauhty Grace; cum, fye, an' ha' dun;
You'st ha' th'·mare, or th' money, whether yo' won."
So Grace geet th' money, an' whomwards hoo's gone;
But hoo keeps it hursel' an' gies Gilbert Scott none.

"TEN THOUSAND POUNDS FOR A CHARACTER"

H ORNBY CASTLE once belonged to a man who said he would gladly pay ten thousand pounds for a good character. This was Francis Charteris, a member of a Scottish family of high position, but who was so utterly unprincipled that early in his career he was drummed out of the Army. He served beyond doubt or question, whereupon his sword was broken in halves before his face and he was dismissed from the Army with ignominy and disgrace, being ordered to leave Brussels on the instant.

Charteris had no money for the journey to England, so resorted to a device, which was typical of the man, to obtain the

HORNBY CASTLE

under the great Duke of Marlborough in the Low Countries during the reign of Queen Anne, and whilst stationed at Brussels was detected cheating his brother officers at cards. The Duke ordered his arrest, and Charteris was brought before a court-martial so that he might have the opportunity of clearing his character. But the court-martial proved his guilt necessary funds. On the road between Brussels and Mechlin he threw away a portion of his clothing, and buttoning his long military cloak from top to bottom so that it entirely covered him, went to an inn for the night. The landlord treated him with the greatest deference as one of the officers of the conquering English Army, and showed him to one of his best bedrooms, where a dinner, the best the house could produce, was served. Early on the following morning Charteris roused the house with curses and lamentations, declaring that his clothes had been stolen during the night. In vain the landlord protested his innocence, Charteris stormed and raved, saying that not only his clothes but a ring, and notes and gold to a large amount, had likewise been stolen, that he would bring the matter before the British General, who would see that the landlord was properly punished for robbing a British officer ; or, if he was not the guilty person, for harbouring thieves in his house. The poor landlord was terrified out of his wits, for the country was under martial law and offences against the English army were treated with great severity. The sum declared by Charteris to have been stolen was far beyond the landlord's means, so hurrying to a neighbouring convent with Charteris' threats of having him hanged in front of his own inn door ringing in his ears, he borrowed the necessary amount from the nuns. Returning to the inn he implored Charteris to accept the money. That gentleman showed a well-simulated reluctance, whereupon the landlord renewed his entreaties and Charteris finally gave way, being graciously pleased to say, as he took the money, that he would " say no more on the matter."

Armed with the spoils of this robbery Charteris made his way to Scotland. News in those days travelled slowly, therefore when he arrived in Edinburgh his disgrace was still unknown, and he was made colonel of a regiment of horse. He took to card-playing again, and likewise to cheating. One night at a party at the house of the Duchess of Queensberry, he cleverly contrived to place the Duchess, with whom he was playing, in front of a large mirror in which he could see reflected all the cards she held. This clever knavery resulted in the Duchess losing three thousand pounds to Colonel Charteris that evening.

About the same time news of his dismissal from the army reached Edinburgh, and, Scotland being now too hot to hold him, Charteris went to London, where, after a short and extremely successful career as a card-sharper, he set up in business as a money-lender. He amassed a huge fortune and gained an evil character. Buying Hornby Castle, he settled there, making vain attempts to be accepted as a respectable member of society. It was at this time he made the remark that he would give ten thousand pounds for a good character.

Charteris was so universally detested by his fellow-countrymen that when supplies were needed during the march through Lancashire of the Pretender's troops in 1715, it was deemed prudent that no Highlanders should be amongst the party sent to Hornby Castle in search of supplies. Such was the feeling against Charteris that Scottish soldiers would have sacked his house. A small English party, under the command of Colonel Oxburgh, therefore was sent. Charteris had fled to Lancaster. Colonel Oxburgh took some wine, beer, and provender for the horses, and although Charteris ought to have been grateful that his house was not burned to the ground, he sent Colonel Oxburgh a bill for three pounds six shillings and eightpence for " the entertainment afforded at Hornby to man and beast." In reply to this insolent demand Oxburgh sent Charteris a note of hand for the amount " payable when his master's (the Pretender's) concerns should be settled."

Charteris married the daughter of Lord Mersington, and their only child, Janet, married the fifth Earl of Wemyss.

LANCASHIRE CASTLES BESIEGED

QUEEN HENRIETTA MARIA, the wife of Charles I., in a letter to James, Earl of Derby, after the outbreak of the Civil War, described Lancashire as "this lost county." And lost it certainly was to the royal cause, for, at the time she wrote, Lathom House in the south, Thurland Castle in the north-west, and Hornby Castle alone were held for Charles.

that they had been obliged to sell their estates. Thurland Castle consequently had come into the possession of Sir John Girlington, a staunch Roman Catholic and devoted Royalist. He garrisoned Thurland for the King, many of the neighbouring ladies and gentlemen devoted to the same cause seeking shelter within the walls. The Parliamentary Colonel Rigby, who in the following year laid un-

THURLAND CASTLE AS DEMOLISHED BY THE PARLIAMENT

The Parliament decided upon the capture of these three Royalist strongholds.

Thurland, lying close to the Westmoreland border, was originally the home of the Tunstalls, of whom Sir Brian Tunstall has come down to history as the "stainless knight" of Flodden Field. The Tunstalls were devout Roman Catholics and long before the Civil War they had suffered so severely from fines and sequestrations for their faith's sake,

successful siege to Lathom, was dispatched against Thurland. For eleven weeks he prosecuted a vigorous siege with little avail, so strong was Sir John Girlington's defence. During these weeks of attack, however, no help came from the King's forces, which actually lay encamped within view of the Castle walls. So desperate became the position of the besieged that finally a great effort was made to relieve them, and the Westmoreland and Cumberland Royalist force, uniting with those of

Cartmel and Furness, assembled on the sands under Colonel Huddlestone, to the number of sixteen hundred men. This was in the middle of October 1643. Colonel Rigby, perceiving this manœuvre and the danger he ran of being hemmed in between the Royalist force and the besieged, drew off a strong detachment of his army before Thurland Castle and marched them into Furness. This was on a Saturday. On the following morning he committed his troop to the protection of God in a lengthy prayer and then commanded them to attack the enemy. As they rushed to the engagement the Royalists cried " In with Queen Mary," to which the Parliamentarians made answer, "God with us." But instead of a battle, it was a rout. For some unknown reason the Royalists were seized with a sudden panic and fled in wild disorder, their leader falling prisoner into Rigby's hands. The Puritan Rigby sent the following dispatch concerning the affair to the Speaker of the House of Commons :—

"At our first appearance, God so struck the hearts of these our enemies with terrour, that before a blow was given, their horse began to retreat, our foot gave a great shout, our horse pursued, theirs fled ; their foot dispersed and fled ; they all trusted more to their feet than their hands, they threw away their arms and their colours, deserted their magazine drawn with eight oxen, and were totally routed in one quarter of an hour's time ; our horse slew some few of them in the pursuit and drove many of them into the sea ; we took their Colonel Huddleston, of Millan, two captains and an ensign, and about foure hundred prisoners, six foot colours, and one horse colour ; and their magazin, and some horses, and more arms than men ; and all this without the losse of any man of ours ; wee had only one man hurt by the enemy, and only another hurt by himself with his own pistoll, but neither mortally ; upon the close of the business, all our men with a great shout cryed out ' Glory be to God ' ; and wee all, except one troop of horse and one foot company, which I left to quiet the countrey, returned forthwith towards our siege at Thurland."

Rigby thereupon pressed the siege of the Castle so vigorously that the defenders, knowing they had now no hope of relief or succour, were obliged to yield, and the Parliamentarians captured " much money and plate, with many disaffected ladies and gentlemen." The fortress was then demolished and it remained in ruins until the reign of George III., when it was rebuilt from designs by Sir James Wyatt.

Hornby Castle also had been strongly garrisoned by the Royalists. From its position it was deemed impregnable, as it was inaccessible from three sides. Colonel Assheton headed the Parliamentary forces sent to besiege Hornby. Some accounts say it was a deserter from the Castle who showed him how it could be taken ; other accounts say that it was one of his own soldiers who formerly had been well acquainted with the place. But whoever was the informant, a few days after the siege had begun Assheton made the pretence of an attack upon the weak side of the Castle. But previously he had put a large number of his men under the guidance of his informer. Following this man they climbed up a precipice, and whilst the besieged were repelling Assheton's attack in front they suddenly found themselves set upon by their enemies in the very rooms from which they were firing. Scaling the precipice the men had crept through a window unperceived by the Royalists, who had no alternative but to surrender. The Parliament then ordered that "the Castle of Hornby be any further use thereof to the annoyance of the inhabitants."

HORNBY CASTLE AS DEMOLISHED BY THE PARLIAMENT

forthwith so defaced, or demolished, that the enemy may be prevented from making The order was carried out, but Hornby, like Thurland, was afterwards restored.

TRIPPET

THIS ancient game, which was very popular in East Lancashire some seventy years ago, is still played by colliers in the district. The game is not unlike that of tipcat, which is played at Burnley. A smooth boulder, with a gently sloping side, is chosen by the players, and upon this the "trippet"—a piece of holly-wood about two inches long, and an inch in diameter in the middle, sloping off at either end in a conical shape—is placed, one point overhanging. The player taps the end of the "trippet" with a long, flexible, heavy-headed club, and as it rises he strikes it with all his force. The one who can send the "trippet" the greatest distance in a certain number of strokes, wins the game.

POSSESSED OF A DEVIL

IN modern times there would be a simple explanation of the following amazing story of seven persons belonging to the same family being "possessed" by evil spirits at one and the same time. Mesmerism on the part of the man Hartlay would immediately be suspected. But in 1594 there was a firmly-rooted belief in the existence of evil spirits and in witchcraft amongst all classes, and it was upon this belief and the prevailing ignorance of the will power one person may exercise upon another, that men of the type of Hartlay traded. The bitter religious differences then existing between Protestants and Roman Catholics gave these "conjurors," as Hartlay and his fellows were called, a still wider scope for their wicked dealings. A Mr. Nicholas Starkie[1] of Huntroyd, in the parish of Whalley, had married an heiress who had inherited Cleworth (now called Clayworth) from her father, John Parr. Two children, a boy and a girl, called John and Anne, were born to the Starkies. Suddenly in 1594, these two children became possessed by evil spirits, and a famous "conjuror of spirits," named Hartlay, was summoned to give them relief. This he speedily brought about by the use of various charms, and by drawing a magical circle with four crosses upon the ground near the house.

Hartlay found himself in very pleasant quarters, and had no wish to leave the substantial comforts of a country gentleman's house for his own poor lodgings. By a variety of devices, and by playing upon the ignorance and credulity of his host he succeeded in proving to him that only by his presence in the house could a return of the evil spirits be prevented. But after nearly three years of this easy

[1] See "Peg o' th' Well."

existence, believing himself to be indispensable, Hartlay grew more exacting in his demands. Mr. Starkie, probably weary of his self-imposed visitor, probably also grown suspicious after so long an acquaintance, refused the demands made upon him. There was a quarrel, and Hartlay left the house, but not before the two children again became "possessed," and with them three girls who were wards of Mr. Starkie, as well as a visitor, and two of the maidservants.

This wholesale "possession" was at once attributed to Hartlay, for, according to the narrative, "it was judged in the house that whomsoever he kissed, on them he breathed the devil." The seven "possessed" people, "sending forth a strange and supernatural voice of loud shouting," turned poor Mr. Starkie's house into a perfect bedlam. John Starkie, the son, was "as fierce as a mad man or a mad dog," his sister Anne was little better. Of Mr. Starkie's three wards, Margaret Hardman, a gay and sprightly girl, suddenly aspired after all the splendid attire of a woman of fashion, calling for one extravagant thing after another, and telling her "lad," as she called her unseen "familiar," that she would be finer than him. Ellinor, her sister, and the third ward, Ellen Holland, were also "troubled." The visitor, Margaret Byron, of Salford, who was a woman of thirty-three, "became giddy and partook of the general malady. They all sang and danced and talked at such a rate that nothing could be heard but themselves, and then they would suddenly fall down as if they were dead." Under the advice of the great Dr. Dee, the warden of Manchester College, and a famous exorciser of spirits, some "godly preachers" were called in, whereupon Margaret Hardman ran under a bed and began to make a hole in the wall so that her "lad" might come to her; she also tried to jump out of the window.

It was observed when their "fits" were upon them these unfortunate people had not the use of their tongues and their feet at the same time; if they danced or ran about they could not speak; if they spoke they could not move their legs. Margaret Byron seems to have been more heavily afflicted than the others. She thought there was a calf in her inside which lay always upon her left side, and when it rose up towards her heart, she thought "the head and nose thereof had been full of nails, wherewith being pricked, she was compelled to shriek aloud with very pain and fear; sometimes she barked and howled, and at others she so much quaked that her teeth chattered in her head." When she was confronted with Hartlay she fell down speechless and saw a great black dog with a monstrous tail and a long chain running at her open-mouthed. Two of the ministers, George More and John Darrall, the latter of whom wrote a full narrative of these proceedings, then appeared on the scene, and afterwards testified to having themselves witnessed all these manifestations. Jane Ashton, the maidservant, they said, howled in a supernatural manner; it afterwards transpired that Hartlay had kissed her, and had promised to marry her.

The seven "demoniacs," as they were called, were placed on couches in a large parlour, and for a whole day the two ministers, assisted by a third named Dickens (the vicar of the parish) and thirty other people, prayed and fasted. Throughout the day the unfortunate seven "remained in their fits," but towards the evening "every one of them, with voice and hands lifted up, cried to God for mercy, and he was pleased to

hear them, so that six of them were shortly dispossessed, and Jane Ashton in the course of the next day experienced the same deliverance. At the moment of dispossession, some of them were miserably rent, and the blood gushed out both at the nose and mouth."

Each of the dispossessed seven had the satisfaction of seeing the creature that had been tormenting them, but there is little doubt that their heated imaginations were acting on the suggestion of the minister Darrall. Margaret Byron described her spirit as an ugly black man with shoulders higher than his head; she declared that she felt it come up her throat, and that it gave her "a sore tug" when it left her body, and then went out of the window with a flash of fire. But she was the only person who saw this phenomenon. Jack Starkie said his spirit was an ugly man with a hunch in his back. Ellinor Hardman's spirit was like an urchin. Two days later, according to Darrall, the evil spirits returned and would have re-entered their victims' bodies if they had not been visited by that holy man. When the spirits could not succeed either by bribes or entreaties, they threw some of the dispossessed ones violently to the ground, and deprived others of the use of their legs and arms. But finally victory lay with the preachers, and all the devils were for ever banished from Mr. Starkie's household.

Hartlay, after being examined by two magistrates, was committed to Lancaster Castle, where he was shortly afterwards tried for witchcraft. On the evidence of Mr. Starkie and his family he was convicted and sentenced to death, his principal offence being the drawing of the magic circle. Hartlay was clearly a quack, with some knowledge of mesmerism and thought transference, a knowledge he had used to impose upon the ignorant

Mr. Starkie. He protested his innocence even on the scaffold, but the rope breaking when he was drawn up, he confessed his guilt—a new rope was procured, and Hartlay was strung up to die—a victim of his own knavery and the gross superstition of the days in which he lived.

Not content with his success in the "dispossession" of the Starkie household of its devils, the Rev. John Darrall must needs write a long *Narrative* relating all the details and the part he himself had played at Cleworth. His book brought upon him consequences he little anticipated. It gave rise to a long controversy on the subject of demonology, which ended in Darrall being roundly accused by the Rev. Samuel Harsnet, afterwards Bishop of Chichester and Norwich, and Archbishop of York, of making a trade of casting out devils, and instructing the "possessed" how to conduct themselves in order to aid him in carrying on his imposition. Shortly afterwards Darrall was examined by Queen Elizabeth's Commissioners, and after all the evidence was heard, by full agreement of the whole court he was condemned as an impostor, driven from the Church, and ordered to prison, there to remain for further punishment. His partner in the Starkie exorcising, George More, some time later wrote "A Discourse Concerning the Possession and the Dispossession of Seven Persons in One Family in Lancashire." He admits that he "was a prisoner in the Clinke for nearly two years" because he had borne witness to the facts stated by Darrall as having occurred in the Starkie household, and, ignoring the part Hartlay played, he makes a particularly malicious and unfounded charge against some of Mrs. Starkie's relatives. He says that Mr. Starkie married the widow of Thomas Barton, of Smithells Hall, and that this lady being the heiress of Cleworth, her estate would go at her death to the male children of her first marriage. Some of her relatives were Roman Catholics, and these "partly for religion and partly because the estate descended but to heirs male—prayed for the perishing of her issue. Four sons by her first marriage pined away and died, and Mrs. Starkie hearing of the prayers of these relatives, and seeing their accomplishment in the deaths of her children, left her lands to her husband and his heirs failing issue of her own body. A son and daughter were born to Mr. and Mrs. Starkie, "who prospered well until they became possessed." The wicked inference, of course, is that the prayers of the Roman Catholic relatives were once more being directed against Mrs. Starkie's children, and that they were responsible for the two children being "possessed." This charge against Mrs. Starkie's relatives falls to the ground, for the simple reason that Nicholas Starkie was her first husband, and Thurstan Barton of Smithells her second.

The boy John Starkie, who was "as fierce as a mad man or a mad dog," ultimately became Sheriff of Lancashire; his sister, Anne, married a Yorkshire gentleman.

THE PRAISE OF LANCASHIRE MEN

OR

A few lines which here is penn'd
Wherein they Lancashire lads commend.

This ballad, the authorship of which is unknown, was written in the reign of the first or second King James.

YOU Muses all assist my pen,
    I earnestly require,
      To write the praise of the young men
Born in Lancashire :
They are both comely, stout and tall,
    And of most mild behaviour ;
Fair maids, I do intreat you all
    To yield to them your favour.

When a Lancashire lad doth feel the dart
    Of Cupid's bow and quiver,
And aims to take a fair maid's part,
    I'm sure he'll not deceive her :
Unto their promise they will stand,
    Which they to you propounded ;
They will not break for house or land,
    If love their hearts have wounded.

There is knights' sons and gentlemen,
    That is born in Lancashire,
That will be merry now and then,
    If need it do require :
The plowman likewise is our friend,
    Who doth use plow and harrow ;
He freely will his money spend
    When he meets with his marrow.[1]

In Lancashire there's brisk young lads
    As are within our nation,
Most of them of several trades,
    Or of some occupation ;
That their wives they can well maintain,
    And bring them store of treasure ;
All by their labour and their pain,
    They live with joy and pleasure.

[1] Marrow stands for a mate, a companion, a lover, or a match.

It is a most delightful thing,
    And pleasure for to hear,
These boys their songs and catches sing
    When they drink their ale and beer :
They will be merry, great and small,
    When they do meet together ;
And freely pay for what they call—
    A fig for wind and weather.

At pleasant sports and football play
    They will be blithe and jolly ;
Their money they will freely lay,
    And cast off melancholy.
When Lancashire lads of several trades,
    They have a jovial meeting,
Each man a glass unto the maids
    Will drink unto his sweeting.

Brave Lancashire lads are soldiers stout,
    Whose valour has been tryed
At sea and land in many a bout
    When thousands brave men died ;
And always scornèd for to yield
    Although the foes were plenty
If they're but ten men on the field,
    They surely will fight twenty.

Great James our King they will defend
    As well as any shire ;
To England they will prove a friend,
    If need it do require.
They loyal subjects still have been,
    And most of them stout-hearted,
Who still will fight for king and queen,
    And never from them started.

Now to conclude and make an end
    Of this my harmless sonnet ;
I hope no man I do offend ;
    Each man put off his bonnet,
And drink a health to James our King,
    And to our English nation ;
God us defend in everything,
    And keep us from invasion !

HARTSHEAD PIKE

TOWARDS the end of the eighteenth century the view from Hartshead Hill, near Staly- Haslingden and Horwich Moor, Stockport, Manchester and the Welsh hills could be clearly seen. To-day the view

OLD HARTSHEAD PIKE

bridge, upon the top of which stood the Pike, was described by Dr. Aikin as being "most delightful." A hundred years ago Butterworth said that on a clear day consists entirely of tall chimneys, factories and the refuse heaps of coal-pits.

Dr. Aikin also says it was generally supposed that the Pike was a "sea mark," but it was actually a beacon, such as were scattered over the whole country to be used as signals in time of war. How all England was warned of the coming of the Spanish Armada by these beacon fires is told in Macaulay's *The Armada*—

" From Eddystone to Berwick bounds, from Lynn to Milford Bay,
That time of slumber was as bright and busy as the day ;
For swift to east and swift to west the ghastly war-flame spread,
High on St. Michael's Mount it shone : it shone on Beachy Head.
Far on the deep the Spaniard saw, along each southern shire,
Cape beyond cape, in endless range, those twinkling points of fire."

From London the fires sent the signals to the north—

"And on and on, without a pause, untired they bounded still :
All night from tower to tower they sprang ; they sprang from hill to hill."

The fiery message doubtless came to Hartshead and was sent on towards Lancaster, whence

" . . . Skiddaw saw the fire that burned on Gaunt's embattled pile,
And the red glare on Skiddaw roused the burghers of Carlisle."

The tower shown in the illustration was built in 1758 upon the site of the old beacon. It was used for heliographing. Upon its western side was this inscription—

Look me well before you go,
And see you nothing at me throw.

This Pike was erected by public subscription in 1758.

Some forty years later the building split from top to bottom, " near half a yard in width," and speedily fell into ruins. There was a general desire that the Pike should be rebuilt, but nothing was done—although a few pounds would have sufficed for its repair when the split first appeared—until 1863. In that year the foundations of a new tower were laid with much ceremony and circumstance.

An inscription on the present Pike states that it was " Re-erected by Public Subscription to commemorate the marriage of H.R.H. Albert Edward, Prince of Wales, to H.R.H. Princess Alexandra of Denmark and to restore the Ancient Land Mark of Hartshead Pike." In 1912 the Pike, together with nearly two acres of ground around it, was given to the Hartshead Parish Council by the Trustees of the Earl of Stamford and Warrington for the use of the public.

A TRAFFORD AND A BYRON FEUD

BY

THOMAS BARRITT

IN our Fourth Edward's fickle days
A serious quarrel, story says,
Took place near Rochdale, we are told,
'Twixt Trafford and a Byron bold.
The cause was this, we understand,
About some privilege of land.
Oliver Chadwick from Chadwick Hall,
On Byron's part that day did fall ;
But afterwards it came to pass,
Lord Stanley arbitrator was,
Who fixed it upon this ground,
Trafford should pay full sixty pound,
In holy church at Manchester ;
And from this contract not to err,
To Chadwick's heirs, to keep them quiet,
And never more to move a riot :
Ten marks at birth-day of St. John,
And ten at Martin's day upon
Each year until the whole was paid ;
And to be friends again, he said.

CHOWBENT IN THE EIGHTEENTH CENTURY

IN the year 1787 a certain Mr. Durning Rasbotham sat him down and wrote some notes upon Chowbent, little thinking he was preserving a picture of life and its ways and means in his own time, for the interest and perhaps the wonder of the people of a hundred and twenty-five years later.

" In this township " (of Atherton), he says, " there is a very considerable village, which, from a bent or common, is denominated from one Chew or Chow, and now known by the name of Chowbent. It hath an Episcopal Chapel and a Dissenting (or Presbyterian) meeting-house. The chapel is a small brick edifice, and was built in the year 1648, originally for the tenants and domestics of the Atherton family. The Dissenters made use of it as their place of worship till the year 1720, when, upon a change of principles in the family, it was taken from them and consecrated by Dr. Wilson, at that time Bishop of the Isle of Man, and the patronage of it is now in the Atherton family. The last minister of the Dissenting persuasion who preached there was James Woods. . . . During the Rebellion of 1715 Mr. Woods, at that time minister of the chapel, by virtue of a commission under the hand of General Wills, marched to Preston at the head of about eighty of his hearers armed with implements of husbandry, in support of the present government. By the General's orders he took his post upon the south side of the Ribble, for the defence of the ford which leads from Penwortham to Preston. His situation did not allow him to take any active part in the victory which immediately succeeded, but he is said to have drawn his sword upon one of his men, who showed some signs of fear, and to have sworn (which he constantly denied) that he would run the first man through who betrayed any sign of timidity. The oldest branch of the family of the Morts were at that time High Churchmen. One of them had left the annual sum of fifty-five pounds to the orthodox minister of the place. Woods was deemed a schismatic, and the payment had been withheld until the sum due amounted to three hundred pounds. One Mort, a councillor, by whose advice the money had been withheld, and in whose hands it was at this time, died. His successor, less scrupulous, paid the whole to Woods, and it was this sum which enabled him to march his men to Preston. As a reward for his conduct he received a gratuity of one hundred pounds from His Majesty, which he generously distributed amongst his men, and which was expended in the erection of the Dissenting meeting-house. It was built in the year 1722, upon the alienation of what is now the Episcopal Chapel. It is an extensive brick building, hath a bell, a large burying ground, and a congregation of about one thousand persons." Great efforts were made in the building of this chapel, and it is related that " General " Woods, as he was always called after the Battle of Preston, went to Squire Hulton and asked him for twenty oaks from Hulton Park for the building.

" Nay, man, " said the Squire, " but I'll give you ten."

" Thank you, " answered Woods. " Just the number I want ; for I knew you would only give me half of what I asked."

" Woods was not an eloquent preacher," continues Mr. Rasbotham, " but ' though he could not preach, ' he was wont to say, ' he could tell his hearers a story and that did as well.' He lived so as to be esteemed even by those against whom he had taken arms, and hath his memory even now revered by some of the most inveterate of the enemies of the cause he espoused. He died at the age of eighty-six or eighty-seven. . . .

"The wages of the common labourer are from 18*d.* to 20*d.* a day, and he expects to receive a cup of ale twice a day. A carpenter's wages are 2*s.* a day, a brick-setter receives the same, but till this year was content with 20*d.* Coals sell in this township at 2½*d.* per hundred, and is carried to the most distant part of it at 3½*d.* There is a good market at Chowbent for butcher's meat, for the consumption of which seven or eight cows, in the spring fourteen or fifteen, and from Midsummer to March about three calves, and through-out the year perhaps a dozen sheep are weekly killed. Every branch of the old fustian manufacture (in which, however, I do not mean to include muslins, the manu-facture of which is trifling) is carried on here. Here also is a very considerable factory of nails, and several families have acquired fortunes by making spinning-jennies and carding machines, which they send into Scotland, Ireland and different parts of the kingdom. Some of the mechanics do not keep less than thirty journeymen employed in this business."

In the eighteenth century the Bishops apparently had the ordering of the census, for ten years before Mr. Rasbotham wrote these notes, Chowbent had been numbered by the direction of the Bishop of Chester. The inhabitants then numbered two thousand two hundred. And here we have an instance of the survival of the belief in witchcraft so late as the beginning of the eighteenth century. "In the beginning of this century," says Mr. Rasbotham, "one Katherine Walkden, an old woman of this township, was committed to Lancaster as a witch. She was exam-ined at Hulton Hall, where the magistrate then resided, by a jury of matrons, by whom a private teat was discovered, and upon this and other evidence (I suppose of equal importance) her mittimus was made out, but she died in gaol before the ensuing assizes.

"Very few of the common people here go by the proper names of their families, a singularity (if it can in this part of Lancashire be called such) probably owing to there being many persons of the same name in the township. This may be in-stanced in the Smiths, Aldreds, Huttons, etc., and their common denominations are usually taken from their trades, peculiarity in their features or manners, or other accidental circumstances."

Housewives will read the following prices with envy, but it must be remem-bered that although the price of food has risen manyfold during the past hundred years, money was then of more value than it is to-day. "Beef upon the average of the whole year, sells at 4*d.* per pound; veal and mutton at about the same rate; a goose at 5*d.* per pound; new milk at 1*d.* per quart; butter from 8*d.* to 10*d.* or 11*d.* per pound; and the very best potatoes at 20*d.* a bushel. The fuel is coal and cannel. The general wages of men-servants are £10 a year. Women may be hired from £5 to £6 a year. The rod consists of eight yards. Land lets from 50*s.* to £6 an acre; and the prices of farms, which are chiefly small, vary from £15 a year to £100. The common manures are lime, brought from Worsley, the carriage of which amounts to 2½*d.* a basket, and soaper's waste, which is brought from Warrington, and dung. Eight quarts make a peck, four pecks a bushel or strike, Winchester measure. The bushel is called by the country people a measure, and four bushels constitute a load."

"Here is coal," says Mr. Rasbotham in conclusion. "Iron hath been formerly gotten, as appears from the cinders yet remaining, and there are quarries of stone fit for building. The coal mines have long been worked. In the deepest part they do not lie more than sixty yards from the surface; they are freed from water by pumps, and are not liable to damps. The cotton manufacture was established here about the beginning of the century, but only low-priced goods were at that time made. It hath risen upon the ruins of the iron trade, which hath decreased in proportion to its rise."

Since the worthy Mr. Rasbotham, who must have been an observant and painstaking man, wrote these notes on the Chowbent of 1787, the iron trade has been revived. After this time too silk weaving became a profitable industry, but it decayed. Nail-making is still carried on, but it is no longer the principal business of the place. Cotton spinning employs a large number of the inhabitants to-day.

COPY OF A HANDBILL OF 1820

—THE—
PACKET BOATS
BETWEEN
KENDAL AND PRESTON,
ARE INTENDED TO COMMENCE SAILING FROM THESE TOWNS,
ON MONDAY, THE 1ST OF MAY,
AT SIX O'CLOCK IN THE MORNING,
And will continue to Sail Daily during the Summer.

————•————

The Boat from Kendal to Preston will arrive at the Locks at nine o'clock, at Lancaster at one o'clock, at Garstang at four o'clock, and at Preston at eight o'clock.

The Boat from Preston to Kendal will arrive at Garstang at ten o'clock, at Lancaster at one o'clock, at the Locks at four o'clock, and at Kendal at eight o'clock.

Passengers the whole length, Fore-cabin 6s. After-cabin 4s.—between Lancaster and Preston, or Lancaster and Kendal, Fore-cabin 3s. After-cabin 2s. —for shorter distances, Fore-cabin 1½d. After-cabin 1d. per mile.—Tea, Coffee, and refreshments provided.

The Coaches for the North leave Kendal soon after the arrival of the Packet.
Parcels and Packages will be carried on reasonable terms, and delivered free of Porterage.

Canal Office, Lancaster, April 13, 1820.
————————

Printed by M. & R. Branthwaite, Fish-Market, Kendal.

THE THREE SISTERS

THERE was a king of the north
    countree,
    Bow down, bow down, bow down!
There was a king of the north countree,
And he had daughters, one, two, three.
  I'll be true to my love, and my love'll be
    true to me.

To the eldest he gave a beaver hat,
  Bow down, bow down, bow down!
To the eldest he gave a beaver hat,
And the youngest she thought much of that.
  I'll be true to my love, and my love'll be
    true to me.

To the youngest he gave a gay gold chain,
  Bow down, bow down, bow down!
To the youngest he gave a gay gold chain,
And the eldest she thought much of the
    same.
  I'll be true to my love, and my love'll be
    true to me.

These sisters were walking on the bryn,[1]
  Bow down, bow down, bow down!
These sisters were walking on the bryn,
And the eldest pushed the younger in.
  I'll be true to my love, and my love'll be
    true to me.

Oh, sister! oh, sister. oh, lend me your
    hand!
  Bow down, bow down, bow down!
Oh, sister! oh, sister! oh, lend me your
    hand!
And I will give you both houses and land.
  I'll be true to my love, and my love'll be
    true to me.

I'll neither give you my hand nor glove,
  Bow down, bow down, bow down!
I'll neither give you my hand nor glove
Unless you give me your (own) true love.
  I'll be true to my love, and my love'll be
    true to me.

Away she sank, away she swam,
  Bow down, bow down, bow down!

---

[1] Brink of a river, a craggy slope.

Away she sank, away she swam,
Until she came to the miller's dam.
  I'll be true to my love, and my love'll be
    true to me.

The miller and daughter stood at the door,
  Bow down, bow down, bow down!
The miller and daughter stood at the door,
And watched her floating down the shore.
  I'll be true to my love, and my love'll be
    true to me.

Oh, father! oh, father! I see a white swan,
  Bow down, bow down, bow down!
Oh, father! oh, father! I see a white swan,
Or else it is a fair wo-man.
  I'll be true to my love, and my love'll be
    true to me.

The miller he took up his long crook,
  Bow down, bow down, bow down!
The miller he took up his long crook,
And the maiden up from the stream he
    took.
  I'll be true to my love, and my love'll be
    true to me.

The miller he took the gay gold chain,
  Bow down, bow down, bow down!
The miller he took the gay gold chain,
And he pushed her into the water again.
  I'll be true to my love, and my love'll be
    true to me.

The miller was hang'd on his high gate,
  Bow down, bow down, bow down!
The miller was hang'd on his high gate,
For drowning our poor sister Kate.
  I'll be true to my love, and my love'll be
    true to me.

The cat's behind the buttery shelf,
  Bow down, bow down, bow down!
The cat's behind the buttery shelf;
If you want any more you may sing it your-
    self.
  I'll be true to my love, and my love'll be
    true to me.

A CLEVER TRICK

SUPERINTENDENT BENT, in his reminiscences of forty-two years as a police officer in Lancashire, tells an amusing story of how he prevented the escape of three prisoners. One Monday morning when he was stationed at Newton Heath, the Superintendent found that three warehousemen had been locked up the previous night for being drunk and disorderly. " At that time," he says, " Mr. Trafford, the stipendiary magistrate, always expected a prisoner to be handcuffed, no matter with what offence he was charged." The three men all had families, and earnestly begged the Superintendent that they might be spared the disgrace of being taken handcuffed through the streets. At first he said he could not interfere, but when they told him they would lose their situations if it came to the knowledge of their employers that they had been locked up for drunkenness, he thought the matter over. He " looked at their trousers," he says, " and finding they were all pretty widely made round the waist," he told the men he would take them to the court without handcuffing them on one condition, and that was that they should let him have their braces, " for I knew very well," he adds, " that it would be impossible for them to run and hold up their trousers at the same time." The men agreed, and were not handcuffed. " Each man put his hands in his trousers pockets," says Superintendent Bent, " and we started off to the court, and they did not make the least attempt to give me the slip." On the way to the court they met Mr. Trafford going in the opposite direction. When the case was over the magistrate called the Superintendent into the witness-box and said, " Bent, those three men I have just fined were not handcuffed." " No, sir," replied the Superintendent, " they were not." " Well then," Mr. Trafford asked, " do you know what would have happened if any of them had escaped?" " I know the responsibility I have taken upon myself," the Superintendent answered, " and that they could not have run very far without being apprehended."

" What, young men like them not run," exclaimed Mr. Trafford; " what would prevent them?"

" Well, sir," the Superintendent answered, " they pleaded so earnestly not to be handcuffed that I agreed not to do so if each would give me his braces. You may depend upon one thing, sir, they would not run very far nor very quick without their suspenders."